"The Red Watch"

Colonel J.A. Currie

"The Red Watch"

With the First Canadian Division in Flanders During the Great War

J.A. Currie

"The Red Watch"
With the First Canadian Division in Flanders During the Great War
by J.A. Currie

First published under the title
"The Red Watch" with the First Canadian Division in Flanders

Leonaur is an imprint of Oakpast Ltd

ISBN: 978-0-85706-649-7 (hardcover)
ISBN: 978-0-85706-650-3 (softcover)

http://www.leonaur.com

Publisher's Notes

The opinions of the authors represent a view of events in which he was a participant related from his own perspective, as such the text is relevant as an historical document.

The views expressed in this book are not necessarily those of the publisher.

Contents

DEDICATED TO THE MEMORY
OF THE CANADIAN SOLDIERS
WHO FELL IN FLANDERS

These for the Empire stood in war array,
Barring the Hun invader on his way;
Into the battle rushed at Duty's call,
Resolved to hold their trenches or to fall;
That Britons ne'er to tyrants bend the knee
But live as they were born, unyoked and free.
Now, in the bosom of a distant land
These warriors sleep, for such is God's command.
The Fates in all decree, and have their will,
And mortals must their destiny fulfil.

J.A. Currie, M.P.,
Colonel.

Preface

The kind reception given to the rough notes from the Author's Diary, which appeared first in the daily papers in Canada, encouraged the production of this book. These notes, in order to make them more readable, have been put in narrative form. There is no pretence that this is a history of the war. It is only a string of pen pictures describing life and incidents of the campaign common to almost every corps in the field.

Where anything is omitted it must be borne in mind that the author cannot give any information of a military character which might assist the enemy while the war is in progress.

Opinions and observations on military matters are omitted. Discussions on the merits of the various arms, equipments, rifles, work of the staff, errors, omissions and criticisms of the manner in which the war is conducted, must wait for a future volume.

It is hoped that this publication will encourage all young men to "take their places in the ranks" and bear arms for the King and Empire, regardless of whether our military system be volunteering, conscription or National service.

It is more evident every day that there is need for the mobilization and consolidation of all the resources of the Empire. Consolidated and mobilized the Empire is self-sustaining and invincible. Its military and financial powers would be quadrupled. There is nothing to justify any delay in accomplishing this object except political expediency. In union there would be not only immediate strength, but confidence and harmony.

The world is just as full of brave deeds and stirring events as ever. The British Empire is yet a lump of clay unfashioned and formless on the wheel of the potter. That is the colonial view. It is for us to help "Mould it nearer to our heart's desire."

It is a great privilege to live in this age when such glorious deeds are being performed and history is being written. It is better still to be permitted to die, doing brave deeds, that our Empire may live, greater, freer and happier than ever.

Toronto, October 2nd, 1916.

Chapter 1

Kilties in Canada

With this book as with many others the first chapter should be read last. The reason it is placed first is that the chronological order must be maintained. Besides, when stirring deeds by brave men are recalled, it matters not how briefly, they demand better treatment than being embalmed in an appendix.

This chapter deals with the first appearance of the Highland soldier in Canada. That appearance was both interesting and tragic. The stories and legends surrounding the campaigns of these brave men have furnished many themes for the poet and novelist. This chapter can only briefly refer to them.

If you search the great plains and rugged mountains of Canada from end to end, you will find many beautiful plants and flowers, but not a single spray of heather. Only in one spot in the whole vast Dominion will you find the plant that is so characteristically Scottish, growing naturally, and that is in Point Pleasant Park, Halifax. Tradition has it that on this spot, in 1757, the soldiers of the "Black Watch[1]," the 42nd Highlanders, first set foot on Canadian soil. Here in this park, one of the most beautiful in America, the visitor is shown a plot of Scottish heather, flourishing vigorously in spite of souvenir hunters and vandals.

The Black Watch arrived at Halifax in the spring of 1757 to take part in the expedition against Louisburg, under General Abercrombie. Some say that the men of the Regiment, desirous of perpetuating the badge of so many of their clansmen, planted the heather seed where it now grows. Others, that the palliasses or mattresses of the soldiers were emptied here after the voyage, and the heather with which they

1. *The History of the Black Watch* by Archibald Forbes, also published by Leonaur.

had been filled in Scotland provided the seed from which this plot grew. It matters very little how it came. The heather still flourishes on the spot where the Black Watch first pitched its tent in Canada.

The expedition against Louisburg was abandoned, but the following year the regiment took part in the operations against the French under Montcalm at Lake George. Visitors there are shown the ruins of the ramparts of Ticonderoga. Around these ruins cling many legends and stories, but the name of Ticonderoga will live forever in the weird tale immortalized by Sir Thomas Dick Lauder, Parkman and the poem of Robert Louis Stevenson. It is told how on the eve of the battle there appeared to Duncan Campbell, of Inverawe, Major of the Black Watch, the wraith of a relative, murdered by a man to whom Campbell had granted sanctuary. This wraith had years previously appeared to him and warned him that he would meet him at "Ticonderoga." The following day Major Campbell died at the head of the assaulting columns of the Black Watch, and that brave regiment lost 655 officers and men, nearly equalling the losses of the "Red Watch," the 48th Highlanders of Canada, at the Battle of St. Julian in Flanders, when their roll showed 691 casualties.

The charge of the Black Watch at Ticonderoga was one of the bravest exploits of British arms. The gallant Highlanders advanced against the log redoubts and abattis of the French under Montcalm, hacking at the branches with their broadswords, climbing the ramparts with the assistance of their comrades, only to be hurled back, torn and bleeding, with the grape shot from hidden guns and musket-fire from many loopholes. They assaulted again and again, and finally had to be withdrawn.

For their gallant conduct at Ticonderoga[2] the "Black Watch" were made a "Royal" regiment by the King.

The Black Watch was quartered for many years afterwards in Canada and quite a few of the descendants of these old warriors helped to make history for the Canadians in this latest and "Greatest War."

The second appearance of the armed Highlander in Canada was characteristically dramatic. They came in the persons of Fraser's Highlanders, hard on the heels of the gallant Black Watch. This regiment, known as the old 78th, was celebrated in many ways. This is the corps raised by Lord Lovat, that Pitt was said to have had in mind when in the British House of Commons he delivered the famous panegyric on

---

2. *The Black Watch at Ticonderoga* by Frederick B. Richards, also published by Leonaur.

the Highland troops.

This regiment distinguished itself first at the taking of Louisburg. It was the first to climb the Heights of Abraham and its fame has come down through history with that of Wolfe's victory at Quebec. The fierce charge of this regiment at Quebec which broke through the French line as if it were paper, is accounted for by the story that the Highlanders were rendered frantic by the fall of Wolfe whom they idolized, as the young staff officer who, on the day after Culloden, dared the anger of his Commander by refusing to pistol a wounded Highlander. A Canadian poet, Mr. Duncan Anderson, in describing the Battle of the Plains of Abraham, refers to the Frasers thus:

And the shrill pipe its coronach that wailed,
On dark Culloden moor, o'er trampled dead,
Now sounds the 'Onset' that each clansman knows,
Still leads the foremost rank where noblest blood is shed.

While Fraser's regiment were in garrison in Quebec, an incident occurred that was later on duplicated in Flanders. Owing to the inclement weather in Quebec, some of the officers in authority decided that the men should discard their kilts and don trousers. The officers and men of the regiment would not hear of it, and the historian of the regiment says that the kilt was retained winter and summer and that "in the course of six years the doctors learned that in the coldest of winters the men clad in the Highland garb were more healthy than those regiments that wore breeches and warm clothing."

In the trenches at Neuve Chapelle an agitation arose to give the kilted Canadian soldier in the trenches trousers. With the snow on the ground and half an inch of ice on the water pails in the morning, they would not hear of anything but the kilt. Their health was similarly good, colds being unknown.

Along with Fraser's regiment there came also the Montgomery Highlanders, the 77th, raised by Hon. Arch. Montgomery, son of the Earl of Eglington. This regiment took its full share of the operations against the French at Fort Duquesne and elsewhere.

Romantic interest clings around the memories of the Montgomery Highlanders. This regiment was known as the "Lost Regiment." The legend says that one of its gallant leaders, Major Charteris, fell in love with a young woman of his native parish of Perth before he went to the War. She promised to wait till he returned when he would have carved a name for himself with his good broadsword, which was his only fortune. Whilst his regiment was in America his letters failed to reach her, and finally the troop ship on which Charteris sailed for home was driven ashore and his regiment took eight months to make the voyage. All hands were given up as lost, and Major Charteris' sweetheart consented to marry another officer, a "slacker" who had not gone to the war. While the wedding bells were ringing, the regiment marched into Perth, but half an hour too late. Charteris returned to America and died the death of a soldier. His name is still perpetuated in that of a town in Illinois, Ft. Charteris.

The first Highland Regiment to be enlisted in Canada was the Royal Highland Emigrants, still known in the army list as the 84th. No regiment ever embodied in the British service deserves kindlier remembrance in Canada than this gallant corps. The name and number has been perpetuated in the British Army List. Its exploits will never be forgotten and should be cherished by all Canadians. This regiment was enlisted in 1775 when the Revolutionary War broke out, from the Highlanders of Fraser's, Montgomery's and the Black Watch regiments that had settled in America.

When the Revolutionary War broke out Lieut.-Col. Allan McLean, of Torlousk, and Capt. John Small of Strathardle, in Athole, proceeded to embody the members of the Highland regiments that had settled in America. These old Highlanders rallied to the colours of the new battalions, two in number, and they served with great distinction throughout the revolutionary period. McLean raised one battalion in the States among the loyal Highlanders of Virginia and the Carolinas. He was assisted by Capt. McLeod, a former officer in Fraser's regiment. Through many perils and devious routes the men who enlisted found their way to the battalion rendezvous, and when they had all gathered they marched to Quebec, and virtually took charge of the stirring defence of that famous fortress against the American army under Montgomery and Arnold. Throughout the siege, the order and gallantry of the Highlanders animated the garrison and it was before the muskets of the Royal Highland Emigrants that Montgomery fell at the barrier beneath the citadel.

No greater service was ever given to the British Crown than that given at Quebec by the Royal Highland Emigrants, during the second siege. Their undaunted conduct stirred to emulation the brave French-Canadians who mustered to assist the British, and by their joint efforts the American invasion and siege came to an end.

The second battalion served in Nova Scotia during the war. Five of the companies accompanied Lord Cornwallis in his operations in New York and the Southern coast States. Later the two battalions were formed into the 84th Regiment, Sir Henry Clinton being appointed Colonel-in-Chief.

History repeats itself and the descendants of the gallant Royal Highland Emigrants, more than a hundred years later, in the ranks of the "Red Watch," or 48th Highlanders of Canada, fought side by side in the same brigade in Flanders with the gallant Royal Montreal Regiment, composed largely of French-Canadians.

When the Royal Emigrants were disbanded in Canada after the war, the men returned to their farms. Colonel McLean's battalion settled chiefly in Ontario. Many of their descendants still live on their original homesteads and have filled honourable positions in the public and private life of their country. The members of Small's battalion settled in Nova Scotia, and their descendants were in evidence when a Highland corps was organized by Lieut.-Col. Struan Robertson of Pictou, to take part in the "Greatest War."

During the War of 1812, a regiment was raised amongst the Highlanders of the County of Glengarry, Ontario, known as the Glengarry Fencibles. Descendants of these soldiers were amongst the first to offer their services for Flanders in 1914. One gallant officer of the 48th, Captain Archibald McGregor, who gave his life at the Battle of St. Julien, was a descendant of these men of Glengarry.

The Glengarry Fencibles fought amongst the foremost at the Battle of Lundy's Lane alongside the 100th Prince of Wales Regiment, which at that period was uniformed in kilts.

Many distinguished highland regiments served in Canada during the nineteenth century. Amongst those that are still held in kindly remembrance are the following: The Highland Light Infantry, the 73rd, 74th, 78th, 79th and 93rd. Many of the officers and men of these regiments bought out in Canada or else settled in the country at the end of their period of service.

Thus it will be seen that the kilted soldiers have played a prominent part in the pioneer life and settlement of Canada, where men of Scottish blood have always found a congenial home. The highest offices in the gift of the people have gone to the men of Scottish origin like Sir John Macdonald, Alexander Mackenzie, George Brown and Sir Oliver Mowat, whose genius for organization and government made possible Confederation. In the financial and industrial life of the country the names of Lord Strathcona, Sir James Drummond and many other Scots will always be cherished.

It matters not whether the Scottish lad comes from the "dim shieling" or the ancestral castle, when he reaches the shores of Canada he finds the Field Marshal's baton in his pocket, and he can be a leader in whatever sphere of life he chooses.

Chapter 2

The "Red Watch" or 48th Highlanders

It was while doing duty in Scotland, shortly after the Jacobite rising, that the 42nd Highlanders came to be called the "Black Watch." The sombre colour of their kilts and the work in which they were engaged combined to give them this nickname, which has clung to this famous regiment ever since. The 48th Highlanders of Canada wore a sombre tartan like the "Black Watch," interwoven with a broad red check, and it was whilst doing duty as patrol over a steel plant at Sault Ste. Marie that some striking Scotchmen first called the Canadian Regiment the "Red Watch." The name has been accepted and alternates with the "48th" in describing this corps. The brave Seaforths have a light grey check in their tartans, the gay Gordons a brilliant golden check, but the 48th have this check in red, and when the kilts are properly made the stripe comes on the fold of the tartan and gives a peculiar shimmering effect to the swaying kilts while the men are on the march.

The nickname of the "Red Watch" is not as well known as that of the "Black Watch," but the Imperial Battalion of the "Red Watch" loyally earned the name at the great salient at Ypres, where they watched at the post of honour and halted the German masses in their second great drive to Calais. This story has most to tell about these stirring days, but a word about the Canadian Militia and this regiment in particular may be in order.

Reference in the foregoing chapter has been made to the Highland regiments that served in the Colonial Wars. These troops were regular troops, but always serving with or against them were the Canadian Militia.

From the very beginning of the Colonies there was a Canadian

Militia. From its inception during the Indian wars down to the time of writing, this Militia has been distinguished for bravery. It came into being in the days of the early French settlement, and the Canadian Militia helped Montcalm to fight at Ticonderoga, Detroit and Fort DuQuesne. During the Seven Years' War, the Canadian Militia served continuously. At the capitulation of Canada it was stipulated that the Provincial Militia were to be allowed to return unmolested to their farms. They marched out of the fallen fortresses with all the honours of war, with arms and badges, drums beating, colours flying and matches lit. When Canada became British, the militia was incorporated into the new State organization. It distinguished itself again during the War of 1812 at Chateauguay, Detroit, Queenston Heights, Chippewa and Lundy's Lane. On numerous occasions the Imperial authorities commended the gallant conduct of the Canadian Militia.

When the Confederation of the Canadian Colonies was accomplished, in 1866, it was decided that the defence of the country should be left largely to the Militia, and a condition of Confederation was that this force was to be retained and strengthened, and a certain sum of money should be spent upon it annually.

When an invasion was threatened from the United States in 1866, the Canadian Militia sprang to arms and manned the frontiers. When General Louis Riel raised the banner of rebellion in the North-West Territories of Canada on two occasions, it was the civilian soldiers that suppressed the uprising. When the British power under Lord Wolseley went to the assistance of General Gordon in the Soudan, a contingent of Canadians, under Colonel Frederick Denison, C.B., M.P., helped to pilot the Nile barges up that historic river. Again when war broke out in South Africa, the Canadian contingent covered itself with glory on the hard won field of Paardeburg, helping materially to win the first decisive victory in South Africa for the British Army.

The 48th Highlanders Regiment in the Canadian Militia was formed in 1891. A number of enthusiastic Scotchmen met in the City of Toronto and decided to organize a Militia Regiment wearing the tartan kilt and feather bonnet. Committees were formed and in a very short time sufficient funds were raised to enable the regiment to be uniformed. Sir George E. Foster, then Minister of Finance for the Dominion of Canada, Sir John A. Macdonald, the Prime Minister, and Sir Oliver Mowat, the Premier of the Province of Ontario, lent their patronage to the movement. The writer was associated in the work, and appeared in the first *Gazette* as a captain of the new corps. The first Commanding Officer, Lieutenant-Colonel J.I. Davidson, Lieutenant-Colonel A.M. Cosby, Lieutenant-Colonel W.C. Macdonald, Lieutenant-Colonel Robertson and Lieutenant-Colonel William Hendrie were on the original committees of the regiment. At the time of writing this book, the regiment had one Colonel and five lieutenant-colonels on active service, namely, Colonel Currie, M.P., Lieutenant-Colonels Marshall, Hendrie, Dansereau, Miller and Chisholm.

One of the leading spirits in the formation of the corps was Hon. Lt.-Colonel Dr. Alexander Fraser, Ph.D., A.D.C., the noted Celtic scholar and antiquarian. The tartan chosen was the old Davidson tartan in honour of its first colonel. The badge was the Celtic motto "*Dileas Gu Brath.*" It was given the number "48" in the Canadian Militia list, which number on its bonnets and badges it has since proudly worn on two continents and in three countries, on tented ground and hard fought field. In the South African War the regiment sent its quota and the men served with much distinction.

Many Highland gatherings in Canada were held under the auspices of this regiment. A bayonet team was sent to the Royal Military tournament, at Islington, in June, 1897, and this team carried off the three principal events, *viz.*: the Colonial Individual Competition, the All-Comers' Individual Championship and the Team Championship. Private George Stewart it was that won the Championship, and a great reception was tendered him when he came home to Canada.

The regiment had always paid a great deal of attention to musketry and in 1913, the year the writer became commanding officer, the blue ribbon of Rifle shooting, the King's Prize, was won at Bisley by a member of the corps, Sergeant Hawkins. In that year the Colonel-in-Chief of the regiment, General Sir Ian Hamilton, arrived in Canada on a tour of inspection of the Overseas Forces of the Crown. He reviewed the regiment and expressed himself as well pleased. This visit was considered a great honour.

Early in the year 1914, the strength of the regiment was raised to a peace establishment of 867, rank and file, and the field training of the corps took place at Petawawa, where Lord Brooke had command of the Canadian forces in training. The regiment behaved well and showed evidence of the high standard of efficiency which it subsequently reached. The greatest enthusiasm prevailed, and the corps was in excellent form when the war was declared in August, 1914. It was the first to volunteer as a unit for Overseas service.

CHAPTER 3

The Newer Colonial Policy

"I suppose now that Great Britain has declared war on Germany, Canada will throw in her lot with the United States," so laughingly spoke an American friend that I met the day Great Britain declared war on Germany.

"Not a bit of it," I said. "Before the week is over you will hear the drums beating and see recruits foregathering here. Canada is at war as well as Great Britain."

"But won't you have difficulties with Quebec?"

"Nothing of the kind. Depend upon it, the last gun in favour of British connection in Canada will, if necessary, be fired by a French-Canadian. They marry young and may be a trifle slow in volunteering on that account. It requires a great effort for a man to tear himself away from a young, helpless wife and a large small family, but they come of good fighting stock, and when it comes to war, blood will tell."

"Well, you can depend on the Monroe-doctrine anyway."

"Yes, we believe in the Monroe-doctrine just the same as you do. We are going to fight for it on the Plains of Flanders."

"But you don't mean that Canada is going to take an active part in the war?"

"Certainly."

"Well, nobody ever thought you would."

In this he was expressing the traditional view of Colonial connection. At the time of the break with the American colonies, Turgot, the great French economist, coined a phrase which has been accepted by the chancelleries of Europe as a truism: "Colonies are like fruit, when they become ripe they drop from the parent stem."

When Germany decided to cross the Meuse into Belgium the Emperor had been assured by his foreign office that Great Britain would not take part in the war. There were the disturbing questions of Home Rule for Ireland, Socialism and anti-Militarism, and the Colonies had grown in wealth and population to such an extent that they were ready to drop from the parent stem if ever they would do so. Would Great Britain risk civil war at home and the loss of her Colonies abroad in order to vindicate her pledge given years before, to keep inviolate the frontiers of Belgium? The answer was the prompt declaration of war on Germany, the cessation of political warfare at home, abroad the splendid enthusiasm of the Colonies with offers of men and money.

Previous to the break with the American Colonies, Great Britain had adopted a colonial policy very much on what we would call Imperial lines. The Navigation Laws of Cromwell gave her virtually command of all trade by sea, protective tariffs and bounties built up inter-Imperial and home trade.

At the end of the Seven Years' War, the Empire, judged from the world's standard, was far greater than it is now. The Colonies were vaster and comparatively more powerful. The general impression now is that Britain's Colonies in America were in those days managed the same as Germany managed her African Colonies, that they were oppressed and had nothing to say about how they were governed and that the mother country played the part of a despot. Such was not the case. The constitutions of the American Provinces were most democratic, more so than many colonial constitutions of today. All the provinces in America possessed a parliament elected by the people, and three of them, Connecticut, Rhode Island and Massachusetts, elected an upper House or Senate. Rhode Island and Connecticut elected their own Governors, and these two provinces, along with Maryland, could enact laws without the veto or interference of British legislators or the Crown.

In 1762 Great Britain had 337,000 men under arms, and of these over 25,000 were Colonials from America. Fifteen thousand New England seamen volunteered for the Spanish War, and during the Seven Years' War the Colonials manned over 400 privateers or ships of war, and the State of Pennsylvania spent £440,000, a great sum of money in those days, for military purposes.

With the Colonies so loyal and so willing to assist Great Britain in time of trouble and danger, how was it that in a decade the Empire was shattered and the major portion of the Colonies were busy building up a nation of their own? At this distance of time it is still hard to view the question dispassionately.

Who was responsible for this great criminal folly?

Was it some individual?

Was it the old Colonial policy?

Or, was it petty parish politics?

The trend of political thought in the Colonies has generally been the antithesis of political thought in Great Britain. Colonial thought has always been an enigma to the British. Of recent years it has been both disturbing and confusing. The Colonial, who, with his own eyes, within the span of a few years in his own country, views the transition of a bit of landscape from barbarism to civilization, the hunter giving way to the shepherd, the herder to the farmer, cities and towns springing up over night with factories and banking established in a few months, seldom arrives at the same political conclusion as the theorist who tries to conjure up the genesis of political economy from books and musty documents. His is the school of hard experience, which teaches lessons that fine-spun theories cannot upset. It is so with his Colonial theories of economics and government. The dead weight of tradition does not hang around his neck where State affairs are concerned and precedent only counts when it is right and just.

Governor Pownall, of New Jersey, immediately previous to the time of the Revolutionary war, wrote a book, entitled: *The Administration of the British Colonies*. In this work he pointed out the necessity of closer political union between the Colonies and the mother country; in fact, he outlined an Imperial constitution. He pointed out that there had always existed two lines of thought among English-speaking people. One favoured unity, centralization, Imperialism, the other disunion, or individualism, claiming that in the absolute independence of each small unit of the Empire rested liberty and freedom. This struggle is still on.

Had Pitt followed up his idea of uniting the Colonies into a Dominion, or into an even greater union such as he was pressed then to do, the American Revolution would in all probability have been averted.

But Pitt's energies were turned to the war then being carried on in Germany, and the Colonies were for the time-being neglected with disastrous results.

The historical philosophers of modern Germany cherished the delusion that history would repeat itself.

Ever since the American Revolution, Great Britain had adopted a

Captain R. Clifford Darling, Adjutant

different Colonial policy from the policy of Pitt. The navigation laws had been repealed, protection and bounties had been withdrawn, the doctrine of *laisser faire* prevailed.

When the American Colonies secured their independence, each colony of the thirteen was a helpless independent unit. They had united for the war of Independence, but the union was one of sentiment, there was no constitution, no common ground on which they could unite for political action. Fortunately, the war had produced such wise patriotic men as Washington, Franklin and Hamilton, and through their efforts a political union of the Colonies was accomplished. It took the better part of ten years to do this. It was part of the policy of reconstruction. Later on, the Colonies in Canada followed suit. They united under a constitution which, at the same time, guaranteed the autonomy of the provinces within and solidarity in external affairs. Australia and South Africa followed suit. The policy of Imperial unity had been gathering force and momentum, but when the great war came it had not yet reached that point where the pressing of a button would set machinery at work which would marshal all the financial, mechanical, political and military resources of the Empire. That day will come.

The example of the Colonies in rallying immediately to the aid of the mother country proved the saying that after all it is the horse, not the harness, that pulls the load. The Imperial harness is an aggregation of shreds and patches, not yet even a conception, but when the time of trial came, the Imperial spirit rose superior to all obstacles, surprising the German Emperor and the whole world.

In vain were the seeds of sedition sown in various parts of the Empire and in neutral countries.

An old Irish woman voiced the Home Rule sentiment abroad thus: "The English have not used the Irish right, but we will forget that for the moment, for we will never be able to lift our heads again in New York if we let the Germans bate us."

The most preposterous thing in connection with the German program was the propaganda of anti-militarism preached among the British people, and the most amazing thing was that the British were so lacking in self-respect that they would listen to such doctrines. A noble and unsullied past has given the British people the right to be in the highest sense a military nation. For a century the sun has never risen, but its rays have fallen on the face of a Briton who has died for liberty. Wherever Britain has been compelled to draw the sword there has followed freedom and peace. There is the record of India, Canada, of Egypt and of South Africa to point to. No person unless steeped to the eye-brows in pro-Germanism can, in the face of that record, assert that Great Britain ever used her military power to oppress the weak, or tyrannize over the people she, of necessity, had to conquer. Why then should Britain be asked to disarm and turn over the business of maintaining the world's peace to the Hun and the Turk? To preach anti-militarism to a British people is to insult their intelligence.

Britain alone of all nations has brought peace with her sword. The interests of Christianity, of humanity and of civilization demand that she be always a great military power. Had she not listened to the pro-German pleas of the so-called anti-militarists, Austria-Germany would not have dared to dream of conquering the world. Much suffering would have been avoided, and life and treasure would have been saved. This war is fairly laid at the door of those who practised and preached anti-militarism in the British Empire. If Great Britain had possessed a national army of half a million men in 1913, there would have been no war.

Somebody has to police the world and the best policeman is the man who wears khaki and speaks the English tongue.

Chapter 4

The Call to Arms

In the War of 1870, the Germans advanced across the Rhine on the frontier of France. The independent State of Luxemburg and the Kingdom of Belgium were not disturbed. The Germans at that time respected the neutrality of these countries. They kept the treaties that had been made years before, guaranteeing these countries from invasion in case of war. Bismarck, although a man of "blood" and "iron," as a rule, respected treaties.

With the French frontier bristling with guns, fortresses and entrenchments that had been deliberately prepared in advance, the Germans, in 1914, stood a good chance of being beaten in the first round if they had attacked the eastern frontier of France on the declaration of war. Behind a ring of entrenchments the French Generals could deliberately mass their armies, and the battle front could be narrowed to such an extent that the preponderance of numbers which the Germans could put in the field could not count.

For some years, however, German military writers had been advocating that the German army of invasion should march through Belgium and Luxemburg. It was known that the latter country could not object, but with Belgium it was different. The Belgians had been warned, and were busy arming, under the leadership of their ruler, who was universally beloved. The Belgians are a proud people, and since the days of Caesar they had on numerous occasions hurled the invading Germans back and held their homes and frontiers inviolate. The Germans, however, imagined, that once their vast armies crossed the Meuse and began a march on Namur and Charleroi, the martial ardour of the Belgians would cool and that beyond a formal protest, no resistance would be offered.

As France and Belgium had been on terms of friendship for many years, the Franco-Belgian frontier had not been protected by fortresses. The German frontier of Belgium, however, had been fortified some years before under the direction of a famous Belgian engineer, named Brailmont, who was the successor of other eminent military Belgian engineers, such as Vauban, who had taught the art of fortification to a previous age.

On August 2nd, 1914, the Germans declared war on France, and the First field army of Austro-Germans crossed the Meuse near Liege. For two weeks the Germans delayed before Liege, expecting that the French would send several armies into Belgium and thus weaken the forces before Metz. The French generals refused the bait, and were ready when the German main army struck along the old road from Metz to Paris. The Germans were defeated and left 40,000 dead on the battlefield. This was the greatest battle in the history of the world.

Great Britain declared war on Germany for violating the neutrality of Belgium and the war feeling in Canada became intense. It was realized that Canada must participate. The only question was what form aid would take.

For a number of years the question of the "German Peril" had been discussed, but a great many people imagined that the anti-German talk was a mild form of Jingoism. It soon became known that Great Britain would accept the defence of the sea as her share of the war, and that only a small field army would be sent abroad. The great question for a few days was, would Canada be allowed to send a contingent to serve with the Allies? Again, as in the case of the South African war, the armchair critics were in favour of drafting a number of Canadians to serve with the British regiments. Sir Robert Borden, however, was not long in making it known that a contingent of Canadians would be enlisted and that they would serve abroad as a unit, under their own officers. Then there was much rejoicing.

The next question that arose was whether the unit was to be composed of regiments of militia, drafts from militia regiments, or recruits from outside the militia. The Minister of Militia and Defence promptly announced that he would accept battalions or units from Militia regiments and that the men would serve under their own officers. This was highly satisfactory.

The guiding hand of his Royal Highness the Duke of Connaught, Governor-General, the first soldier of Europe, was seen everywhere, at the beginning and throughout the war. It was a fortunate matter for Canada that he was Governor-General at the time.

To the Prime Minister, Sir Robert Borden, was due the splendid response to the call to arms of the Canadian people. He put duty before public applause of petty politics like a true Canadian. Future generations will do full credit to his unselfishness.

Sir Wilfrid Laurier, the leader of the Opposition, brushing aside all partisanship, earnestly seconded the efforts of the Government. His splendid patriotism never rose to greater heights than in this trying time.

A meeting of the 48th Highlanders was immediately called at the Officers' quarters, and they were asked to say whether they desired the regiment to go as a complete battalion. The first man to say "yes" was the regimental surgeon, Major MacKenzie, whose subsequent services at Flanders were of great value. Other officers tendered their services and it was seen at once that there would be plenty of officers; as for the men, numbers were available, and it was decided then and there that the regiment would go as a unit. Some officers could not see their way to go. Business and family ties prevented them. Happy is that militia regiment whose senior officers are at all times ready to sacrifice their business as well as their lives in the service of the country.

It was my duty as the Commanding Officer to see the Minister of Militia at once and tender the services of the 48th Highlanders as a unit. Those were strenuous days for the Minister. At Ottawa I found him surrounded by his staff, with sleeves rolled up, dealing with heaps of correspondence and a long row of people outside in the ante-room waiting to see him. I asked him if he would take the Regiment, kilts and all, and he promptly said he would, that in a few hours orders would be issued for the Militia to enlist for foreign service and that a great camp of instruction would be formed at Valcartier, where they would all be prepared for overseas service. In the meantime, the units enlisting or volunteering would be drilled at local Headquarters, and the 48th and the Toronto units would go into camp at Long Branch for a few weeks. The announcement was made in the press that the 48th had volunteered, under my command, and on my return I ordered a parade of the regiment on Friday, August 8th, to start work for overseas and open recruit classes.

On Friday evening, the battalion paraded nine hundred and fifty-three strong. The great armories were thronged with people and hundreds had to be refused permission to enter. The people were filled with the war spirit and the excitement was intense. The two bands were on hand, the brass with forty-five musicians and the pipes with twenty pipers. The battalion marched through the streets, and all along the line of march for over a mile the streets were so thronged with a cheering crowd that it was almost impossible for the men in fours to march through. Thousands of flags waved and the people were much excited. Someone for a joke waved the German flag at the head of the regiment and in a moment it was torn from his hand and trampled to pieces by the crowd. The joker had a narrow escape with his life. That night, three hundred and fifty-five recruits joined for overseas service. Many men in the regiment had served for years and in some instances father and son stood side by side in the ranks.

It was felt it would not be fair to take many men of middle age along. This was going to be a long war and required young men, and the age limit was put at thirty years, the height at five feet eight inches and the chest measurement at thirty-eight inches. These were the limits given to the recruiting sergeants, and with lots of men offering, we knew that we would have no difficulty in getting all we required.

Orders for the mobilization, on the 15th of August, of the Canadian Militia, were issued. Instructions for the Toronto Corps to go into training at Long Branch were also given and I was instructed that whilst at Long Branch I would have to officiate as Brigadier. On the 17th of August the 48th Highlanders paraded at the armories and, headed by the pipers playing "*We will take the High Road*," they marched to the Union Station and entrained for Long Branch Camp.

Long Branch is located about twelve miles west of the City of Toronto. Here there is an excellent Rifle Range and ample accommodation for four or five thousand men. Major Sweny, a Canadian officer in the British Army, who was attached to the Canadian instructional staff, and Major Dixon, acted as Brigade staff officers, and very soon the camp was in running order.

The first night the battalion spent in camp there was a terrible thunder-storm, one of the worst in years. It was our first night on active service and no doubt many wondered if this presaged the future of the "Red Watch" in Flanders.

There was not much sleep for the Commanding Officer that night. What with the terrific storm which lit up the landscape as light as day, and the newly-acquired responsibility of drilling and disciplining a battalion of raw troops for the war, the outlook spelt much hard work. Drilling a battalion of Militia once a week was fun compared with such work, for besides the foot and arm drill there was the field training, and worst of all, the training of the men and non-commissioned officers in the duties of a soldier in quarters and in the field. The material was of the very best quality, comprising college men, business men, and men associated with the industrial life of the country. The responsibility of its form and future rested on its commanding officer. The officers and non-commissioned officers had to be trained from the beginning. In the British army the tradition of the duties of officers and non-commissioned officers,—the interior economy of the regiment—descends from generation to generation as unwritten laws or rules.

Certain things are done in a certain way, often differently from other corps, in memory of some event in the history of the regiment. We had no standing orders and no regimental traditions. In a regular regiment a non-com. learns how to "carry on" his work from practical experience and seeing other non-coms. doing their work. Long before he becomes a "duty" non-com., he knows what to do. In our case these duties would have to be taught by means of lectures. This would be difficult. The first morning we were in camp, classes for the officers and non-commissioned officers were started. The adjutant, Captain Darling, and Lieutenant Warren, who was made assistant adjutant, rendered very valuable services at this juncture, as did also Sergeant-Major Grant, Sergeant Alex. Sinclair, who was given a commission, and Sergeant Radcliffe, who subsequently became a Company Commander in one of the battalions of the Staffordshire regiment, and was wounded at the Dardanelles. The men were turned over for musketry instruction to Captain McGregor. Fortunately, we had several good musketry instructors, among them Sergeant Hawkins, winner of the King's prize at Bisley, Sergeant Graham and Sergeant Williams, bayonet instructor.

All young men who desired to qualify as non-coms. and instructors were asked to join these classes, and they responded in large numbers. They became highly efficient, and when we went to England, quite a few transferred to the New Army as instructional officers and rose very rapidly in the British service.

The organization and discipline of the Light Division in the Peninsular War, trained by Sir John Moore and General Crauford, has always been noted as a model for future armies. It was decided to follow as closely as possible this system, and the Standing Orders of the Light Division, that served with such distinction under the Duke of Wellington in Spain, Portugal and France, became the basis of the standing orders of our new Highland Battalion. The instructional classes, once established, ran on very smoothly. Great stress was laid upon acquiring a good clear, decisive and loud word of command. There is nothing that will galvanize a Highland Battalion into action like a sharp word of command with the "rs" well sounded.

The duties of Brigadier at Long Branch did not prove as onerous as expected, as the units that went out for training there were officered by experienced instructors who were accustomed to training camps at Niagara, so the work of hammering the various troops into shape proceeded very rapidly. The anti-militarists, however, were very busy and persisted in anonymously calling me up by telephone and pointing out to me what a terrible thing it was to take up arms against the *Kaiser* and to take so many fine men off with me to the war. Others wrote annoying anonymous letters calling down the wrath of Heaven on my head for trying to mix Canada in the war, whilst a third faction suffering from the Celtic gift of second sight described how mysterious falling stars and meteors flashing across the sky at night, and other portents, presaged dire disaster to the British arms in the war, and more particularly to the 48th Highlanders.

Staff officers, Majors Dixon and Sweny, were both soon called to Valcartier to help organize the first contingent. Later, Major Sweny left for England to join his regiment, which had been ordered to the Front. Had Major Sweny remained in Canada he no doubt would have been given a command high up on the staff, and very rapid promotion, but he chose to play the manlier part, and joined his own regiment in England when called. The war gave him well deserved promotion.

On August the 18th, the House of Commons met in Ottawa and the Speech from the Throne was read by His Royal Highness the Duke of Connaught, khaki being the uniform of the military men present. A short visit to Ottawa to say goodbye to colleagues in the House of Commons, a brief trip to Collingwood in my constituency to lay the corner stone of a new post-office building, and I was back again at the work of preparing for Flanders. The soldiers were hardly settled in camp at Long Branch, when orders were given that every man would have to be inoculated against typhoid, and the process began on a Saturday. The men lined up cheerfully and let the regimental surgeon, Major MacKenzie, jab a needle and the serum into their arms.

The following Sunday there was a Church parade. The sermon was preached by Rev. Major Crawford Brown, the regimental Chaplain. The various units in camp paraded at a small natural amphitheatre near the lines. Many people motored out from Toronto to attend the service. The band of the regiment, under Lieut. John Slatter, came out and supplied the music for the service. The day was beautifully bright and a trifle warm. After the sermon had commenced, many of the men began to feel the effects of the serum and a few toppled over, and for the first time the new battalion heard the call of "stretcher bearer." The men were all ordered to sit down. The effect of the inoculation is to make one have real typhoid for a few hours, after that there is a quick recovery, and the absence of typhoid among the men subsequently spoke volumes for the efficacy of the preventative.

Every evening the battalion had a camp fire and "sing-song," and hundreds of people came out from Toronto to join in the fun, which consisted of band music, choruses and Highland dancing. The days passed very pleasantly and quickly. On August 27th, orders arrived for the battalion to go to Valcartier to join the contingent being formed there for overseas service, and an advance party left for that camp at once. The date for the departure of the battalion was fixed for Saturday, August 29th. That was to be the first march on the road to Flanders.

Chapter 5

Organizing Imperial Battalions

The work of organizing and equipping the Canadian Imperial Battalions for overseas service was taken up with great vigour by the Minister of Militia, Major-General Sir Sam Hughes, and the officers of his department.

Owing to the influence of the churches the best class of youth in the country came forward in large numbers. The clergy appealed to the athletes that had been trained in the gymnasiums of the Y.M.C.A., and the ranks soon contained a large sprinkling of Canadian lacrosse and hockey players. It was afterwards to be shown that the manly and strenuous native Canadian sports, lacrosse and hockey, practised by almost every boy in the country from the time he is able to walk, are of a character admirably suited to produce bold and courageous soldiers. Boys who have been accustomed to handle lacrosse and hockey sticks, develop arm and shoulder muscles that make the carrying and use of the rifle easy. Firing for hours during a hot and sustained engagement does not fatigue nor exhaust them as it otherwise would.

In the rough work of the bayonet charge, they keep their heads, and have confidence in their ability at close quarters to overcome their antagonist. They do not dread a blow or a bayonet, for they have been accustomed to roughing it all their lives. When it comes to "cold steel," it is the man who has the courage and confidence in himself that wins, for nineteen times out of twenty the other man is dominated before blades are crossed, and at once either throws up his hands or runs.

The moral character and influence of these men permeated the first contingent, with the result that never since the days of Cromwell's New Army did the Empire possess a more athletic, courageous or God-fearing army than the First Canadian Contingent. The work of carving the name of "Canada" in the annals of the war was entrusted to the hands of these clean, sober, religious, athletic young men. How they kept this trust history in future ages will tell in letters of gold. Many clergymen of various denominations who had been foremost in preaching pacifism, upon hearing of the ruthless invasion of Belgium, realized the hollow sham of German culture, and saw the Hun in his true light. With the Empire plunged into a great war, it was not a time to consider the ancient and pampered ideas of consistency. Until the German was destroyed there could be no peace of any kind. To their eternal credit, be it said, they flung themselves whole-heartedly into the cause, and none equalled them in preaching resistance, recruiting and working night and day for the Red Cross Society and various other patriotic and national organizations.

With such vast numbers of men coming forward there was a good deal of discussion as to who should be first taken, the arguments being very much in favour of the veterans or "ribbon" men who had seen service in previous campaigns. About two thousand of the men who had gone from Canada to the South African war were still living, and a great many veterans from the Old Country had immigrated to Canada, and with few exceptions they unhesitatingly offered their services. If they passed the surgeon they were taken on, and afterwards they did good service. They were especially numerous in the Princess Pats, the British Columbian and Western Regiments. These men, although foreign born, prided themselves on being "Canadians." They increased, however, the percentage of those in the first contingent born outside of Canada, but the officers of the first contingent almost to a man were Canadians.

On Saturday, August 29th, 1914, our Battalion paraded early in the morning and bade farewell to Long Branch Camp. The night before we left we had a "sing-song" or concert. Arrangements had been made for us to take cars for Toronto in the morning and rendezvous at the armories during the noon-hour, when the men would be allowed to see their friends or sweethearts. We entrained safely and made a brave show as we marched up Queen Street to the armories, the pipes playing "*Highland Laddie.*" Shortly after one o'clock the people began to gather and they soon filled the drill hall. There was very little gloom and everybody was cheerful.

As we fell in, the Lieutenant-Governor, Sir John Gibson, and Lady Gibson, arrived and they spoke to me of their son, Lieutenant Frank Gibson, who was one of my officers, expressing their pleasure at his being an officer of the corps. A gallant young soldier he was, indeed; a graduate of the Royal Military College, and always wearing a pleasant smile. Other parents spoke of their sons to me. Some of the older officers of the garrison were afraid that my officers were too young and that we did not have enough officers of mature years, but experience was to show that age does not give a monopoly of courage or bravery, nor of fortitude and good judgment.

Memorable addresses were delivered by the Lieutenant-Governor, the Mayor of the City, Mr. Hocken, and by the Chaplain Major, the Rev. Crawford Brown. His excellent address was full of comfort and cheer for the men. He told them it was a great honour to be permitted to go to the front and that their country would always esteem them and owe them a debt of gratitude. The armories rang with cheers as the pipes struck up the war tune, "*Well take the High Road,*" and the battalion swung out of the doors and into the drizzling rain that was falling, but in spite of which, thousands of people lined the streets. Every step we took the excitement became more intense, and by the time we reached the Don Station where we were to entrain for Valcartier, almost all semblance of order was gone from the ranks.

Young ladies carried the men's rifles, others decorated them with flowers, others clung to their arms and the sidewalks were a mass of excited cheering humanity. Friends and relations came from all over the Province of Ontario to see the regiment off for the front. I have seen many crowds in my life, and excited ones at that, but the crowd that covered the Don Bridge above the station and every available vantage point and avenue that led to our train that afternoon was by long odds the largest. It was estimated that 100,000 gathered to see us off. The farewell the people gave us was very touching. There were no tears, no wailing, but cheers, earnestness and good will, and a hearty send-off. In spite of the crowd the men found their way to their respective cars, and we pulled out of the station on the second lap of our journey to the front, on time.

Lieutenant Barwick acted as transport officer and the parade state showed 970 men and officers.

We had an excellent run on the Canadian Northern Railway to Quebec, but lost a little time there and were late in reaching Valcartier. The men had their blankets, rifles, and equipment complete with them. They were fitted out ready for the field with everything but ammunition.

When we arrived at Valcartier it was still raining, but the troops already there turned out and lined the roadway to cheer and see us march in. The Minister of Militia met us at the station, together with Lt.-Colonel Murphy of Ottawa, and guides led us to the lines where we were to be quartered for the night.

Nature has done much to adorn Valcartier and every mile along the road from Quebec to this beautiful valley is rich in historic associations. First, there is the St. Charles River, whose shallows and mud flats foiled General Wolfe in his first assault upon Quebec. A few miles along we came near to the ruins of the famous Chateau Noir or Hermitage of Intendant Bigot, made famous in story by Kirby in *Le Chien D'Or*; by Sir Gilbert Parker in *The Seats of the Mighty*; by W.D. Howells and by Joseph Marinette. Only a heap of ruins are left. The famous maze is gone, chopped into firewood, no doubt. Still nightly the spirit of Caroline, according to local traditions, haunts the spot where she was murdered by her jealous rival, Madame Pean. Further on, there is the village of Loretto where hundreds of years ago the first mission to the Indians was established in Canada. Here are living today the last of that mighty Indian tribe, the Hurons, who in the beginning cast in their lot with the French settlers, and paid for it later by being annihilated by the fierce Iroquois, the Allies of the British. For over two hundred years, since 1697, this remnant have lived in security within the sound of Loretto Falls, and worshipped for over one hundred and fifty years in the Mission Church of Loretto, which is a replica of the Santa Casa of Loretto and contains a copy of the Loretto figure of the Virgin.

Further on, the road leads to where, through a deep gash in the mighty Laurentian Mountains, the Jacques Cartier River makes its troubled way to the broad St. Lawrence. There, in a beautiful wide valley, amid high mountains rising in graceful terraces from the river and overlooking the St. Lawrence, about one hundred years ago, a number of veterans that had followed Wellington to Waterloo formed a settlement, and beat their swords into ploughshares. They sleep now in the village churchyard, unmindful of drum or trumpet. Their descendents lived there only yesterday, but now their lands had been bought out to provide the grounds for Valcartier Camp.

The outlook for us was not very inviting after the clean camps pitched in the green fields at Long Branch, but the department had done wonders during the time at its disposal. In less than three weeks a swamp had been cleared up, streets laid out with water mains, and even in some places sidewalks were laid. Mount Roby resounded to

OFFICERS OF THE 48TH HIGHLANDERS

From Left to Right—Top Row: Lt. J.A.M. Livingstone, (W); Lt. W.P. Malone; Lt. L.V. Jones, (G.P.); Lt. H.M. Scott, (G); Lt. G.P. Taylor, (K); Lt. R.H. Davidson; Lt. Q.T. Langmuir,(K); Hon. Capt. Moffat, Chaplain; Lt. H.A. Barwick,(G.P.); Lt. F.M. Gibson,(K).

Second Row Standing: Lt. A.J. Sinclair, (W); Lt. E.W. Bickle, (W.G.); Lt. A.E. Muir, (K); Lt. C.V. Fessenden, (G.P.); Lt. E.O. Bath, (G.P.); Lt. W.B. Lawson; Lt. F.H.C. MacDonald, (G.P.); Lt. F.J. Smith, (G.P.); Lt. J.A. Dansereau (W.G.); Lt. W.W. Jago, (W); Lt. W. Mavor, (G.W. 3); Lt. P.G. Campbell; Lt. P.P. Acland, M.C., (W).

Sitting Down; Capt. Frank Perry; Capt. A.M. Daniels, (K); Capt. C.H. Musgrove, (W); Capt. F.G.M. Alexander, M.C., (G.P.); Surgeon Major A.J. MacKenzie; Lt. Col. Wm. Hendrie, (Divisional Remount Officer); Col. J.A. Currie, M.P., (G), (Commanding Officer); Major W.R. Marshall, D.S.O., (K); Major J.E.K. Osborne, (W.G.P.): Capt. G.H. McLaren, (G.); Capt. A.R. McGregor, (K.); Capt. R.R. McKessock, (G.W.P.).

the shrill blast of the bugle, the rattle of rifles and the roar of field guns. The work of making a camp on a large scale was being carried out by hundreds of workmen, under foremen skilled in laying out cities and towns in Western Canada. The day after we arrived we were given our own lines and we settled down to hard work.

We transferred to our battalion enough men to fill our ranks up to the Imperial Establishment of 1,170 rank and file, including the base company and the transport. In order to accomplish this small detachments were taken from the 95th regiment, Cobalt and Sudbury, composed of miners and prospectors, also from the 31st Regiment, of Grey County, and the 13th Scottish Dragoons.

The 48th Highlanders, the "Red Watch," became the 15th Battalion of the First Canadian Division, C.E.F. It was subsequently, with all its officers, N.C.O.'s and men, granted the status of a Regular Imperial Regiment and given its name, "48th Highlanders," in the British Army List.

The regiment was turned over by the commanding officer, fully uniformed and equipped for the field as a regular Highland battalion without expense to the Crown except for rifles, bayonets and knapsacks, thus saving the country $25,000.

The camp was under the command of Colonel Victor Williams. It was no small task to clothe, equip and drill, ready for active warfare, some thirty-three thousand men. No liquor was allowed in the camp and there was very little difficulty with the men.

On Sunday, September 7th, the Division was reviewed by the Duke of Connaught. The battalions marched past in lines of half-battalions and made a very good showing.

Night and day the officers and men were hard at it. One of the greatest of many difficulties that were met was the selection of the officers and men for the contingent.

At first it was suggested that all the officers should be examined as to their fitness, and a Board was appointed to look them over, but in a few days this Board threw up its hands and the matter of selection was left to the commanding officers.

Many who had never served in the Militia were clamouring for commands and the Minister of Militia had some work on his hands. The contingent was formed into brigades and our battalion was put into the Highland Brigade, which consisted of our Regiment, the Royal Highlanders of Canada, Montreal, the Royal Regiment of Montreal, made up principally of French-Canadians, and the 16th battalion, subsequently called the Canadian Scottish, a composite corps consisting of Highland Companies from Victoria and Vancouver, B.C., from Winnipeg, Manitoba, and from Hamilton, Ontario. Each company wore a different tartan, but that did not interfere with their efficiency. Colonel Turner, V.C., was given the command.

On the 14th of September we were again reviewed by His Royal Highness, in the presence of General Crozier, an American officer. Rain to some extent interfered, as it had with the previous review. On Sunday, September 20th, Canon Scott, of Quebec, preached a field sermon to the Division. A platform had been erected and His Excellency and his staff took part in the service and subsequently reviewed the troops. The Prime Minister, Sir Robert Borden, arrived in the morning and called on our battalion. Our officers were all introduced. He was accompanied by Lady Borden. The transports were already beginning to gather in the St. Lawrence that were to carry the contingent to England. Our equipment was very nearly complete and enough drill had been given to make us fairly respectable. We all thought we were fit for the field. We learnt differently afterwards.

It is very strange how the idea seems to get hold of a man, the minute he gets into khaki uniform, that he is a fully-trained soldier. In Canada, for years, we had no regular soldiers, and the training generally was of a kind patterned after the South African War. Straw hats and overalls were worn by the infantry, and the irregular cavalry swagger was the fashion. It was fondly imagined that any Canadian who could shoot straight and who had a week's training could take his place in the ranks and would be just as good a soldier as a regular of the King's First Army. No sooner was a man in uniform than everybody began asking him the question "When are you going to the front?" assuming that was a question he could settle himself, and that he would be anything but in the way and a nuisance at the front, owing to his lack of discipline and training.

The public in this way made the men's and officers' lives very miserable. It was almost impossible to settle down to a hard course of training. Lord Kitchener had placed the period necessary for getting a man into shape as a soldier at six months. By great effort that period might be shortened, but from the experience we gained nine months would be nearer the mark. The training could be hurried by giving two months of foot and arm drill, two months' special training of the men in special units, such as signallers, stretcher bearers, machine gunners, bomb throwers, etc., and two months in hard field-training with lots of night work. But the press of the country was clamouring for us to go to the front, and public opinion said "hurry." The battalions were all organized and orders came for us to move on the 29th of September.

There was a slight drizzle of rain in the morning when we paraded for the march out. Our transport waggons had to move out early and march to Quebec, and it was a difficult job to get them started.

I had done everything in my power to suppress gambling and swearing among the men, and on several occasions when individuals were paraded before me for using bad language, I had reprimanded them and informed them that the use of strong language was always left to the officer commanding. This particular morning some choice words had to be used to get the transport moving. They moved, however, to the tick of the clock and Sergeant-Major Grant, with a grin on his face, suggested that from now on there would be no more swearing in the ranks, as everybody was quite satisfied with the Commanding officer's qualifications in that regard.

Again the pipes struck up "*We'll take the High Road,*" and after a march of about a mile and a half to a siding, we entrained in two sections for Quebec.

At Quebec we had not long to wait. The transport *Megantic*, one of the finest ships on the North Atlantic, was hauled up at the pier with long planks out to take our regiment on board. The horses and waggons were to go on a separate ship, although there was plenty of room for them on board. We were all glad to get away, for it was becoming monotonous having everybody we met asking "When are you going away?"

CHAPTER 6

The New Armada

The St. Lawrence River at Quebec presented a busy scene. Never since the days of the *tercentennial* of the discovery of the river by Jacques Cartier, when King George and the British fleet, headed by H.M.S. *The Indomitable,* were present, was there so much activity, or so many ships in the harbour. As soon as each transport was loaded it pulled away from the pier and dropped anchor in the stream. When all our troops were on board the *Megantic* we cast loose, pulled up the stream off Cape Diamond, and "dropped our hook," as a landsman in the ranks was heard to remark. The hotels and boarding houses of the City were filled with friends of the men who had come on excursions to bid the soldiers goodbye. The city was full of life and activity and brilliantly lighted up and the scene at night was very beautiful.

Old Cape Diamond wearing its crown and sparkling with thousands of electric lights looked its name. In its shadow on the evening before he climbed the heights at Ainse d'Fulon Cove, now dim and silent in the distance, to win the immortal battle of the Plains of Abraham, General Wolfe had recited Gray's *Elegy* and unconsciously the prophetic words *The Paths of Glory lead but to the Grave* arose in the mind. In these shadows Wolfe had brooded over those plans which on a succeeding morrow were to mature and lead to three of the greatest epochs in the history of the world—the fall of Quebec, which placed in the hands of Britannia the trident of the world's naval supremacy, destroying the foundations of the ancient regime of France, and laying the corner stone of the great American Republic.

Someone among the crew was humming the refrain of the old anchor-hoisting song, "*Le Chien d'Or*—I love your Daughter;" a melody that has haunted the River St. Lawrence since the day when his comrades forcibly carried off Admiral Nelson, then a "middy," from the wiles and fascinations of the daughter of the landlord of "*Le Chien d'Or*."

The distant tramp of battalions, the rumble of battery after battery as they marched through the crooked streets, came faintly from the shore. The slumbers of a hundred years of peace had been rudely broken. Europe was ablaze. The hands of the clock of civilization had been turned back a century. The Empire was again threatened and Canada was at war.

We lay in the river off Quebec from Saturday night until Tuesday evening, when we pulled up to the pier again and took on fresh water. The Captain had asked me if the bar was to be opened. I said, "No, close it up," which he did most cheerfully, remarking that it was the first time in twenty-seven years that the White Star line had sailed a "dry ship." He had thought he had plenty of water to take us to England, but after three days' experience with a lot of dry Highlanders he came to the conclusion he was mistaken, so he pulled up alongside of the dock again, and a miserable stream of water trickled slowly into the tanks, all afternoon and evening.

Colonel Penhale of the Divisional Ammunition Column was on board and entitled to seniority. I was very glad to be rid of the responsibility of ship management, with its round of inspections at all hours and in all weathers.

We had no sooner got settled on board than I asked the captain to give us a plan of his lifeboat stations so that the men could assemble if necessary, without any confusion, at their posts at the lifeboats in the shortest possible time. I got this plan and then the trouble began. The orderly room began to attach the men to their stations by lists and I waited patiently for a day and there was still nothing but confusion, showing how difficult it is for an office to run a gang of men, something I had learned long ago. The adjutant said "Rush," and every time a list was made out it was found that some names were missing and then fresh lists had to be made over again. Finally I took the sketch of the ship, showing the position of the boats, called the captains of the companies and divided up the boat space among them, and told them to first place the men of their companies at the different stations with their life belts on, call the rolls of each boat squad, then dismiss them, and that in an hour or so I was going to "beat" the troops "to quarters."

In an hour I caused the alarm bugle to sound and there was some scrambling, but I inspected the decks and found every man at his post with his life-belt on. The first time it took twenty-five minutes. We did this turn three times, so that the men soon knew the direct road from their berths to the lifeboats and were able to get into position in ten minutes, which is considered very good.

A time table of physical drill was prepared and carried out every morning and evening. From 9 to 10.30 the right half battalion practised first twenty minutes' run round the deck, then the balance of the time they spent at physical drill. This was repeated again in the afternoon, and the men were all fit when we landed. Officers and all had to go the round.

We pulled out of Quebec on Wednesday night at 10.15 and very soon everybody settled down to sleep. The night was dark and still as we floated down past Cape Diamond. We had a splendid ship, and every day our admiration of her increased. Even if there was a gale outside, the ship was as steady as a church. Every three men had a room and there was a berth for each one. They lived like millionaires. As for the officers and sergeants they had every comfort.

Our captain was a very fine man by the name of James. He was an Englishman from Liverpool, with an aristocratic air, but quite modest, a gentleman and a seaman every inch of him.

Finally, we pulled into the stream and departed for parts unknown. We had a beautiful trip down the St. Lawrence. The sun was shining next day, and on the shore we could see the outlines of the French-Canadian villages, the long narrow farms and big churches. As we neared Gaspe Peninsula the mountains in the distant background were covered with snow. One by one we overhauled the steamers that left before us. In the evening we were off Flame Point, having dropped our pilot. At Flame Point they burned blue rockets or flares on the shore at dusk to give us a send-off. Gradually we swung around Gaspe Peninsula as dusk closed in. It was then we learned that sealed orders had been given the captain to rendezvous at Gaspe Basin. Soon we came in sight of the lights that mark the entrance to this harbour. The captain had his sounding-line going, and I was on the upper deck with the signallers.

Pretty soon we made out the outlines of a small ship shrouded in darkness. We turned our signalling lamp on her and asked her name. In a moment came the answer "British Warship, don't go into the harbour until daylight." The captain could not find bottom with his anchor with one hundred fathoms of chain out, so he had to stay outside, backing and going ahead, all night. We all went to bed feeling secure, with that cruiser lying a short distance away. When I woke up in the morning the bugles were sounding the "Officers' Call" to breakfast. I looked out of my cabin window and after dressing, hastily scrambled on deck. The sight in Gaspe Basin was one never to be forgotten. Twenty-eight transports were swinging at anchor, many of them the flower of the North Atlantic merchant fleet. The ship we were on was the finest of the White Star Line, the *Megantic*. Some distance away was her sister ship the *Laurentic*, also the *Franconia*, the *Allonia*, the *Royal* George, and the *Royal Edward*, all first-class ships. The weather was bright, clear and warm, and the water of the Basin as smooth as oil.

Some of our officers got letters before they left Quebec, stating that on the previous Sunday prayers had been offered up in the churches for the safety of the contingent, which was supposed to be at sea, while it was riding quietly at anchor in Quebec harbour. We were waiting for the last of the transports to come before we left. About ten o'clock I was on the bridge, when I heard cheering, and someone calling my name. I ran down the deck, and saw the Minister of Militia, who had come on alongside on a tug. He was going the rounds of the fleet. He spent a day among the ships, and there was a good deal of talk about his going on board one of the transports, but he did not. We all expected to see him waiting for us when we landed in England. The day passed quietly.

No one was allowed ashore. The ship's gig went down to see some of the other ships of the White Star fleet and we got some of our belated mail. On Saturday we were to sail with the ebb tide. All the transports had come in and there was assembled in Gaspe Basin the greatest Armada that ever set sail for British shores. We were going in this great Armada to assist the Mother Country to maintain the *Pax Britannicum*. There were over twenty-five thousand men in thirty-one transports. They were anchored in the harbour in lines, and as the tide rose and fell they shifted about, now heading one way, and after the lapse of a few hours, in another direction. The Government had kindly issued to the officers Colt automatic pistols and high power field glasses. My glasses were of a very high power, and I could pick out the figures of the women and men working about the farm houses five miles away. The British warships in the basin were obsolete small cruisers of slow speed, the *Diana*, the *Eclipse*, the *Talbot* and the *Charybdis*. The latter was the flagship of the Admiral.

We looked upon these ships with a good deal of apprehension. The *Dresden* or *Karlsruhe*, the German ships in the Atlantic, would only have a mouthful in any one of them, in fact in the whole four. They all anchored apart in a separate part of the harbour, and the signaller on the Admiral's ship amused himself by signalling, "Is your bar open?" "How is the Scotch?" Our men answered back in kind. This mosquito fleet appeared to have a big job on its hands to convoy this Armada across. Presently a naval "gent," or "hossifer" as some of the crew called him, came aboard, and gave the captain his secret instructions, that is, the formation of the convoy, and a rendezvous for each day in case the convoy was scattered by fog, storm or other cause. The captain said we were to sail at three o'clock, in three columns, right, centre and left line, with some ten ships in each line.

The speed was to be ten knots. We were to lead the left line, with H.M.S. *Eclipse* four cable lengths ahead. The *Charybdis* was to lead the centre, and the *Diana* the left of the line, while the *Talbot* acted as a rear guard. Our ship started out first. The captain of the *Eclipse* sent the height of his mast back to our captain and we kept the distance constantly by the officer of the deck reading off the proper angle with the sextant. In and out our line threaded, and then began to zigzag, until by-and-bye we were out of sight of Gaspe Cape and all three lines were abreast.

On the afternoon of the last day before we left a black gas boat filled with people came away from the shore. I scanned them carefully with my glasses. They came within a couple of hundred yards of our ship and after halting, went past, looking over the rest of the fleet. The crew were men and women, evidently fisherfolk, all except one woman, who sat huddled in the stern. She looked very much like a German and under her rough coat she had a fine blouse and good clothes. I had my suspicions and could not help thinking she was either a newspaper woman or a German spy. I was surprised to find that when I mentioned this boat to the captain at the dinner table, he said she had a suspicious passenger on board, like a "German woman."

He was some observer, was Captain James, R.N.R. He said "My word, we had one like her on board the last passage over. I set sail north for Greenland, keeping out of the way and coming in by Belle Isle. This woman had a basket on her arm when she came on board. I noticed her basket, and the pigeons in it soon found their way to the pot. I took them from her. She raised a storm, but I did not want any carrier pigeons on board. They made good pie."

Now I should say a word about this country before we leave it. The Basin where we rendezvoused was beautiful and well protected.

A number of fishing boats flew white sails and proclaimed the principal industry of the villagers. French-Canadians reside on the shore. The most prominent objects on the horizon were the great churches that have the customary gilded spire and the clusters of white cottages about them. The shore rises steeply and the farms taper back into the forests that crown the hills of the background, which rise fully one thousand feet above the sea. On our left hand as we left the Basin were huge clay or sandstone cliffs cut away by the fierce swells of the Gulf. A lighthouse crowned the Point, with a flag staff from which a Union Jack stood out in the wind as stiff as a board. On the left there were masses of rock to mark the shore line, and several small islands. In one place we could plainly see an arched rock called "Pierced Rock," where the sea passed below a natural bridge.

The moon came up brightly as we sailed out into the Gulf. By-and-bye clouds fleeced about it and formed a peculiar halo resembling a cross. We took that for a good omen. We were speculating whether we were to go by Belle Isle or Cape Ray, but about nine o'clock the three lines set their course southeast and then we knew we were to take the southern route. The weather was all that could be desired, and the water as smooth as a mill pond. It was slightly cool, as the breezes always are from Newfoundland. In the morning we could see that ancient Colony, Cape Ray, with its lighthouse and wireless station. We had wireless on board, but were not allowed to use it except to intercept messages.

When the captain took his observation at noon, October 4th, we were in Lat. N. 47° 36', Long. W. 59° 51'. On a chart at the main companion way each day's run was recorded with the latitude and longitude. We had what they called north-easterly gales and fine weather. Along about noon we caught a glimpse of Cape Breton in the distance. Nothing occurred all day. It was cloudy to the north and west and clear to the south, with the sun shining. We had started a dry canteen when we left Quebec, and it was doing a land office business. No drinks of an intoxicating nature were sold on board.

When the captain took his observation we had only sailed 190 miles from Gaspe. The next day was fine. In the morning we saw a ship loom up on our left and the cruiser flew out to "speak" her. Evidently she was all right, *The Bruce*, bound from Newfoundland to Sydney. When she saw us first she started to run away, for the sight of our Armada was a very impressive one. The chase lasted only a short time when she discovered we were friends. Then in a very strange way a large grey battleship slid in from the horizon on our left and was etched against the bright sky. Volumes of smoke rose from her large funnels and two big masts with fighting tops made her look quite formidable. She had been out of sight just beyond the horizon all the time. We found that she was H.M.S. *Glory*, a dreadnought. It felt very comfortable to have her there, speed twenty-three knots and four twelve-inch guns.

Along in the afternoon two whales spouting water came along and had a look at the fleet. They kept with us for some time but presently got tired.

At noon on the 5th, we were in Lat. 46° 17', Long. 35° 03', having sailed 213 miles in the 24 hours. The transport *Monmouth* had been giving us trouble, by constantly dropping back. The next day we would be out of sight of Newfoundland, and we wondered what weather we would get. The men were kept busy drilling and exercising, so were the officers. I was made Hon. President of the ship's Y.M.C.A., and a concert held on board netted a neat sum for the Patriotic fund. We had four preachers on board. We were to have had a priest, but in some way he did not turn up. Today another steamer was chased by the *Charybdis* but she gave us the slip. She had the "legs" on us all, as the captain said, and disappeared into a bank of fog to the north. Then we got clear of Cape Race, which we did not see. The wind changed to southwest, and began breaking up the nasty swell that came down the Atlantic. We had made in the twenty-four hours only 210 knots, our position being Lat. N. 45° 36', Long. W. 50° 11'. During the night the rudder gear jammed and our ship began to run amuck among the fleet. We all slept through it, but the captain had to stay on deck till it was fixed. No harm done.

The next day was also fine. There had always been a storm behind us, but it had not yet caught up. On the 7th of October at noon we were Lat. 46° 46' N., Long. 45° 25' W., another 210 miles to our credit, and we were due about the 20th in Southampton at this rate. In the evening we were amused by a school of dolphins that chased each other about the ship, jumping out of the water, and acting up generally. We expected very soon to be in the Gulf stream, where the weather would be milder. The electric heater in my room was hardly large enough to cope with the chill in the air. On the 8th we made 214 miles and the *Monmouth*, which was still giving trouble, was ordered up to the front and signalled by the Admiral to "stoke up." The Admiral had all the captains scared stiff. Along in the afternoon we got into the Gulf stream. A man threw a green canvas pail overboard, dipped it full and took the temperature of the water. It was 56°. Next day at noon it was 62°.

On the 9th we made 250 miles, which was a record run. The *Monmouth* had found her second wind and was going strong. Some of the ships were tossing but not very much. I forgot to say that on the 7th, a soldier on the ship astern of us died. He was a reservist going home to rejoin his regiment. The ship dropped out of the line and lowered her flag to half mast, and tolled her bell, whilst they buried him at sea.

All this time the weather was all that could be desired, with bright sunny days, a mackerel sky and moonlight nights, the moon being at its full.

The first night out, the captain called my attention to a comet which was showing to the north, and according to traditions said to be a harbinger of war, but when we went to look for it with our glasses it had gone down. We saw it on the evening of the 7th just south of the second star in the tail of the "Dipper" or Great Bear. Looking through my glasses, which were the most powerful on board, being more so than the ship's telescopes, I could see it quite clearly with a great tail stretching to the northeast. In a week or so it would be quite large. The weather continued bright and all the time a storm hung on behind us, but never caught up.

On the 8th we got well into the Gulf stream, and the temperature of the water registered 62° to 65°. The nights had been so cold before this that I had to get out my eiderdown, but when we got into the warm water, that had to be discarded. We had a bit of a swell from the north, and we all felt a shade miserable but not enough to be really sick. During the day a large six-masted schooner, with a barge ahead of her, hove in sight and started down the line. The *Eclipse* went after her and led her out of the convoy line. "My," said the captain to me, "that fellow will have his ticket taken from him for not keeping out of the way of a convoy." I found that a complaint from a naval officer can take away the papers of an officer of the merchant service.

On Saturday the 10th, when I got up, and looked out of my window, there on the port bow was another big warship. When I had a good look at her, I recognized that she was of what they call the Superdreadnought class. It turned out that she was the *Princess Royal*, nicknamed H.M.S. *Hellfire*. She has a speed of 34 knots an hour, and carried eight 13-½" guns, besides being very heavily armoured. God help the German that she marked down, for she was one of the most powerful fighting machines afloat.

On Saturday afternoon I gave the men a half-holiday, which they appreciated very much. The officers spent their spare time playing shuffle board, and other games such as are practised on board ship.

I gave lectures in the afternoons to officers on map reading and topography. They were apparently very interested and a number of the outside officers asked leave to attend. There was only one set of instruments for fifty officers so the class was carried on with difficulty. Much had to be left till we got ashore. On Sunday religious services were held by the various denominations.

I forgot to say that on the morning of the 5th, off Cape Race, there was an alarm in the convoy, a "man overboard." The ships began sounding their horns, and the *Royal Edward*, with the *Princess Pats* on board, turned out of the line and began lowering her boats, at the same time flying her flags. The next ship astern dropped a boat also, and the man was picked up after being in the chilly water for about fifteen minutes. Then the Admiral sent a message back that the men were not to climb the rigging.

On Sunday the *Allonia* left the convoy and went on ahead with the Admiral. It was rumoured they had gone to try and get the British Government to send the contingent over to recover Antwerp, which we learned by wireless had fallen on Sunday. The gale continued all day Monday with a misty fog from the north. We would be off Land's End in the morning.

On Sunday afternoon another warship of the Dreadnought class quietly took her place ahead of us. It was H.M.S. *Majestic*. The sailors said that this was the finest voyage they had ever had at this time of the year.

On Monday, the 12th, we had a signalling competition amongst the companies. Each company had been teaching all the men the semaphore code. It is a good thing to start with, but at the Front they use only the Morse system. About seventy-five *per cent.* of the men of the regiment could read the semaphore alphabet very readily. When a warship sent a signal everybody on board read it. "H" Company won the signalling competition.

The same evening we had a concert given by "F" Company, commanded by Captain Osborne. I was asked to attend and did so. It was a great success.

I was wakened Monday morning by someone pounding on the door telling me that land was in sight. I got up and dressed, had some

Group Non-commissioned Officers. 48th Highlanders

tea and buns and went on deck. There was Lizard Point ahead in the mist. It was blowing a gale, but the sea was not very heavy.

We detached from the convoy about ten o'clock on the 12th, and the swifter ships started to sail on, but still no one knew what our destination would be. Last evening the signallers brought us a message from our general, whoever that might be, saying "dye white haversacks" "and carry a day's rations, on disembarkation." He did not know that dye and coffee had run out so that the men could not dye their white haversacks. Somebody suggested to flag back, "send along some dye by wireless." Our men's haversacks, however, were dyed drab when we got them, so we were all right.

A case of measles developed on board, suspected to be German,—another case of German "frightfulness." In the evening the water was calm and warm and the night very dark. I went on deck to see the wonderful phosphorescent display. The ship seemed to be floating in a sea of gold, or rather sunshine. It was wonderful.

We took a good look at Lizard's Point when we were passing about ten miles off. There was a big white castle on a cliff and nice green farms.

Before closing this chapter reference should be made to the good conduct of all the officers and men. Our men on the signalling staff had a hard time but they did their duty well. The men and officers went ashore in the pink of condition.

We got our first real glimpse of England on the 14th. Off Eddystone Light the pilot came on board. He was a very large portly man and very nervous about being dropped into the sea. I should judge he weighed at least two hundred and fifty pounds. The ladder he had to climb was made of rope with the rungs woven in, and he made them heave him a line which he fastened about his body.

When he came on board we were informed for the first time that our original destination was to have been Southampton, and that it had been changed, by a wireless message from Eddystone Lighthouse that morning, to Plymouth. The evening before, the warship *Princess Royal* came steaming down the line. She was on our left. She crossed our column about half way down—dressed her decks and spars—her crew all in white—and passed upon the right of our column so close that you could toss a biscuit on her deck. She is a magnificent fighting machine. Our men all lined the decks and every available space and cheered themselves hoarse. That ship is the fastest warship afloat. The ordinary Dreadnoughts sail twenty-one knots. The *Emden* and the

Karlsruhe, the German *corsairs*, sailed twenty-six knots, but the *Princess Royal* can reel off thirty-four knots. Our ship was at the head of our column and she swung past our bow to again take her station as if we were standing still, so quickly and easily did she answer her helm. Her decks were cleared for action, her 13-½" guns run out. All her metal work in the setting sun shone like gold. She looked like a great grey yacht. This convoy had been wonderfully cared for. It seemed that all the time we were being convoyed by four great battleships and five light cruisers.

The battleships were always below the horizon till we saw the *Glory* on the right. That was off Cape Breton. Truly the British Navy is wonderful, and ever up to its traditions. We were sailing up the Channel and going to land at Plymouth, the port from which sailed the great Admirals who gave Great Britain command of the sea. The day was lovely, the autumn sun shining brightly, and the shores of England shimmered a ruddy bronze brown. The trees were in full foliage, but the colour scheme as seen from the sea was a much more vivid green than the Canadian landscape. In the early part of the day we could see a wireless tower and life saving stations at the Lizard. The shore was steep, a huge line of chalk cliffs.

Fourteen miles from Plymouth we passed Eddystone Lighthouse. This is one of the most noted lighthouses in the world. The first light was erected here on a submerged reef in 1697. Six years after it was washed away during a great storm. It was rebuilt in wood and the structure stood the buffeting of the Atlantic until it was burned down in 1755. The third, or as it was called the Smeaton Tower, was erected in 1757. It was built of masonry and stood until 1882, over a hundred years. Part of this wonderful old light, I was told by our captain, is still in use in Plymouth. The present light is 135 feet high, and was built by Sir James W. Douglas at a cost of $400,000. In the summer, excursion steamers run out from Plymouth, but very few of the passengers land.

As we gradually drew nearer the harbour we began to meet the sharp-nosed destroyers and torpedo boats that guard the harbour, and as we neared the entrance we were delighted with the view of a vast park and grounds with a castle peeping out from the trees. This park is known as Mount Edgecombe, the seat of Earl Edgecombe. The park is one of the most beautiful in England and occupies the whole of one side of the Sound. Through our glasses we could see beautiful lawns, walks and tropical palm trees growing here in the open air. Soon we could distinguish the great breakwater that almost closes the entrance to the Sound. On all sides we could see from grimy walls and caverns the black gaping mouths of cannon. The shore outlines rose about five hundred feet on each side and great batteries and the white tents of some of Kitchener's army were to be seen almost everywhere. There was certainly no doubt about England being at war. As we drew near the breakwater a shoal of paddle wheel tugs rushed out to welcome us with their sirens blowing to pilot us safely into the most noted harbour in the world.

From this port sailed such great captains as Drake, Hawkins and Cooke, who first circumnavigated the globe. From this port emerged William Longsword when he defeated the French when they desired to land an expedition to defeat King John. Here it was where Sir Howard Effingham and Drake lingered on the Hoe, a hill which we could clearly see, to finish their famous game of bowls (every bowler knows the story) before emerging to fall upon the Spanish Armada. Here Blake, equally famous, the father and organizer of the British Navy, made his *depôt*, and in the church of St. Andrew's, in the city behind the Hoe, is deposited his stout heart. From this Sound emerged the *Mayflower* to land the Pilgrim Fathers in America, there to lay the foundations of yet greater nations, and re-establish that *Pax Britannicum* for which we were here to fight, and which has given a century of peace in the new world.

Nearer and near we came, and soon passed the breakwater, guarded by a huge steel tower girded with long lean gun barrels. The town seemed to wake up and the open spaces began to fill with people. The sailors and cadets on Drake Island poured out from the casements like rabbits from a warren. With our glasses we could see the dense crowd on the Hoe, which is now a public park. We could see the colossal statue of Sir Francis Drake towering aloft over the Hoe, speaking trumpet in hand, as if welcoming us, for certainly this was a great Armada that was entering the Sound, a peaceful Armada, greater than that of King Philip; this second Armada composed largely of the second and third generations of pioneers coming back to give to the Mother Country what she had so freely given to the Colonies and the civilized world.

What would old Sir Francis have said at this sight if he had lived today? Back from Plymouth in a country manor near Tavistock, some descendant guards the ancient drum with which Drake beat his crews to their quarters. It was said that on his deathbed, when he bequeathed this drum, he left directions that it was not to be beaten unless the shores of England were endangered, and if it were beaten, England would produce a great man or something great would occur that would meet the emergency. Twice only had the drum been beaten, and assistance came, first in the persons of the great Admiral Blake and then Admiral Nelson. Someone must have given it a sly tap to bring the Canadian contingent.

Gradually we drew into the inner harbour. The white streaks on the shore and on the warships in the harbour resolved themselves into naval cadets and "tars" "dressing" ship. We had seen this before on the decks of the *Princess Royal*. Here were hundreds and thousands of them. Certainly England did not show any slackness in the number of sailors. We could hear the cheering from the shore, and our pipes struck up "*The Cock o' the North*." The men cheered themselves hoarse in reply. Then we could hear the civilians on the shore giving out something like a college yell. We listened and it came across "Are we down-hearted? No." It never seemed to strike our men that way. We had not heard the latest London Music Hall slang borrowed from "Joe" Chamberlain, so our men called back, "Cheer up, the worst is yet to come" and everybody roared with laughter.

Slowly the *Megantic* threaded her way in and out between buoys, through mines loaded with enough dynamite to blow her to smithereens. The inner harbour is called the Hamoaze. As we passed Drake Island, we were under the guns of the citadel which was built in 1670 and is still occupied; we passed the great naval victualling yard, a large establishment built in 1835 for victualling the navy. Then we entered that part of the Sound known as Devonport, the headquarters of the Royal Navy. Devonport is one of the great naval yards, and there is situated one of the huge naval shipbuilding plants. Huge steam derricks rear their arms along the masonry walls of the harbour on the left, and in several places the huge ribs of warships in course of erection disclose their nakedness.

On the wharves could be seen enormous guns like giant pine logs heaped up ready to be put on board the warships when ready. Several large men-of-war were in the dock, among them one that had knocked a few plates off its bottom in running over a German submarine in the North Sea. Further and further we went until finally our cable was tied to a huge buoy and we were at our moorings. Orders were issued that no one was to go ashore, so I slipped a cable for home, to the pilot, also a gold sovereign. He said he had no change, but I told him the change was his. He was the assistant of our big pilot. He stared for a minute, then he vanished over the rail like a blue streak, down the ladder, over the tender, alongside he hailed another tender that was passing, and before our cable chain was out I could see him climbing up the landing stairs and I guess he is running yet. Gold has its fascination here as elsewhere and spells service. The cable went through all right.

The appearance of the fleet seemed to stir up everybody and the wharves and quays were thronged all evening. The bugles blow Retreat on a beautiful spring-like evening, and after the "First Post" the pipers discoursed those ancient melodies that sounded years ago amid the brown heath and shaggy wood, and that are now calling the descendants of those ancient warriors from farm, city and many peaceful and cheerful firesides to fight for King and Country like their ancestors, and if need be to die that the Empire may live. The men sang themselves to sleep that night. I could hear their songs long after "Lights Out" had sounded.

The voyage was over, and we can thank an All Wise and merciful Providence that we had all come safely so far. Never did a commanding officer have a finer lot of men than mine. Never did a commanding officer have less trouble—the conduct of everybody was so good. We would land eleven hundred and fifty-seven strong and only one man sick. The rest, thanks to continual physical drill, were in the pink of condition, ready and fit to go anywhere. I had only one regret and that was that that some of them might never return. Still, the price of Empire and power, as Bismarck said, must be paid, not in talk nor treaties, nor promises nor golden tribute, but in "blood and iron."

Chapter 7

Salisbury and the Stones of Stonehenge

On Thursday, the 14th of October, orders came to disembark. All the ships of the Canadian fleet were there. We learned that we had been sent to Plymouth at the last minute and that train transport had to be provided for us. All kinds of rumours were afloat; one that we were to go at once to France, disembarking at Rouen, and then by train to the south of France; others said that we were to go to Egypt; and many said that was all right, if the Turks got into the war.

I went ashore with Company Sergeant-Major Radcliffe of my regiment, who is a Plymouth man. It was only when I got ashore that I learned that his bride-to-be lived in Plymouth. We drove all over the town and part of the country. This is Devonshire, the country of cider and cream. I tried them both; they are excellent. It felt good to get ashore, but the voyage was so pleasant that we were sorry to part with our good ship and our captain. We found that in England the people had been very much depressed by the war, but were recovering their spirits. The shipyards were busy, but there was hardly a home in Plymouth, Stonehouse or Devonport (three towns in one), but had someone afloat in the navy, keeping convoy, or keeping guard in the North Sea. I met the editor of one of the Plymouth papers, a very fine man. From him I learned that the Mayor and Corporation of the town had arranged a public reception for the Canadians, but that Lord Kitchener had vetoed the proposal. He also told me of the loss of some ships on the East coast, and some German losses at sea, but said the censor would not permit publication even of our arrival.

We were beginning to learn that there was a big man somewhere about who was doing things, and that his address was not far from the War Office. On the streets we met hundreds of young men route marching, some of them with arms, some in uniform, the majority without either. They were all singing "Tipperary" with its Celtic croon and minor tones. So far apparently, the war had not produced a great war poet or musician, nothing had been written anything like "Tommy Atkins" or "Soldiers of the Queen." Surely war songs were not all "Made in Germany."

Every square, and park and private lawn had its quota of soldiers drilling, all young men and all in deadly earnest. We learned also that the day we arrived some young men from Quebec, speaking French, and a Servian from Winnipeg had strayed ashore, and the announcement was made in the press that the contingent consisted principally of French Canadians and Servians who were coming to fight for the Allies. After the war is over I suppose someone will be giving the Chinese all the credit for what the Canadians did.

So far so good. We remained on board all day. The rivetters on board a huge Dreadnought, that was being built close by, chalked in huge letters on the plating a message for us, "Bravo Canadians." Our men, who were very good with semaphore signals, soon established a wireless connection with the shore and a very animated conversation was carried on between them all day. In the afternoon we presented Captain James with a memento of our voyage, expressing our pleasure in having such a good commander. We bought him the silver when we got ashore.

The next morning an officer came aboard from the staff, and we learned for the first time that General Alderson had been appointed to command the Canadian Expeditionary Force. We could see an officer on shore with a staff cap, who looked very much like General Hughes, but it turned out to be Colonel Davidson of Toronto. About noon our ship pulled into the dock, and the gangways were put out, and disembarkation began. We were ordered to move in two detachments, so I gave the right half battalion to Major Marshall with my blessing, and remained with the left half myself to see that all our stores were landed safely. We learned a good deal about transporting troops. One thing that should be looked after in future contingents is to see that each unit has its own waggons, horses and carts on its own ship.

When we were embarked at Quebec our horses and waggons were taken away from us. The horses were put on board one ship, the harness on another, the waggons on another, the wheels on another, etc. It took weeks to sort everything out, and all the work done at Valcartier had been wasted.

Another thing, the men should not be sent abroad without a good equipment like the Webb. The Oliver equipment was a joke. With our facilities for producing good leather, canvas and woollen stuff in Canada there is no reason why we cannot produce an equipment just as good, if not better, than the Webb. All ammunition is now packed in clips in canvas bandoliers holding fifty rounds, and there is very little necessity for the big ammunition pouches with which equipments were burdened. An equipment made out of green chrome leather with as few straps as possible, or out of good stout drab canvas made in Canada and treated with a solution of soap and alum, so as to make it waterproof, would do just as well as the Webb. Fortunately our regiment had been given an excellent Webb equipment and it was expected the equipment for the rest of the force would be issued in England. The Division outside of our Brigade had been busy for several days staining their Oliver haversacks and kit bags with tea and making a very poor job of it.

The right half battalion shouldered their blankets, kit bags and knapsacks and started off for the station a mile away. Our rifles were boxed and would follow us. We left later on at six in the evening. It was dusk as we marched through Plymouth to the station where we had to wait an hour for our train to be made up. Soon quite a crowd gathered at the station, and everybody wanted to give my men bottles of whiskey and gin. I stopped it as well as I could, but a few who had not had a drink for two months fell by the wayside, not just then but later on. We should have tried out our men in Canada, and given them a free hand, so that the drinkers would be weeded out before coming over.

Our train came in about eight o'clock and we were told our destination was Patney Station, and that our camp was near the station. Off we started and arrived at Patney about one o'clock at night. The men enjoyed the run very much. At every station as we passed the people gathered and cheered themselves hoarse till we all thought we were real heroes. We made only about two stops till we came to Patney, one at Exeter which is one of the oldest towns in England dating from the Roman occupation. This city was the Iscea of Vaspasian's time. It was always a fortified city, previous even to the Romans, and boasts of a beautiful cathedral.

The other stop we made was at Newton Abbot. Here William of Orange was first proclaimed King of England, if I remember right, on a stone in the market square.

At Patney station we found on the station platform Major Marshall and several officers, among them Captain McGregor. They informed us that on the way up a number of the men of "A" Company (Captain McGregor's) had been taken ill, with ptomaine or some other form of poisoning, and were in a bad way. We suspected at once that someone had handed them something. We found thirty-five of them down with colic and very severe pains. Blankets had been laid in the station for them, and Dr. MacKenzie, our surgeon, did not take long getting busy attending to them. He informed me that he did not consider any cases serious, although the poor fellows were suffering much pain. We marched the left half of the battalion over the track on an overhead bridge, and found our right half waiting for us, and for transport waggons which were supposed to be on hand, to take our kit bags and blankets. The night was as dark as a wolf's mouth and the dim lights of a few lanterns showed the men standing in solid lines between the green walls of the hedges of an English lane.

A traction transport arrived and the men began hoisting their kit bags into the two large vans that constituted this traction outfit. Several county policemen were on hand to guide us to our camp which we were told was eleven miles away. That was cheerful. There was no transport for the kit bags and blankets of my half battalion, so that after a while Marshall got all his kits aboard and said good-bye and started off into blank space with his half battalion less the thirty-five sick left at the station. The pipes struck up bravely, "*We'll take the High Road*," the marching-out tune of all Highland Regiments, and soon the black darkness swallowed up the end of his detachment.

The prospect of a night march of eleven miles was not very cheerful for the rest of us. We stood about on the road waiting for another traction engine and waggons to get our kits carried for us. One hour passed, no transport, two hours, no transport. We heard that our transport had gone to Lavington station by mistake, and was on the way back for us. At a quarter to three the officers and non-commissioned officers decided that we had better start and get to camp carrying our own kit bags and blankets. The men said they would rather go than sit around waiting for morning, so a constable with a lantern and a bicycle volunteered to guide us. I gave the command to shoulder kit-bags and blankets and we were off.

Each man carried his knapsack and complete equipment, three blankets, a rubber sheet and a kit bag, full of boots, clothing and all like effects. Some of the men were carrying fully one hundred to one hundred and twenty-five pounds. Sergeant-Major W. Grant slipped up alongside of me at the head of the column, and we marched out into total darkness. At first it was so dark that a person could almost feel it. The road was firm and flinty under foot, and pretty soon someone started up "The Army of today is all Right," and everybody joined in the chorus. We set a slow pace, stepping short and easy so that the end of the column in charge of Captain Warren could keep up. A wonderful man was young Warren, never tired, always cheerful, always knowing what to do. We were blessed with two good field officers in Captains Darling and Warren. At the end of fifteen minutes we halted between two hedges and rows of tall trees. The policeman told me the men could sit against the banks of the hedges, so that first rest was good. In ten minutes we were off again. The road seemed to wind in and out in serpentine curves. The land on either side was taken up with truck and vegetable farming.

In spite of the darkness it was an ideal night for marching, neither too hot nor too cold. The men were standing up to the marching well. After about another quarter of an hour Sergeant Hermitage, my orderly room sergeant, ran up from the rear to tell me to halt the column, as a man had slipped into a culvert and was stuck in the mud. In fishing him out the sergeant had got stung with nettles. This made him hot. It did not mend matters when I suggested that his country was getting even with him for wearing kilts. However, we slowed up. This going was splendid practice as we would no doubt have plenty of night marching of this kind in Flanders. The men stood up to the march with their heavy loads splendidly, thanks to the excellent physical training they had undergone on board ship.

At the first halt a number lit up cigarettes, and as soon as they started a chorus of coughs showed where the seductive weed was getting in its deadly work on the lungs and bronchial tubes. The commanding officers passed the word along to try and not smoke, and not to use the water bottles, and the men did their best for the rest of the march. About an hour before we came to our camp we ran full tilt into a traction train and I commandeered it at once. I turned it around and got the men to load their kit bags into the big vans, which they did most cheerfully, as this lightened their loads. When we reached the great Salisbury Plains, after a steep climb, it was cold and foggy, the kind of weather to take the courage out of a man, about five o'clock in the morning. It was daylight when we reached our tents. There was hot tea ready for the men, and it did not take us very long to roll up in a blanket on the ground and go to sleep.

I made the eleven miles carrying my great coat, sword and equipment, and how I blessed my boots. Not a chafe nor an ache, they were just splendid. From three o'clock till seven ten is not bad for eleven miles on a pitch dark night. We all knew very little of what happened for the rest of the day. Captain Donaldson saw that the officers' luggage was sent in, and by the evening we were quite comfortable, and had a good sleep on Saturday night.

The first work we did on our arrival at Salisbury Plains was to attend an open air church service on Sunday. All the photographers of the London papers were on hand to get snapshots of us. We were warned to be careful of suspicious characters, and some of the gentlemen with cameras were questioned closely. We at last had leisure to look about us. Salisbury Plains, where we had been sent for our training, is in Wiltshire and is a chalk plateau, high up in the middle of England. It is noted for its historical associations and its bad climate. Two great trunk line railways run, one on the north, the other to the south of these Plains which are fully twenty-five miles from north to south and twenty-five miles from east to west. Most of the land is taken over by the Crown for military purposes, but at the cross-roads there are still small English villages nestling in the hollows, whilst on the Plains themselves the game and shooting privileges still remain in the hands of the Lords of the Manor.

The country is very much like the foot-hills of the Rockies near Calgary in appearance. The slopes are generally to the north. We were not by any means the first armed men to tread the heath here. There is no part of England so rich in legend and history. We could see ruins and monuments on every side.

In the middle of the Downs, within plain view of our camp, there arose the most ancient ruins in the British Isles, and the most interesting prehistoric edifice in the whole of Europe—Stonehenge. To speak of Stonehenge or to try to conjure up its past is to deal with people who lived on these plains and enjoyed their cruder methods of civilization and religion in a period more remote than that in which the great Pyramids of Egypt were fashioned. Here in a circle, about one hundred feet in diameter, are reared a series of great pillars of granite, a stone which cannot be found within hundreds of miles from the spot, in fact the north of France is the nearest. Each slab is about twenty feet in height and they are fashioned rudely in the form of a temple. It is said that in the design geometrical figures were used, and that some sun cult was practised by those who reared them, for the sun's shadow passes through various points only on Midsummer and on May Day.

The Druids are supposed to have used this as the great shrine of their faith, and worshippers came from all over Europe every year to take part in the religious ceremonies. Be that as it may this country must have been the centre of a very powerful Celtic or British race, for here and there over the Plains are piled up huge barrows, said to be the burial places of ancient kings. A barrow or *tumulus* is about fifteen to twenty feet high and seventy to a hundred feet in diameter. A great many *tumuluii* are dotted here and there over the Plains. The next people to these Druidical Celts to occupy these plains were Britons and the ruins of some of their villages are still to be found. Then came the Romans, and as usual they left their mark. North of the stones of Stonehenge, about a quarter of a mile, is still to be found the ruins of a chariot race course recalling scenes from *Ben Hur*. Over one end of the course, oaks, centuries old, have grown.

Not far away, about a mile and half east of Stonehenge, there is the huge earthwork walls ofVespasians' Camp. From here it is said the Great Roman general marched to the conquest of Palestine. About four miles south, crowning a high hill, there are the ruins of Old Sarum, at one time a Roman City. From the ramparts of Sarum, each of them a day's march away, can be seen the ruins of seven great Roman Camps. The Romans occupied Britain about four hundred years, a period more remote than if we count from now back beyond the Discovery of America. Everywhere are marks of their civilization, showing that the country during their occupation must have been rich and populous. No less than four of their generals left these Plains to assume the Imperial purple. What stirring times those must have been. Past old Sarum wound the road to Bath where the rich Romans and Britons were carried by slaves on their litters to take the medicinal waters of that ancient well, now found to contain that marvellous nerve-stimulating mineral—radium. Every stone, every hill on these Plains could tell a wonderful story.

After the Romans came the Saxons, and good King Alfred was not unknown to these Plains while he was moulding his kingdom and driving out the Danes. The Norman Conqueror then came and took Sarum as one of his strongholds. And it is admirably suited for defence even today. He established a See or Bishopric at Sarum which later was removed to the City of Salisbury. Sarum then declined and ran to seed, and was gradually abandoned. It registered a last kick, however, when its half a dozen voters, as it was the most noted of the "Rotten" Boroughs, won immortality by sending to Parliament a young Coronet of Horse, Pitt the Elder, afterwards Lord Chatham. It then ceased to be anything but a geographical expression.

If you seek the remainder of the history of this remarkable spot, look for it in Salisbury Cathedral, one of the most charming specimens of late Gothic architecture to be found in the world. There you will find the tomb of William Longsword and other brave crusaders. You will find that Oliver Goldsmith lived in Salisbury, and there wrote the novel *The Vicar of Wakefield*, and that Gay wrote the *Beggar's Opera*, at Amesbury, the village that lies a few miles east of Stonehenge. But of all that we saw that which impressed us most were the Roman ruins, recalling the iron discipline of those unconquerable legionaries, and the great monuments of our Celtic ancestors, the sublime stones of Stonehenge.

Chapter 8

Under Field Marshal Earl Roberts

We had to settle down for a few days to await our arms and equipment, and in the meantime a meeting of the officers was called by General Alderson, our divisional commander.

The chief topic of discussion was the question of having "wet" canteens in the lines. The result of the meeting was that they were shortly installed by contractors for the war office, and gave us a great deal of trouble, and gave a few men who misbehaved themselves a chance to get a quick return ticket to Canada.

In spite of temptation on every side, to the credit of the Canadians be it said they behaved themselves exceedingly well. Fully eighty *per cent.* of them were total abstainers. About ten *per cent.*, chiefly the older men, took an occasional drink, and not more than about three *per cent.* drank to any extent. For these latter, life soon became a burden.

This good behaviour followed the troops to Flanders. Shortly after we crossed and went into the trenches the French Government prohibited the sale of all spirits to soldiers. Any saloon keeper in France who sells hard liquor to a soldier is very severely punished. The only liquor they are allowed to sell to the soldiers is a light beer, about three *per cent.* alcohol, which is manufactured in small home-made breweries at every cross-road and is consumed by the Flemish people in lieu of the water, which is very bad in the low country, and only fit for cooking, also a light native wine with about the strength of ginger-ale, and the taste of vinegar. We found that light beers, wines and fermented liquors are licensed separately in France from spirits. This method has given good satisfaction.

Strong liquors or spirits are given to the soldiers only on a doctor's order. There is no regular issue of rum, and the stories circulated by Jane Adams, a Chicago pacifist, and others that the soldiers are filled up with rum and "dope" to keep up their courage, were deliberate lies as far as the British, French and Canadian troops are concerned. Strong drink of any kind was treated as a drug, not as a beverage. The beer and wine sold had about the same alcoholic content as ginger beer or newly-made bakers' bread. The army in Flanders was not producing "drunken heroes." Those who cannot cut out liquor are better left at home. They are of no value whatever in any war.

We also learned, at this meeting, with great pleasure that Lord Roberts had become the Honorary Commander in Chief of the Canadian Army, and that in a few days he was coming to review us, as was also His Majesty the King and Lord Kitchener. We worked very hard to get into shape for these important events. In the meantime the Minister of Militia from Canada arrived and visited our camp, also several other eminent men, among them Mr. R. Reid, who represents the Province of Ontario in London.

Our lay-out for camp was not as fine as at Valcartier. The tents had been pitched during the summer and occupied by successive territorial battalions, and they were not of the thick water-proof cotton canvas variety that we had in Canada. They were the linen kind such as we used to have in Canada in the Eighties, and they were so thin you could count the stars through them, but were all right for summer use.

We were solemnly cautioned not to make any excavations in the turf, especially ditches around the tents to carry off the rain, or even holes in the ground in which to build our cooking fires, as the land is hunted over, and any stray holes in the ground might break a horseman's collar bone or a horse's leg.

The division was divided up and put in various camps, about a brigade in each camp, which were a mile or so apart. The First Brigade under General Mercer were at Bustard Camp. The Second under General Currie and the Third under General Turner, V.C., were at West Down South. The artillery under Colonel Burstall were with the First Brigade whilst the cavalry were at Sling plantation, and Divisional Headquarters at Bustard Camp.

Earl Roberts came out to review us on Saturday, the 27th of October. I had not seen the hero of Kandahar since the day he marched past the King, resplendent in the scarlet and gold of a Field-Marshal on the Plains of Abraham, at Quebec. Since then he had retired from active duty with the army to devote himself to the cause of National Service.

The important day arrived and the brigades were drawn up in lines

Aboard Ship in Winter Garb

of battalions in mass along the brow of a slope south of our camp. Battalion after battalion, battery after battery, squadron after squadron for nearly two miles the line stretched. It was a magnificent array of men that greeted the brave old veteran in the first review of the Canadians which proved to be his last command.

On his arrival he was received with the general salute. He then rode in a big grey car in front of the line, the officers having been all called out to the front. As he reached each separate battalion the car stopped, General Hughes introduced the commanding officers, and Lord Roberts spoke graciously to them. Some of the officers' horses behaved badly as the big grey car came up to them and some seats were lost that day, but my big charger behaved splendidly. She looked into the big car and wanted to poke her nose into it to see if the driver had any candy or apples. General Hughes, the Minister of Militia, sat in the seat beside Earl Roberts. Age had dealt very kindly with the veteran of Kandahar and South Africa. Although a consistent water drinker, Lord Roberts had a very florid complexion, which was just as bright and ruddy as that of a subaltern of twenty, despite his extreme age. This kind of complexion makes it difficult for a man to gain admission to a temperance club in Canada.

His voice was clear and resonant. "Colonel Currie," he said, "How many men of this kind have you with you? They are indeed a splendid lot, and the Empire owes a debt of gratitude to these gallant soldiers for coming in the hour of need."

I answered, "Eleven hundred and seventy, Sir."

"They are a fine lot and when fully trained should give a good account of themselves," he said.

I thanked him, and he was gone.

It began to drizzle and rain, and as we moved off we had the first taste of that disagreeable weather which clung to us until we left the Plains. Many a time afterwards the lines of R.H. Barham, the author of *Ingoldsby Legends*, came to my mind.

Oh Salisbury Plain is bleak and bare,
At least so I've heard many people declare,
Tho' I must confess that I've never been there.
Not a shrub, not a bush nor tree can you see,
No hedges, no ditches, no gates, no stiles,
Much less a house or a cottage for miles,
It's a very bad thing to be caught in the rain,

When night's coming on, on Salisbury Plain.

On Sunday, the 25th, the men of the division heard a sermon from Bishop Taylor Smith, who visited Salisbury Plain with Dr. McNamara, M.P.

The London press had been very enthusiastic over the Canadian Division. The illustrated papers had photographs of the various corps and officers. Their kindness was very much appreciated.

Lord Roberts issued an Order of the Day, in which he praised us very highly. He said:

> The prompt resolve of Canada to give us such valuable assistance has touched us deeply. That resolve has been galvanized into action in what I consider a marvellously short period of time, under the excellent organization and driving power of your Minister of Militia, my old friend Major General Hughes. In less than three months from the declaration of war I am able to greet this fine body of soldiers on English soil.

Stirring events were happening in Flanders. About this time we learned with much regret that Colonel Lowther, who had served on the staff of His Royal Highness the Duke of Connaught in Canada, had been badly wounded. Also that Major Rivers-Bulkley of the Scots Guards, who had also been on His Royal Highness' staff, had been killed. The latter had, scarcely a year before, been married to Miss Pelly, one of the ladies-in-waiting to Her Royal Highness the Duchess of Connaught in Ottawa.

The German invaders on the western front had swept on past Liege. A great battle had been fought at Waterloo or Charleroi, another at Mons and at Le Cateau. The French Government had left Paris. The greatest battle in the history of the world had taken place near Metz. The Crown Prince's Army had been shattered and General Von Kluck's march on Paris had been stayed at the Marne[1]. Then the Allies had assumed the offensive, and driven the Germans back to the Aisne. Ypres, Hazebrouck, Estairs and Armentieres[2] had been retaken

---

1. *1914: The Marne and the Aisne* Two Accounts of the Early Battles of the First Year of the First World War, *The Battles of the Marne and the Aisne* by H.W. Carless-Davis and *Troyon—an Engagement in the Battle of the Aisne* by A. Neville Hilditch, also published by Leonaur.
2. *1914: Early Battles* by H.W. Carless-Davis Two Accounts of the Battles of the First Year of the First World War, *The Retreat From Mons* and *The Battle of Ypres-Armentieres* also published by Leonaur.

on the Western frontier of Belgium and France. The huge Austrian siege guns, 42 centimetres, had proven too much for the antique concrete of the Belgian and French forts, but the tide of invasion had been stayed.

A few days later, October 29th, a dinner was given in London by Hon. Lieutenant-Colonel Grant Morden in the Royal Automobile Club in honour of the Minister of Militia, Major-General the Honourable Sam Hughes, and the officers commanding the Canadian contingent. Amongst other officers I was invited to be present, and the dinner was one of the most notable I have ever attended. Not so much on account of the number of prominent men who attended, but because it was the last occasion in which Lord Roberts spoke in public. Among others present were Lord Islington, Lord Iverclyde, Sir A. Trevor Dawson, Sir Gilbert Parker, Sir Joseph Lawrence, Sir George Armstrong, Lord Charles Beresford, Sir John Curtis, Sir Edward Carson, Rt. Hon. Walter H. Long, Sir Reginald McLeod, Colonel Sir Edward W. Ward, Sir Vincent Callard and Monsieur R. Thien de la Chaume of the French Embassy.

The toast to Canada was proposed by Sir Charles Beresford in a fine speech, in which he referred to the valuable services of the Canadians in previous wars. The toast was responded to by Sir George Parley, M.P., acting Canadian High Commissioner. Lord Roberts then proposed the toast to Major General Hughes. He was very warmly received when he rose to propose this toast, and was visibly affected by the splendid demonstration. He spoke with great earnestness for over half an hour. He first paid a glowing tribute to the Canadian troops that had served under him in South Africa. When he took command there the first telegram he sent was to Canada. He then referred to the troops he had reviewed on Salisbury Plains in warmest terms. He had not thought it possible that such a fine steady body of men could be got together in such a short time. He commended the Minister of Militia for having achieved such splendid results so quickly. He praised the deportment of the troops the day he had reviewed them in the rain.

He then turned to the subject of the war and reminded his hearers that they were fighting an enemy that meant business, and the destruction of the British Empire. He predicted that through their preparedness they would give us enormous trouble and he warned us that in his estimation the war would require every man that could be put in the field. Lord Kitchener had not called for a man too many, and every effort should be put forward to enlist and train every available man as soon as possible.

Referring to his travels throughout the Empire, he said that it seemed to him the people of the Colonies were more appreciative of the greatness of the struggle and more patriotic than those at home. He attributed this to education in the schools and regretted that patriotism was not taught more in the schools of the Motherland, and the British Flag flown over the schools as in Canada and the other Colonies.

The audience listened with rapt attention and punctured his remarks again and again with applause.

The Downs were very suitable for drill and work in open order. The turf was good and firm, and so far there was no mud or sand. We took up the new drill of 1914. The battalions for drill purposes were formed into four companies with four platoons per company.

We had been told that as soon as we settled down His Majesty the King and Lord Kitchener were coming out to look us over, so we brisked up as quickly as possible for the big event. We had a rehearsal the day before. The troops took their positions along the main roads leading past their respective brigade camps. Our Camp, West Down South, contained two infantry brigades, ours, the Highland Brigade and the Second Brigade. His Majesty, Lord Kitchener, Earl Roberts and staff were to drive up from Salisbury in motor cars, and we were formed up on the east side of the main road from Salisbury to receive him. The mounted troops were to form up on the west side.

We made a brave show but some of the battalions were not fully equipped as they had not yet received their bayonets. The practise was a great success. Major Beatty, brother of Admiral Beatty, who was officer on General Alderson's staff, took us all in. A general officer from the War Office was to have looked us over, but as he did not show up the genial Major went through the motions, and it was only after each of the battalions in succession had received him with the general salute and presented arms as he walked past in front of us, and we had a look at his badges, that we realized that we had been fooled. Of course as a Major he was junior to the officers in command of the regiments and not entitled to the honours, but he took them with a grin and the rehearsal passed off well.

We had King's weather next day when the King came to West Down South. The Royal Party came promptly to the minute. There was His Majesty the King, Her Majesty the Queen and some ladies-in-waiting; Lord Kitchener, the Secretary of State for War, Earl Roberts, Lord Stamford, Sir Richard McBride and a number of staff officers. We were lined up and made a splendid showing. The King rode up to the line and began the inspection of the artillery and the Divisional Cavalry opposite us. The Royal party was then on foot, and His Majesty greeted each officer, and then passed through the ranks in and out, speaking a word here and there to the men. After he had gone over the mounted troops he crossed the road and started down the line of infantry.

The battalions were in order from right to left. Her Majesty the Queen and her ladies-in-waiting with Sir George Perley followed the King and Lord Kitchener. In a few minutes they were at the right flank of our battalion. I received His Majesty with broadsword at the salute, and was introduced by General Turner, V.C. He asked me about our tartan, and how many men I had in it. I told him the whole regiment wore the tartan. He was introduced to the officers and then, with Sergeant-Major Grant and Lord Kitchener, he started through the ranks. Someone called me back and I was introduced to Her Majesty, who in a plain suit of black with a black hat, as she was in mourning, stood smiling to greet me.

I had not seen Her Majesty since the night of the reception given by the King and Queen, then the Prince and Princess of Wales, in the Parliament Buildings in the City of Toronto in 1902. She had not changed at all and there is no woman in the world who looks the part of a Queen better than Her Majesty Queen Mary. She looked the front line of our battalion over carefully. There was not a man there less than six feet two inches. Youth and intelligence was written all over them but they stood as if carved out of stone.

"What a fine lot of men" was her gracious comment as she passed along the line. "And they all look like professional men and students."

A mention of their patriotism in coming to the war, a prayer that they might be spared to return safely to Canada, and then with a farewell, and "Good luck to you and your Regiment Colonel," the Royal Party passed on down the line to the Canadian Scottish Regiment. That concluded the inspection, and entering the motors they rode off to Sling Plantation Camp to review more soldiers. Our Brigade had advanced to the side of the road, and as they passed on they received cheers that could be heard three miles away. We waited for the return of the Royal Party and lined both sides of the road and gave more cheers. That was our last look at Lord Roberts. A few days later he went to France and died very suddenly at St. Omar while he was visiting the troops under his old Lieutenant, Sir John French. He died as he would have wished, within the sound of the guns. Coincident with his visit there the British had driven the Germans back behind the Yperlee Canal, where the first Canadian Division was to win immortal fame.

Those who heard him speak on National Service and the duty of every man in connection with the war will never forget his earnestness and fervour. His voice will come ringing down the ages calling men of British birth to their duty like the voice of Demosthenes, the Greek patriot, whose constant cry was, "Yet O Athenians, yet there is time. And there is one manner in which you can recover your greatness, or dying fall worthy of your Marathon and Salamis. Yet O Athenians you have it in your power, and the manner of it is this. Cease to hire your armies. Go, yourselves, every man of you, and stand in the ranks, and either a victory, beyond all victories in its glory, awaits you, or falling you shall fall greatly and worthy of your past."

A few days later the officers and men of the First Canadian Contingent were given the status and rank of Imperial troops, that is to say British Regulars. This made all the officers, non-coms. and men senior to officers and non-coms. of the same rank in the Canadian militia or the Home Territorial forces.

Chapter 9

Moulding an Army

"Escort and Prisoner, Right Turn. Quick March," rang out the voice of Sergeant-Major Grant at the door of the orderly tent.

Three men, as in file, came marching through the doorway, and as they reached the camp table at which I sat, the sergeant-major continued, "Halt, Left Turn, Right-Dress."

The men turned smartly, facing me. In the centre stood bareheaded the prisoner, a young man about twenty-two years of age, on each side of him a grim old soldier with a drawn bayonet.

An "Orderly Room" is the court which the commanding officer holds, usually in the morning when men are brought before him, charged with any offences they may have committed, with which the company commanders cannot deal.

It is a very solemn affair, and is a parade which all the officers of the battalion, especially those who have men charged with offences, are supposed to attend. They stand on either side of the officer commanding at "Attention." The adjutant stands rigid on the right hand. The officer commanding alone is seated.

The sergeant-major handed the "Crime Sheet," that is the document in which the nature of the crime and the names of the witnesses are stated, to Adjutant Darling, who read:—

> That on December 10th, at 2 p.m., Private John B—— of the 48th Highlanders was found loitering in the Park at Bournemouth without a pass. That he became violently abusive on being taken into custody. Witnesses, Police constables 'J——' and 'D——' of Bournemouth.

Then followed the evidence of the constables taken down in the presence of an officer at Bournemouth, to the effect:

> That on Dec. 10th, at 2 p.m., I, Police Constable 'J——,' together with Constable 'D——,' was patrolling the Park at Bournemouth when I saw Private B—— of the 15th Battalion sitting on a park seat with two young ladies. As was customary in such cases I asked him if he had a pass. He produced a pass signed by the Commanding Officer of the 15th Battalion, which had expired the day before. When we pointed out that Private B—— was 'absent without leave,' he said he expected an extension by wire that day, from his Commanding Officer. When we told him that it was our duty to take him into custody, he became very abusive, calling us 'Thick-headed John Bulls,' 'Fat-headed Englishmen,' 'Mutton heads,' 'Blasted Britishers,' etc. He had also abused the English people in very violent terms.

The constables had taken charge of him and handed him over to the customary escort sent after him from camp.

When the adjutant had finished reading the "crime sheet," I asked Private B—— if he had anything to say, and if the charge was true.

He had nothing to say. "It is true."

"How long were you out from England before you joined this Battalion," I asked.

"Three years, Sir."

"Do you think that three years' residence in Canada entitles you to abuse your countrymen, and call them 'fat-headed Englishmen'?" I asked.

The humour of the situation seemed to strike him.

"I don't know, Sir."

"Well, your pay during your absence will be forfeited by Royal Warrant, and you are admonished not to use abusive language to your countrymen again."

"Escort and Prisoner, Left Turn, Quick March, Admonished!" roared the sergeant-major as the prisoner left the room, and the officers all broke into a hearty laugh.

Of course the Private's name did not begin with B, but this incident is an example of the spirit that filled the men of the First Canadian Division. As soon as a man donned the bronze shoulder badge with "Canada" on it he became a Canadian, and forgot his hyphen. There was no mention of the British-born, the French-Canadian, or Canadian-born. These great issues had to be left for discussion and settlement to those who stayed at home.

As a matter of fact, there was only one pure bred Canadian in the "Red Watch." He joined as a transport driver at Valcartier. He was a full-blooded Indian and very proud of it. He had left a family and a good farm to go and see some fighting for the King. When he came to see me, he said he knew our regiment would see some fighting and he wanted to go with us. I asked him if he could handle horses. He said he could so I put him into the transport to his great joy. A very humorous incident occurred in regard to him, shortly after he had reached the Salisbury Plains. He had overstayed his leave one night, by a few hours, and was promptly taken in charge by the quarter-guard, who put him in the guard tent.

There was much dismay in the guard-tent at daybreak when it was found that the prisoner had flown. "Breaking out" or "forcing" a guard is a serious offence, so when he was found up in the horse lines a short time later and brought before me at the Orderly Room, matters looked interesting. His explanation, however, was most ingenious, and given with such earnestness that we could not help but accept it. He said that when he woke up before daylight he found himself in a strange tent. He knew it was time for him to go and attend to his horses, so he got out as quietly as possible so as not to disturb his comrades, and had gone about his duties as usual. His story, which was verified, gained him forgiveness. He proved a very good soldier afterwards, and at the Battle of St. Julien, when the transport was shelled out of its quarters at Ypres, and his horses killed, instead of retiring he took a rifle and ammunition, and found his way four miles down into the trenches at the salient, where his comrades were battling with the Huns at close range. He was there wounded, gassed, and taken prisoner. His name was Lickers, and he certainly displayed all the war-like qualities of his race.

When we left Canada we expected to spend some time in England completing our training. Everybody thought that we would be handed over to a lot of crack English drill instructors, and would be placed alongside of British regular regiments so as to acquire the proper polish. This would, no doubt, have been very desirable, but when we reached Salisbury Plains we found the British War Office in the throes of evolving what was known as "Kitchener's Army." The whole country was alive with recruiting committees, bands and patriotic organizations, and in the music halls the songs were all of the "Soldier's Farewell" variety.

Every soldier that could instruct was utilized. Officers who had retired and pensioners were recalled and came gladly. Instead of providing us with officers to instruct and guide us in our training, we were asked to come to the aid of the New Army, and we gave as many officers and instructors as we could spare. Commissions in the new army were offered freely to non-commissioned officers of the Canadian Army, and each battalion gave from ten to twenty of their best. These young men subsequently acquitted themselves with much credit. One of mine won his Military Cross at the Dardanelles.

One of the most difficult things we had to cope with was discipline. At first it was hard for the young Canadian who is brought up in a village or on a farm to realize that he has to obey the orders of his superior officer, if that officer happens to be a comrade who has only the day before been given a corporal's stripes. It is doubly difficult if the command is couched in the language of an order.

On the other hand officers and non-commissioned officers had to be taught that they must not bully or browbeat their subordinates. We did not take long to acquire the new discipline. Everybody was willing.

Now that men have to act largely for themselves, the system of discipline in the British army has been changed. The idea now is that the men must be taught to obey from a sense of duty, not from fear of their superiors. Armies have obeyed their leaders from time immemorial, from various motives. The Roman legions obeyed because of their regard for their citizenship; the soldiers of Cromwell and the Japanese from religious motives, the Germans from fear of their superior officers, and the British and French armies of today from patriotism and a high sense of duty. When a soldier obeys from a sense of duty he will "carry on" even if his officers are killed or disabled. His courage is much higher. In previous wars when a battalion was decimated or had lost ten *per cent.* of its numbers, it was not considered a disgrace to retire, but in this war such losses are not considered. Battalions in the Canadian army have suffered losses as high as seventy *per cent.*, and have still held their ground undaunted, and responded most cheerfully to the orders of their remaining officers to counter-attack and charge with their bayonets.

It took some patience to bring about this discipline. It often took several visits to the orderly room to teach a man that it was one of his first duties to try and keep his "conduct sheet,"—that is the page on the regimental records, which tells of his deeds—clear of any entries for misconduct.

Another troublesome matter was to teach the men that they could not go away from camp without "leave" and a "pass," and that it was wrong to overstay a "pass." When a soldier wants to leave camp he has to get permission from the officer commanding his company. He then gets a "pass" signed by the officer commanding the battalion and armed with this pass he is at liberty for the period named on the pass.

The next big event in which we figured, after the King's visit, was the Lord Mayor's show. The Canadians were to be represented, and there was quite a flutter of excitement and much interest as to who should go to represent each battalion. I gave the honour to Lieutenant Frank Smith, who had worked very hard and had shown much ability.

The Lord Mayor's show is one of the annual events of London, and we were all anxious to see it. I had the good fortune to be invited by Sir Joseph Lawrence to view the procession from a balcony close to Temple Bar. The procession has been described so often that everybody knows all about it. The Canadians made a very fine showing. They were under the command of Colonel Williams. Our Highland detachment, under Lieutenant Frank Smith, looked exceedingly smart and got a full page in a number of the London illustrated dailies next morning.

One thing that struck me very favourably in the parade was the way in which the British regulars covered each other as they marched in fours along the street. Their rifles formed four ribbons of steel. There was no straggling.

The battalion soon settled down to a hard syllabus of training and instruction, beginning with squad drill. It was drill, drill, drill, all day long, rain or shine, and it was almost always rain.

We were much struck at first by the fact that in England farmers paid no attention to the rain. They kept on ploughing in rain, that in Canada would have sent the hired man to the shelter of the barn. After a while it dawned on us that if they did not plough in the rain they would not get any ploughing done at all.

Not only did the battalions give their days to drill but after they got through their squad drill they took two nights a week in training. All this soon began to get the men in shape.

On Thursday, November 19th, the 3rd Brigade had a visit from Mr. Rudyard Kipling. I sat at lunch with him and formed a friendship which I regard very highly. Mr. Kipling is one of the great men of the age, the first Imperialist of the Empire. He said very nice things about the Canadians.

On the 27th of November the Canadian Division was reviewed by General Pitcairn Campbell, Officer Commanding the southern command. The division was drawn up in a long line on the Downs and presented a formidable aspect. It was one of the most inspiring sights I have ever seen. There was plenty of room on the plains and after we had performed a number of evolutions we were formed in line miles long and marched some distance, then formed for an attack upon a ridge crowned by a number of *tumuli*. The earth trembled with the tread of the battalions and the hoofs of the battery horses. Thirty thousand Canadians in battle array is a sight never to be forgotten. Everything passed off well, considering the difficulties with which we had to contend. General Campbell was accompanied by Mr. Walter Long, M.P.

After luncheon he was kind enough to ride over to the 48th and complimented us very highly on our excellent appearance. The field training and hard work was working wonders on the men. Every day they were becoming better soldiers. It was the same with the other battalions. The officers were in earnest and unconsciously they were giving to the men under their command just what they needed. In the ranks there were a number of men born in the British Isles. Most of the officers were of Canadian birth, and the British-born soldier gets on magnificently with Colonial officers. Mutual respect was gradually bringing about efficiency and discipline of a very high order.

There was still much discontent because we were not sent abroad. It was not as bad with us as with Kitchener's Army. The question everybody was asking of the men in khaki was "When are you going to the front?" It is wonderful how the sight of a uniform acts on the people's mind. They think that just as soon as a man dons a uniform he is ready to go to the front. This reacts on the men, and with everyone asking "When are you going to the front?" they become almost frantic with impatience. After a soldier has been drilling a while, however, he realizes there is still something for him to learn. Then when he gets to the Front he discovers that it is not just knowing his drill that made him a soldier but the experience of obeying orders and doing the same things over and over again until he forgets drill and does the right thing without even thinking.

People who ask soldiers when they are going to the "front" forget that it is not the men's fault they do not leave for the front at once. A man that had lost a leg and whose left arm had been shattered at the elbow was invalided home, and he complained to me that because he was in uniform everybody kept asking him when he was going to the front.

In November we learned that the arch *corsair*, the *Emden*, had been caught and put out of business by the Australian cruiser *Sydney*, after a spirited action in which the latter ship upheld the traditions of the British Navy. We also learned that while in England the Canadians were supposed to take a share in the defence of the East coast in case of a German invasion. On two separate occasions I was called at midnight and warned to be ready.

I forgot to mention that the Royal Flying Corps had a school at Lark Hill near Amesbury and that every day the aviators sailed above us. On several places on the Plains monuments have been erected by the Flying Corps in memory of officers who had given their lives in the interests of the new science. Some of the Canadians joined this Corps. Lieut. Lawson of the 48th, an engineer of ability and experience, subsequently joined and served in Mesopotamia. One man in our battalion wanted to join, but when it was pointed out to him that according to the statistics of the war his chances of being killed in a Highland Battalion were much better than in a flying squadron, he decided to stay with the 48th.

Towards Christmas we received an invitation to go to Glasgow and play football against one of the Glasgow battalions. On Christmas Day a number of the Canadian oarsmen in the different regiments had a race for eights in the Thames. We had eight first class men who had belonged to Canadian fast crews, namely, Lieutenants Alex. Sinclair, Acland, Bickell, Muir, Taylor, Bath, Wilson and Campbell. The crews were arranged according to clubs at home. If the crews had been by battalions I am inclined to think we would have won.

Our football team went to Glasgow on New Year's Day and played at Annie's Land. They played a very strong game but were up against new rules that penalized them, so they did not win.

The people of Glasgow were very kind and appreciative.

Our Pullman Coach

Chapter 10

His Majesty the King, and Field Marshal the Right Honourable Viscount Kitchener

"Did they bury him standing on his head, or the other way on?"

We, that is to say, Mr. J.R. Robinson, editor of the *Toronto Telegram*, and I stood in Westminster Abbey at the spot in the hallowed floor where "Rare" Ben Jonson had claimed his foot of ground, and we were playing "*Innocents Abroad*" and having some fun with our guide. He told us that he was a Swiss and that he had shown "Buffalo Bill," "Sir" Thomas Edison, and other famous Americans about the place.

"I guess they stood him up on his feet," answered the guide.

"Was he the man who wrote the dictionary?"

"I guess that is him," answered the guide. "I understand he was a literary man."

"Who was this chap Goldsmith? Was he the first pawnbroker, or the man who invented watches?"

"I think he had something to do with the watches," said our guide, awestricken by our profound knowledge.

"Who was this Salisbury?" we asked. "He must have been somebody important to have such a fine monument?"

"He was some rich lawyer chap," was the answer we received. We were certainly having our money's worth.

We wandered up and down the aisles; beneath whose flagstones rest Britain's honoured dead.

"What strikes me most," said Robinson, "is not the number of tombs and monuments to the great, but the numberless monuments to nonentities that by some means have managed to creep into the shadow of greatness, by crowding upon the tombs of the Immortals in this Holy of Holies, the Temple of Fame of the British race."

After we had grilled our guide to our heart's content, and fed him till he almost fainted, we went around to have a look at Cromwell's monument and the spot in the great hall where Charles I. stood when he received his death sentence. Poor Charles, whose pictures look so much like his descendant William of Germany, the *Kaiser*, who has caused so much trouble for us all.

Of all the public buildings I have ever seen the great Hall of William Rufus at Westminster impressed me most. It is of the Norman order of architecture. The conception and simplicity of the structure is magnificent. King William announced to the banqueting courtiers, according to tradition, that this majestic structure was intended as an ante-room to the great Parliament Buildings which he intended to rear on the banks of the Thames. The person who reads the poetry of the stones inwardly curses the careless archer whose arrow cut short the career of this truly great king, for this is not the only great structure that "William the Red" conceived and commenced during his turbulent reign.

The three distinctive monuments of London are, this Hall of William the Red, the grim dominating lineaments shown in Cromwell's statue, and the noble well balanced head of the great Clive, the foremost of Empire builders.

"London Bridge is falling Down" is the marching-out tune of the "Red Watch," and many other Highland Regiments, although in the Celtic the words of the song say "*Well tak' the High Road*." London Bridge had not fallen down in spite of threatened Zeppelin raids, and from it we had a good look at the Thames with the magnificent vista of buildings along the embankment.

The Thames means a great deal to the Imperialist. I have seen the Missouri River where it joins the Mississippi, the two gigantic streams forming a symphony of liquid mud, the Detroit River rushing between two busy cities laden with hundreds of ships representing liquid commerce, but the Thames,—the Thames represents liquid history.

There was great joy and rejoicing when we were informed that everybody was to have a holiday either at Christmas or New Year, and that His Majesty had decreed that free transportation would be provided for such as wished a holiday to visit friends. A free trip to any place in Great Britain or Ireland meant a great deal to our men. The Government had taken over the British railways on an agreement to pay the proprietors the amount of the earnings in 1913, during the period the roads would be under control. The managers of the railways had been formed into a Board to run the roads, and the whole thing had proved such a great success that the Government was virtually having the work done for nothing. In the language of the London *Statist*, this was "the best bargain" the British government ever made.

The curse of railways is competition. Governments can and have endeavoured to adjust rates so as to cheapen the cost of service and at the same time put a stop to rate cutting, but there is such a thing as competition in service or operation which means running too many trains, where control by the Government ends.

The whole matter, however, turned out to the advantage of the soldiers. Those of our men who had friends in England chose Christmas for their holidays. The Scotchmen selected New Year's, and the Irish chose both and had their way, for what Commanding Officer could deny a man a two weeks' holiday in the Green Isle when the recipient stood a good chance of never seeing the home of his ancestors again?

The pipes of the 48th Highlanders played on New Year's Day in Glasgow, but Scotland was too busy with the war to listen. I spent a few days in the Hebrides. This is not the place for the description of a tour in the Highlands. There is something about the Highland Hills that impresses one very deeply. The peaks are not so majestic as the Saw Tooth Rockies, the Kicking Horse Range, the Cariboo Mountain, or the Range of the Agawa Valley on the northwest shore of Lake Superior which is the most beautiful spot probably in the whole world, but there is something of solemn grandeur in the Scottish Hills that pertains to them alone. They are cathedral-like in their majesty. No wonder they have produced poets and soldiers.

But Scotland was busy arming for the war. Every man of military age was taking to the field. It required no conscription to send the Scots to the war. Ninety-three *per cent.* of the sons of the Scottish Manse had volunteered and gone, and only the lame, the halt and the blind of military age remained. If this war continued very long there would be no Scotch left, except what you get in bottles.

I spent a day in Mull and Iona motoring with a friend who was enlisting men for the naval service. We stopped at a village on our return, and while he went off to see a young man, I was sitting in the automobile opposite a small cottage, at the front gate of which stood a tall, handsome young woman, with two tiny children clinging to her skirts. She managed to pluck up courage to speak to me.

"Perhaps you are from the war, Sir?" she said with a wistful look on her face, and a strong Highland accent.

"My husband is in one of the Highland Regiments, perhaps you have seen his battalion, the Argyles?"

I replied in the negative, adding that I belonged to a Canadian Highland Regiment.

"There are only two young men left in this village who have not gone to the war," she volunteered. "And they will have to be out of here to-morrow, or they will hear from the women."

"You Scotch women are very hard on the men," I said in a half joking way; "You are sending them all to the war. There won't be any left. Why did you, with those two little children, let your husband go to the war?"

This seemed to stagger her for a moment, then she drew herself up scornfully and turning on me, with her eyes fairly blazing, she said:

"I am a Cameron, Sir. I would never have spoken to him again if he had not volunteered to go to the war."

I regretted my remark, and the refrain of the old Jacobite song recurred to me, "A Cameron never can yield." This is an example of the spirit of the Highland Scotch people in the Great War.

It should be considered a duty of every person of Scottish blood to see Scotland and live in it, if only for a short time, and have their children see "Home." The people of Scotland cannot understand why Colonials and Americans of Scottish descent to the second and third generations, especially Canadians, should call Scotland "Home." The reason is easily explained.

In America we are constantly struggling to attain wealth, social or political greatness, or else we are busy all the time fighting to prevent others from achieving success. We were only in Scotland a very short time when the kindly spirit and homely friendship of the people give us a new experience. It is like the feeling of good-will that centres about one's own fireside. As a country Scotland is "Home." Everyone there from the humblest fisherman to the highest born in the land is anxious to show you some kindness and make you feel at home. That is why Scotland is the cradle of soldiers, poets, statesmen and heroes.

As soon as the holiday season was over the Canadians again settled down to Field Training. Every morning we started off with our waggons and enough food to do us for the day. We drilled and fought and put into effect new lessons in tactics. Particular attention was paid to musketry, such as training the men and the squad leaders to name and recognize targets, also to judge distances by practical methods. Every day we were becoming more efficient.

Before the Christmas holidays I had had the good fortune to be able to take the "Hythe" Course and certificate in musketry and machine gun training at Hayling Island. I went there a confirmed adherent to the old Bisley style of deliberate shooting. I left a convert to the new British system of musketry that turned out the formidable riflemen of the First British Army. These soldiers overwhelmed the Germans with the great rapidity and accuracy of their fire. The Germans would hardly believe that the British were not armed with automatic rifles.

On the way back from Hayling Island I met with an accident which luckily had no bad results for me. Accompanied by General Turner, V.C., and Lt.-Colonel Burland, I was being driven in an automobile from Salisbury City to Lark's Hill Camp, when the steering gear of the automobile went wrong and we ran into an embankment, the car turning turtle. I was sitting in the front seat with the driver, and the machine, going at the rate of thirty miles an hour, crashed into the bank. I braced myself, seeing visions ahead of a broken neck and a sudden inglorious end to my campaigning. But Providence saved me from even a scratch, although I was projected with such force against the glass windshield as to smash it to atoms. As the car went over, I had presence of mind enough to grasp the stancheons of the top, and thus saved myself from being thrown out over the front of the car.

General Turner, V.C., who was in the rear seat with Colonel Burland, was buried under the machine, and as I cleared myself from the broken glass and debris I hear him groan, whilst the automobile hind wheels continued to revolve as long as any gasoline was left in the carburettor to feed the engine. We managed to get him out of the wreck and commandeered another automobile to take him back to Salisbury, where it was found that his collar bone and several ribs were broken. He was very cheerful and his only anxiety was lest his injuries might prevent him from going to the Front. As this book was published while I was still "soldiering" my lips were sealed as far as saying anything about my superior officers was concerned. All I dare say is that no braver, better, truer man than General Turner, V.C., ever lived.

Our field training brought our men along very quickly. They were gradually becoming seasoned. They had gone into huts at Lark Hill which they had built themselves, and as these huts were warm and comfortable life began to be a real pleasure.

About the last week in January Hon. Sir George H. Perley and Lord Islington paid us a visit at Lark Hill, and we had the pleasure of their company at an informal luncheon.

Thursday, February 4th, 1915, was one of the greatest days in the history of the regiment. The previous week, when Sir George Perley and Lord Islington visited us in our huts and messed with us on soldiers' fare, the Acting High Commissioner told me that it was probable that His Majesty the King and Lord Kitchener would be down the following week to review the Canadian Division and say goodbye. This put everybody in tune, even the lads who had to stay in England with the surplus officers. On Wednesday afternoon the field officers spent some time in going over the review ground, pegging it out, so it will not be out of place to say a word about the grounds. Lark Hill Camp lies on a gentle slope facing west, and from the door of my hut I could see Stonehenge, that mighty monument to the great race that at one time lived on these plains and raised the enormous *tumuli* monuments to the heroes of their day.

The reviewing ground was selected about a mile and a half west of the camp on the new line of railway which had been built largely by the Canadians. The stand was placed to face north and the long lines, two of them stretched away east and west. About a mile south Stonehenge is visible, and from Signal Mound in the rear of the reviewing grounds the river and Old Sarum can be seen in the distance. All about the plains huge mounds raised by the Druidical Celts rear themselves, of varying sizes, some twenty feet high, others smaller. This must in all ages have been a great military centre. We are not the first comers by any means, and this is truly historic ground that has resounded to the tread of the warrior for thirty centuries. It was fitting that it should be ground chosen by the King on which to review his Canadian troops.

The morning looked very uninviting. It threatened rain, sleet and snow. For a moment it brightened up and then we were ordered to parade with overcoats in packs, but by the time the troops got to the ground it was raining heavily and we were reviewed in overcoats after all.

The troops were placed in two lines, at about two hundred paces distance, the cavalry on the right, then the artillery and the auxiliaries, then the infantry, three brigades of them, the pick of the contingent. They certainly looked well as they marched across the Downs to their appointed stations. The training had had its effect. They looked much better than at the first review, many of them on that occasion being without parts of their uniform, and the drill was rather loose and frayed at the ends.

However, that was an historic occasion for we had Her Gracious Majesty with us then, as well as the King, and Lord Roberts, whose smile was so refulgent it was worth the whole voyage to see it.

The King was to arrive at eleven o'clock, and a few minutes before that hour the whistling of a locomotive was heard as the train wound its way up and down over the hills of Amesbury. The road was built along the sides of the hills without any pretence of grading to a level. It was built by the sturdy Canadians who will leave that monument behind them on Salisbury Plains, more useful if not more ornamental or enduring than Stonehenge, the *tumuli*, or the fallen ramparts and ditches of Celts, Saxons, Normans or Romans.

The train consisted of two locomotives and two coaches. After a few moments it stopped and His Majesty and his Staff stepped out and advanced along a board walk to the platform which had been erected for him to stand on, and over which the Royal Standard was then floating. As he took his place on the stand, a trumpet sounded and as one man the troops came to the salute. Each double line was over a mile in length. His Majesty and Staff, accompanied by General Alderson and Colonel Seely, M.P., now the new Cavalry Commander, started down the first line to the left, then back up the front of the second line to its right. The officers commanding units dismounted as His Majesty left the stand.

My regiment was the second from the left in the second line. His Majesty walked between the line of officers and the front line of men. The most prominent figure on the Staff was Lord Kitchener, who, wonder of wonders, wore a smile like a summer morning. As His Majesty approached the left of the regiment, I met him, saluting. He shook hands with me, and I took my place on his left hand. He asked me very kindly about the health of the men and expressed great pleasure to know that we had almost recovered from the terrible epidemic of influenza and of la grippe that had affected the troops. I assured him that the men did not grumble, they considered it part of their work and were quite content to "do their bit" for His Majesty and the Empire. He repeated that it was altogether too bad that the Canadians had had to put up with disagreeable conditions, but they were going abroad in a few days, and he felt sure they would distinguish themselves. He then shook hands with me, bade me goodbye and wished myself and the regiment "good-luck." Lord Kitchener then shook hands, and with a "Good-luck to you and your fine regiment, Colonel," they passed along to the next battalion. Several of the other officers on the Staff shook hands and chatted for a moment.

His Majesty looked greatly improved in health, and seemed in better spirits than the first time we saw him at West Down South. On that occasion he was showing the effects of the hard work he had been giving to the Army—here today, miles away to-morrow. But those first strenuous days were over. The war was well in hand. The measure of the Germans had been taken, at sea as well as on land.

When the war broke out the one thing the people dreaded was lack of efficient leadership. No one imagined the King would be the strongest and best King the Empire had ever seen. To him alone is to be ascribed the wonderful political solidarity of the British people. The masses always had a latent feeling that King George would make a great King.

His Majesty returned to the stand, and we marched past in double lines, the cavalry eight deep in fours, the artillery two guns abreast, the infantry in double lines of fours, eight men abreast. Then they defiled along the railway four deep to cheer His Majesty as his train passed. The bonnets were placed on the muzzles of the rifles and the men cheered like mad. His Majesty stood at the window of the Royal Coach and waved farewells, and the second review by the King was over. I heard the men say how much they regretted that Her Majesty had not been there, for we enjoyed her first visit very much, and the interest she took in the soldiers.

The frills are now all over and it is get ready to entrain and cross over to France.

It was a great pleasure to learn from time to time that the officers that went to Valcartier supernumerary to our establishment and were transferred to other corps were getting along well. Lieutenants Smith and Ian Sinclair had gone to the Royal Highlanders of Canada, Lieutenant Bell to the 17th Battalion. They all subsequently distinguished themselves in France.

At Salisbury Plains Captain J.W. Moffatt was transferred to our Battalion as Chaplain. He immediately joined the officers' training class and qualified as a combatant officer so that if need be he could transfer to the effectives in Flanders. He was a great favourite with us all.

Chapter 11

Off for France

"Sir! There is a cup of coffee ready for you, and your horse will be at the door in fifteen minutes."

I had thrown myself at ten o'clock on my cot, fully equipped for the first march on the way to France, and had slept soundly till roused at twelve forty-five by a knock on my door, followed by the voice of the orderly room sergeant.

I went to the door of my hut and looked out. The night was dark as a wolf's mouth. The stars in this northern latitude sparkled with unusual brilliancy.

On the evening of the 9th, I had been asked to go to the Headquarters of the Third Brigade, where General Turner, V.C., had informed me that my regiment would march out for France on the 11th.

There was great glee when this became known. The tents hummed with bustle and activity. Everybody got busy polishing and packing up. The spare kits and kit bags were to be left at Salisbury. Many of them would never be claimed.

It seemed almost impossible for us to get ready in time. We had not yet learned to march on an hour's notice, but we were told to cut down our baggage to the regular allowance.

We were not sorry to leave England for we had spent many disagreeable hours on Salisbury Plains with rain a dozen times a day, mud varying from ankle to knee depth, wet clothing and poor tents.

A few undesirables had crept into our Force at Valcartier where they had not been confronted with the wet canteen evil. When these chaps got to England they broke loose and had to be sent back to Canada. They should have been put through the wet canteen test before they sailed. It would have saved Canada a great deal of money. These men caused a lot of talk about the Canadians in London.

London was the Headquarters of a German lie factory and all

kinds of yarns were circulated there about us. For instance, it was told about the Princess Pats that when they went to Flanders they failed to hold their trenches and had to be brought back to London and hidden away "somewhere" to cool their nerves. This was a shameless lie about one of the grandest corps ever raised for the British army, a corps that in holding the "warm corners" in the British line in six months had casualties of over 2,700 men, or about three times its effective strength. The deeds of this gallant corps at Ypres and St. Eloi will live forever in song and story, and the names of Lt. Colonel Farquhar and other gallant leaders will not be forgotten in the future annals of the British Army.

The people of Salisbury were sorry to see us leave for we had spent much money in the town.

The day before we marched out I had visited the city to pay up our bills, see about the storage of baggage and kits, and pay a visit before leaving to the ruins of old Sarum.

Contemplation of these stupendous ruins of a great people recall the fact that it was the Huns that destroyed the civilization of Greece and Rome. Always when the Hun absorbs sufficient civilization from his neighbor to make him efficient in the art of war he becomes seized with a military mania, the madness of Thor, and he seeks to destroy the civilized efforts of ages. Replacing nothing he thus plunges the world into darkness and barbarism. He destroyed the Graeco-Roman civilization and the world reverted to utter darkness for four centuries. Then Charlemagne came and there was a renaissance of civilization and law, and literature. Education and the arts again flourished, but after him came again the conquering Hun and then followed another long era of darkness and barbarism.

I rode out in front of the battalion and could just distinguish the dark outlines of two companies. The other two were getting ready and would march two hours later with Major Marshall in command.

With me was the Quartermaster, Captain Duguid, the Adjutant, Captain Darling, the Transport Officer, Captain Jago, and most of the train. We had a little difficulty in getting the men moving. I asked the transport officer the number of vehicles and animals and he told me he had eleven waggons. I rode to the cross roads, halted the regiment and ordered the transport to lead, counting them.

When I ordered the regiment to march, Captain McGregor's hoarse command "Form fours! right! left wheel! Quick March!" from the darkness, set the column in motion.

I took a final look at Lark Hill Camp and Salisbury Plains. The lights here and there on the Downs showed a glimmer of life. We had spent some happy days in the Lark Hill huts, the happiest we had spent in England.

I carried an electric torch in my hand and led the way. There was a slight frost that made the muddy road better for marching. The adjutant rode ahead to look after the transport, and Sergeant-Major Grant strode at my saddle bow. My horse kept dancing all the way on his hind legs, as if he too was glad to leave and anxious to be over in France. Soon in the distance ahead gleamed the lights of Amesbury, and after a while tall firs closed on either side of the road as we passed the gates of the Manor House of Amesbury.

These gates were built over a hundred years ago and were designed by a celebrated architect Inigo Jones.

In an hour we were at the station. As we approached I rode ahead into the station yard and found that our train had not yet arrived. The regiment marched on the entraining platform, and on looking over the transport I found that my spare riding horse, which was lame and carried my saddle bags, had been left behind on the roadside. I sent Private Gold, one of my orderlies, back to look them up, with instructions to bring them along with the second half of the regiment.

Our train was half an hour late, but when it backed in it did not take us long to load. The English open cars are coupled up close, and the open waggons that take our transport are all loaded from the end of the train the way circus waggons are loaded in America. We entrained horses and waggons in forty minutes. We startled the train people so that they all came to see me when we had finished to tell me how fast we had loaded. The railway transport officer came to my compartment and told me that he had been loading troops for four years there and he had never seen such a fast clean piece of work.

We had to sit for fifteen or twenty minutes before the train moved, as we were ahead of time. Our destination had not been given us. It was very cold in the compartment as there was no steam available, but the train rushed along, and soon we were in Salisbury. On we went west. Fortunately a long course of travel in Canada had given me the habit of sleeping sitting in my seat, and I took advantage of it. At dawn I woke up and found we were nearing Bristol of which Avonmouth is the seaport.

We arrived at our port of embarkation about seven in the morning. The green fields glistened with hoar frost and the distant hills seen through the haze were covered with snow. Through the gaps of the hills here and there could be seen the mounting flames of great blast furnaces. This is the region of coal and iron.

When we reached the station we could see the harbour filled with transports waiting to carry our Division to France.

I disembarked and asked for the R.T.O. who is the official in charge of the handling of the troops. I found that he was uptown having his breakfast. We had to wait about fifteen minutes till he arrived. Then he was apologetic and said he did not expect we would be on time. He then got busy calling for a fatigue party to unload the transport, but after he had blown off a little steam I pointed out to him that the fatigue party was waiting at the head of the column, and had been waiting for him for a quarter of an hour, and that they wanted to be shown to the unloading platform. Then he took a tumble that we "knew our job," and from that time on sugar could not have been sweeter. He told us that our transport was the *Mount Temple*, and showed me the ship, and in a very few minutes we had the men on board. They soon got busy and had the waggons slung into the hold. We found that on the evening before the five-inch gun battery and one unit of an ammunition column under Major McGee had gone on board. They had stowed the big guns in the lower hold, and they had enough lyddite stowed forward to insure a perfectly good explosion provided a submarine plugged us with a torpedo. Our adjutant and the steward soon had us in our cabins.

A couple of hours after we embarked Major Marshall came along with the left half battalion and reported a very successful entraining. The railway company, however, had provided a train with one coach too few, and four horses and eight mules had to be left behind to be brought by the next train. They were in charge of Sergeant Fisher, my transport sergeant, who was a very good man, one of my best non-commissioned officers. Sergeant Gratton, who had been my transport sergeant, took ill before we left Lark Hill. He had to be left behind eating his heart out like a lot of other good officers; non-commissioned officers, and men that I would have liked to have had with me, *viz.*, Lieutenant Davidson, who had bronchial trouble and a bad knee, Lieutenant Lawson had bronchial trouble and a bad throat. Captain Marshall had pneumonia, Lieutenants Campbell, Kay and Wilson each had a touch of pneumonia. Lieutenant Art. Muir was recovering from bronchial pneumonia.

Capt. Musgrave and Lieut. Malone, good steady officers, had to remain with the base company. Lieutenants Acland and Livingston had been sent several weeks before to help drill "Details" and reinforcements for the British troops in France, and they were both at Falmouth working hard putting some polish on the English Tommies. I wrote General Alderson before I left, asking him to let me have Lieutenants Acland and Livingston back, but got "no" for an answer. They were sent to Falmouth while I was in Glasgow at New Year's. If I had been in Camp I would not have parted with them.

We got through loading early in the afternoon and later on the mules arrived in charge of Sergeant Fisher and were safely tucked on board. I had a little trouble keeping people off the dock who were intent on handing liquor to my men.

We were pretty well crowded up and I was informed that this ship had been wrecked once, but the good old C.P.R. flag was floating at the mast head and we took that for an omen of good luck, and it was. During the afternoon I told the men off to the life-boat stations and received the cheerful information that the ship was short a few life belts. I intended to have carried an inner motor cycle tube for my personal use, but forgot to take it along, so would have had to take my chances on a hen coop or a hatch if anything had gone wrong.

The men were in great good humour. They were singing like larks. Some of them had left newly married wives at home in England. One at least, one of my best men, was too much married as he had left two wives behind. He had joined the regiment in Toronto and had given his separation allowance to a wife in Paisley. When we got to Salisbury another woman wrote from Glasgow saying she was his wife and claiming the allowance. In an unfortunate moment he had taken a trip to Paisley and wife No. 1 had pounced on him while he was visiting wife No. 2 and there was a scene. She wrote to me threatening to have him arrested for bigamy. I saw this would not do as there were three interests demanding satisfaction. First, there was his duty to the King.

It had cost a lot of money to train him and bring him so far. He would be no use to the King in gaol for bigamy and would be only a further expense to the country and a good soldier would be lost to the service. So I suggested to Wife No. 1 that she leave him alone till after the war if he gave her an assignment of his pay of twenty dollars a month. Like a sensible Scotch woman she saw the wisdom of Solomon in my suggestion and accepted it. Wife No. 2 received the separation allowance and the King got the services of a first class soldier and all three interests were satisfied.

48th Highlanders at Church Service Under Fire Near Messines,
Rev. F.G. Scott Officiating

We embarked for France with not a dozen men in the regiment with entries on their conduct sheets. A better behaved lot of men it would be hard to find. We had succeeded in instilling in them the iron discipline of duty which was to prove better than the discipline of fear. It was Napoleon who said, "Show me the regiment that has the most punishments and I will show you the regiment that has the worst discipline." He was right.

We sailed during the early hours of the morning. I got up early and after some breakfast went on deck. Colonel Burchall Wood of the Divisional Staff had joined us on the previous afternoon, and as he was my senior officer I reported to him, but he said he preferred to be my guest and for me to take command. The captain who was a Welshman named Griffith told me he wanted a guard of fifty men fore and aft with loaded rifles to look out for submarines. We also mounted two machine guns on the bridge so we pitied the submarine that would come along. The *Mount Temple* could make ten knots in calm weather and the Captain told me that he intended, if a "sub." showed up, to go for it full tilt and run it down.

By ten o'clock we were well out in the British channel. The Welsh Hills were covered with snow and it was a delightful day, hardly a ripple on the surface. Two destroyers, Numbers "1" and "2," kept doing "stunts" back and forward ahead of us all day.

Before dealing with France or anything further, I desire to say that the Canadian Ordnance Officers were very hard worked and had to make "bricks without straw." The death of Colonel Strange made a vacancy which should have gone to Captain Donaldson, a Canadian, my Quartermaster, and no better or more experienced officer ever served the King.

A British officer, however, was called in to do the work. The difference between a British officer of the old school and the Canadian is that when the former is confronted with some work he says, "I'll call my man," that is a non-commissioned officer with a "red tape" training, to do the job. The Canadian takes the responsibility himself and sees that the matter is attended to.

The first evening was bright and clear and I tried my field glasses on the stars. The captain told me the barometer was falling and that we were likely to have a change of weather.

The thirteenth is generally a tough day with everybody and this was no exception. I was aroused shortly after daylight by a loud noise, the banging of furniture and the sound of dishes rattling. Sure enough we were having a storm. The first officer was in the hall. His room was opposite to mine and he was trying to get in, but the drawers and chairs in his room had piled up against the door. I asked him what was wrong and he said he wanted a surgeon as he had hurt his leg. One of the boats had got loose and while fastening it he had his leg jammed. The boat had been carried away. The ship was going like a pendulum, swinging nearly forty-five degrees every jump. One minute I looked down on Major Marshall who was in the top bunk over on the opposite side of our cabin, the next minute the curtains on his bunk hung straight over my head.

Then the ship would take a turn and stand on her head, and the roar of the screw told us there was still plenty of steam in the boilers. Then the screws would submerge and the shock would send a shiver all over the ship. We were in the "chops" of the channel all right. It looked as if the storm would get us if the submarines did not. I told the first officer that the doctor was in a room in the sick bay, and he was helped away limping along the deck. Captain Frank Perry came along as cheerful as a morning in June. He was Officer of the Day and a first class sailor. He came to my room to report that there was a big gale outside, that the men were all right, very few sick, that an artillery horse had broken out of his stall and that he was down and likely dead; also that the waggons were loose in the hold forward with one or two waltzing around. While he was telling this he had to sit on the floor of the cabin. He had split his oil cloth coat up the back, and a stray door speeding the parting guest had slammed on a very tender part of his body, making it difficult for him even to sit down. I laughed till my sides ached.

The admiralty stevedores had stowed the waggons in the hold and a mess they had made of it. I asked him if the big guns were lashed down, fearing that if one got loose in the lower hold it would go through the side of the ship like paper. He assured me that the big gun lashings held, and I ordered him to get a fatigue party and get baled hay and dump it among the waggons to stop the riot, then to lash the waggons. He departed on his errand.

The steward brought me in some Bovril and biscuits, and Major Marshall, who also kept to his bunk on my advice, began feeding upon hard tack to get into trench practice. Bye-and-bye Perry came back and reported that Sergeant McMaster had fallen and broken his arm. Capt. MacLaren was up and he was a good surgeon and hastily set the injured limb. The sergeant had fallen and struck his elbow on the iron deck. The men were all wearing their English boots with heavy iron nails in the soles and they did not hold well on a steel deck. I took a few looks out at the sea and it was a daisy. I saw the captain who came in and reported very bad weather, but he hoped to clear Cape Ushant. Captain Perry reported that the ship was making about half a knot an hour sometimes, sometimes not making anything, wouldn't steer, and half the time in the trough of the sea, if there was any trough to be found, for a cross gale had turned the sea into pyramids. He also informed me that everything had been made fast, that the men were cheerful and that there were no German submarines in sight, and the storm continued with terrible violence all day. The destroyers had sped as soon as we had left the British Coast. Several times during the day the ship took to her beam ends and the crew thought she would not come back, but she did. I took a bite in bed and stayed there all day. Perry looked after the rations and feeding of the men.

I woke up about seven the next morning and still the ship was swinging. Captain Perry came in to say that they had made a good night, another boat had gone by the board and also a bit of the rail. The horse belonging to the artillery was dead. About nine o'clock I got up, and at ten went the rounds of the ship and saw the captain who told me we were bound for St. Nazaire in Western France. This place had been used as a British base before the retreat of the Germans from the Marne.

The weather moderated during the day, and on going the rounds I found the men cheerful and that most of the horses had been moved into the centre of the ship which was some improvement. My horses were all well except the big mare whose leg still gave her trouble. In the afternoon the sun came out and it got so warm that we could go about without overcoats. We were 300 miles south of Salisbury Plains. No wonder the swallows follow the summer. We were not as low yet as the latitude of Sault Ste. Marie. What would it be when we got to the latitude of Toronto?

During the day several ships passed us going in the opposite direction. They were all tramp or troop ships. I forgot to say that the first day out near the Irish Coast we saw a great three-masted full-rigged ship in the distance. She was a magnificent sight with all sails set. What a great sight a fleet of these sailing vessels must have presented in the days of Nelson. Now ships only showed low black platforms and smoke stacks. No novelty nor romance about them.

In the evening the captain said we would soon see the light houses on the French Coast. As soon as it became dark we could see in the sky the double flashes of a great light at Belle Ile forty miles away. This is one of the most wonderful lights in the world. The sea was still high, but we were making good time. The captain told me we would not make the harbour till the following afternoon at four o'clock when the tide was up. We came into the estuary of the Loire and halted, waiting for a pilot. Then the ship began to roll in earnest. I was up on the bridge with the signalmen, and one minute we were up in the air and the next the black sea yawned beneath us.

I had my sea legs by this time. There were two or three lights bobbing about and a very powerful lighthouse light cast a baleful gleam every five seconds. The officer of the deck said we were about twenty miles from our destination and that we would hardly get in until after four in the morning when there was high tide, and if not then, not until the afternoon. Bye-and-bye we saw a light bobbing up and down in the swell and he said that was the pilot. He missed the ship the first round but came about to lee, and in the dim light we saw a cockle shell of a boat with two men in it. In a few minutes a line was thrown to them, the ladder was let down over the rail, the pilot grasped the rungs and began his perilous climb. He was a French sea dog and hung on like grim death and managed to get on deck safely. He went into the wheel house and I went to bed.

I got up early the next morning to see what was doing. I learned that they were going to move the ship to the docks before noon and that we would start disembarking right away. The River Loire was in flood and no tide was necessary to give a sufficient depth of water.

It was a glorious morning and pretty soon we were on the quay. It was a typical French sea port, not very prepossessing, but a busy place. French soldiers of all kinds were about, some on duty, some with their arms done up in slings, some of them apparently loafing. About noon two puffing tugs got us through the lock and tied up to a wharf. A Canadian transport officer and admiralty man came on board. We were told as soon as we were ready we could start unloading, and as soon as the "brows" (the sloping platform or gang planks for the horses) were in place we could start taking off the horses. It did not take us long getting ready. Pickets were put out on the quay and various fatigue parties manned the horses. My big mare was pretty lame but my other horse was in good shape. We had escaped the perils of the Bay of Biscay and were now in Western France.

Towards evening I asked the transport officer what time we would take the train, as we had been told we were to go up country. He said that as soon as we had unloaded he would be able to tell me, as he would then order a train from the French. I then learned that the French had a wonderful system of moving troops. When you want to move troops in France you tell them and they supply you a certain number of box cars, a guard van, an officer's car and a certain number of cars to handle your men, horses and waggons. They tell you what time you are to move out, and you have to be ready to the minute. If you have not finished loading, the train moves just the same. There is no fussing among the French, but a deadly efficiency in all things.

Chapter 12

"Somewhere in Flanders"

Bah! Ba! Ba! Ba-a-a! Moo! Mo! Moo! M-o-o-o! Ugh! Ugh! Ugh! Ba-a-a-a!

I was taking a stroll along the railway platform of a station in Northern France where the engine stopped to coal and water when this chorus of barnyard calls burst from the men packed in the box cars, reminding me of a cattle train. When they saw me halt and turn in astonishment there was a roar of laughter.

"I'm very sorry men, that you are so crowded."

"That's all right, Sir," came back the cheery answer, "that's what we are here for."

No wonder they thus amused themselves, for they had been travelling two nights and a day on the way to the front, and the accommodation; Well! only those who have been there can tell about or realize it.

The French do move troops in a wonderful manner. Each train is made up of a certain number of box cars, flat cars and passenger cars. Into a passenger car of the compartment kind the officers and staff are jammed, eight in a compartment. On the flat cars the waggons, guns and vehicles are run and lashed, and into the box cars the men and horses are crowded. On each box car there is painted the legend "*Cheveaux* 8, *Hommes* 40," which being translated means that the capacity of the car is eight horses or forty men, and we had to put 40 men into each box car which crowded them so that only eight men could lie down at a time while the rest stood up. It was thus a very trying journey, but the men did not grumble. They had to stand 48 hours of this and did it without a murmur.

They expected greater hardships than this when they got to the front, and as a poor shattered warrior said to me later on when I clasped his hand and regretted his terrible wounds, "Don't you mind, Colonel. That's what we came over here for."

When we landed we were told to march for the train at seven in the evening, and we were ready to the minute. We marched silently through the streets of Nazaire, and in a quarter of an hour we were at the station. We found the train all ready, but no crew, no conductor, no engine. An official at a water tank told us that the crew and transport officer were at the cafe dining. They came along presently and we started loading. Barnum & Bailey's circus never loaded a train as fast as we did that one.

When we were loaded I was handed my train orders and a big yellow ticket on which was marked the halts and times to eat. We had at least a twenty-four hour run ahead of us. I was told that when I got to Rouen we would get further orders. We carried three days' rations, so I climbed into my compartment, and was soon asleep. I woke shortly after the train started to find we were travelling through a big city along the banks of the River Loire. We halted about seven in the morning to feed and water the horses and make tea for the men in their dixies or oval camp kettles. It is rather a serious business looking after a thousand men and over sixty horses and mules, but our organization stood the test well. My quartermaster, Captain Duguid, knew his work. I had Lieutenant Dansereau as our scouting and interpreting officer. He was a graduate of the R.M.C. and a good officer.

It is a beautiful country but not really to be compared with Western Ontario. Many large *chateaus* with square doleful looking windows were passed and hillsides covered with vineyards. We were on red clay, soil like that of Devonshire or Niagara. The landscape is punctuated with windmills, most of them old and without sails. At noon we came to Le Mans, a large railway centre, only about forty miles from Paris. We then turned west for Rouen. We stopped at La Hutte for dinner. It was a small wayside station with several large switches. There was an English officer at the platform. The place was right in the country. He informed me that he enjoyed his stay there very much, but that rural France was not like Paris. He said a transport officer up the line kept calling for the 48th.

A beautiful country girl of about twelve years of age came along with a big box of cigarettes which she handed to the men. This was the first demonstration we had had of any kind since we left England. Evidently the people were accustomed to seeing English officers and paid very little attention to us. We were only "*Anglaise*." During the afternoon when we stopped at towns the streets and approaches to the station were crowded with people. About ten o'clock at night we came to Rouen. This was as far as my ticket read. An officer, however, came on board and took my ticket, but returned in a little while with it and another one, sending us on further. We were in for another night on the train. We were now in old Brittany and back in a chalk country. There was not very much to report the next day. We arrived at Bologne about ten o'clock. The Canadian base hospital is stationed here and I did not think we were going further, but we went on. We also passed through Calais which a noted English Queen said would be found written on her heart. They were certainly giving us a trip around the country.

At St. Omar we were told we were to go to Hazebrouck, where we arrived about seven in the evening, and the R.T. Officer who kept asking for us came aboard. It was Lieut. Russell who had sat with myself and officers at the St. Andrew's dinner given at the Queen's Hotel, Toronto, in 1913. He had attended Varsity and knew me and most of our officers. We were delighted to see him again. He told me we had to march out five miles into the country but, if I preferred it, I could stay all night in billets in a new hospital that was in course of erection and was prepared for such use. I chose the hospital, as my men had been standing for two days and nights in box cars. We marched a quarter of a mile through the streets to the hospital, and it did not take us long to get to bed on some straw trusses.

In finding our billets here Sergeant Burness and a piper had dropped through a hole in the floor. Burness was badly hurt and was unable to go any further.

This was the evening of the 17th of February and "it is a strange thing but this regiment has ended most of its big moves on the seventeenth," remarked my orderly room sergeant.

Chapter 13

With Field Marshal Sir John French

"I am the Commander of the British Army in France," said a thick-set ruddy-faced, grey-haired officer in staff cap and uniform.

"Yes, Sir John," I answered, saluting.

"I have had the pleasure of seeing you and your battalion before in Toronto. Have you all the Toronto Highlanders with you?"

"Yes, Sir John," I replied, "most of them."

Our brigade was being reviewed by the commander-in-chief in a hop yard not far from Caestre.

It was raining as usual. We had not yet been reviewed, from the time we first went to Valcartier, that it had not rained.

"Is your establishment complete?"

"Yes, Sir John. In fact we are twenty over strength, and I am afraid you will 'wig' me for it, but we marched out at night and some of the men in the base company, hearing we were leaving, stole away from their quarters, marched five miles and smuggled themselves into the ranks as we marched out into the darkness."

"You will never be wigged by me for bringing such a battalion as this, a few men over strength. We will need them all. Good luck to you, Colonel." We shook hands, and he started over to review the 16th Battalion.

"I am the Officer Commanding the Second Army," and I was saluting and shaking hands with General Sir Horace Smith-Dorrien. With Sir John French[1] were the principal officers of the British Expeditionary Force.

General Sir Horace Smith-Dorrien I had often heard of and he

1. *1914: the Early Campaigns of the Great War by the British Commander* by Sir John French also published by Leonaur.

impressed me more than any officer I had hitherto met. Above medium height, broad-shouldered, with head set square on his shoulders, he seemed the living embodiment of resolution and force. His manner was kind and courteous.

He reminded me that our regiment had sent a detachment to England to the manoeuvres, some years previous, and that he had had the pleasure of meeting some of the officers.

He complimented me upon the fine appearance of the battalion and passed on.

Another officer shook hands. It was Prince Arthur of Connaught.

"Good luck to you, Colonel, and your fine regiment."

Then another officer stopped and shook hands. It was Lord Brooke. He had commanded the Canadian forces at Petawawa the year before when we were there. "I expect to get a command in the Canadians shortly," he informed me. He did. He got a Brigade in the Second Division.

In a few minutes the review was over and we marched back to our billets in Caestre.

Two days before the battalion had marched out of Hazebrouck hospital, leaving a picquet behind to clean up and bring along any stragglers. Thank goodness we were not bothered with many of them, and if it had not been for the bad weather at Salisbury Plains, which accounted for nearly seventy-five good men in the hospitals, we would have had very few weaklings.

We took the main road which turns north from Hazebrouck to Caestre. We were going into billets in the war zone. The place where we were to be billeted was just back of the centre of the line held by the British. East, slightly north, was the famous town of Ypres, due east twelve miles was Armentieres, southwest seventeen miles was La Bassee, south was Bethune, fifteen miles away. East twenty miles, or about as far as Port Credit from Toronto, was the famous fortress of Lille held by the Germans. We were in old French Flanders.

The farmers were ploughing and working in the fields as we marched along the road. The children ran out to look at us. They were all fair and flaxenhaired. It was as peaceful as a Sunday at home, but we were reminded of the war by the trenches running through the fields. The Germans had been here, but left on the big drive from the Marne. The road was a model, made of large stones set about 8×16 inches square and of granite hardness.

Just before we got to Caestre we ran into the Royal Montreal

Regiment halted on the road, and I saw a horseman riding along a side road waving his hand. He joined us and proved to be Colonel Penhale of the Divisional Ammunition Column, who had been with us on the *Megantic.*

I had sent out a billeting officer, Lieut. Dansereau, ahead of us, and when we got within a mile of the town I was joined by General Alderson, who rode Sir Adam Beck's prize winning horse, "Sir James." We rode along for a while and he told me a little about our future programme, just as much as he dared speak about. I rode into the village ahead to find out why we were halted. As I got to the outskirts of the town three horsemen appeared. They were English officers with lots of ribbons on their jackets. We saluted, and as I was going at a good trot, it was only as he passed and smiled and saluted that I recognized His Royal Highness Prince Arthur of Connaught.

When I got into the town I found Captain Pope who had been sent ahead by the Brigadier to divide up the billets among the battalions of the Brigade. My battalion was given the western part of the village. I was interested to know how the billeting would work out. I was put up with a brewer. The brewery was in the back yard. I was shown to my room which contained a large bed, plenty of sideboards and a pair of magnificent bronze lamps on the mantel which were never used.

We very soon got settled down, and mounted a guard and an inlying picquet. We then adopted the plan of making one of the companies furnish the duties every day. One company each day provided all the duty officers, guards, picquets and fatigue parties. This had the advantage that the men are all the time working under their own officers.

On Friday, February 19th, I was sent for to go to Brigade Headquarters. I found Colonel Mitchell of the Toronto artillery there, also the other regimental commanders. Soon a British General dropped in. It was General Campbell of the Ordnance. He was introduced to me and we had quite a chat. He told me that he had belonged to the Gordons, and was so glad we were here. He left, and shortly after another General came in. He told us he was our corps Commander, General Pultney. He had another General with him who sat down beside me and talked for a moment or two. Presently General Alderson came along and then we were told about the review next day.

In the afternoon the Brigadier and I rode out to the field where the review was to take place. There was a quaint old-fashioned churchyard across the road and a brewery further up. Behind us was a Flemish hop yard. This country is full of breweries, broken down wind-mills and hop yards. In the graveyard they said a German Prince was buried. His grave is not marked. The British and Germans had a pretty smart action down the road several months ago. They tell us that six thousand British troops defeated forty thousand Germans and drove them like sheep across the Lye.

We opened the officers' mess in a school room. I tried to keep the officers dining together as long as possible as I knew that as soon as our billets were more open we would have to mess by companies. At this time we were virtually occupying alarm quarters. The men had been behaving splendidly. The inhabitants took to them kindly and of course relieved them of all their spare change. The people of the town are mostly old Flemish. The Flemings have the proverbial long noses, sharp features and have fair complexions. Occasionally a stocky, swarthy individual shows Wallon extraction. Some of the peasants speak nothing but Flemish, which is one of the ancient Gallic languages.

The regiment was up at an early hour next morning and everyone was shaved and cleaned. We had thus far avoided that terrible but famous pest of the soldier that sheds more blood than bullets.

The regiment paraded at the alarm post at ten o'clock. At ten-thirty we marched out and in a few minutes were on the parade ground. We were the first regiment there and were soon formed up *en masse* facing the town. The officers were ordered to be dismounted and I sent my horses back. Shortly after the Brigade staff turned up and all the Brigade formed up in two lines, the 14th Montreal Regiment on the right, the 13th Royal Highlanders on the left of the first line, our regiment on the right of the second line and the Canadian Scottish on the left. The inspecting generals arrived and were accorded the customary salute. The inspection started with the Royal Highlanders, and I noticed that the General who led was a short chunky man with grey hair. He passed up and down the Montreal Regiment and went back and forwards through it. I expected he would go to the left but he headed straight for me, and I recognized the Commander-in-Chief, Sir John French, as already told.

In the afternoon after the review I met Canon Scott, who had lost(?) his way and had come up to the Front with the troops. I asked him to dine with me at a little Flemish restaurant, and we had an excellent Flemish dinner. The proprietress was a very lively creature.

She chattered in French and broken English like a magpie, and flew here and there as lively as if she were on the stage. The canon said the whole affair was like a scene from a French comedy.

Canon Scott was a well known poet and churchman in Canada. His son was an officer in one of the Canadian battalions, and was subsequently wounded. Canon Scott had volunteered as chaplain with the First Contingent, giving up a fashionable congregation in Quebec city. I took him on the strength of our battalion from that night.

The men all behaved very well indeed. It had been given out in divisional orders that several men had fallen out of the line of march for drunkenness, in other regiments, and been shot. The Canadians were all too keen to get to the front for anything like that.

On Sunday, February 21st, I arranged that Canon Scott should preach to the regiment in the morning. We marched out to a green field about a quarter of a mile from the village and formed up in a hollow square. The day was bright and clear, a typical March day in Canada. The ground was very wet and soggy, but the sun shone out bravely. The scene was very impressive. There was no wind and to the northeast of us, about three or four miles away, a terrible battle was going on. The drum fire of the guns shook the earth, and sometimes the good Canon could hardly be heard. He remarked about this unique experience of holding his first service in Flanders within sound of cannon. We sang the hymns quite cheerfully and then he left to attend another service.

I said a few words of thanks to my men, and then we marched back to billets.

Church Steeple Where V.C. was Won

CHAPTER 14

Under Hiex Shells

"I understand that orders have just arrived at the orderly room that we are to march up to the trenches tomorrow. I guess we will have to close the officers' mess till after the war."

This is the greeting I received from Surgeon Major "Alick" MacKenzie when I rode up to the door of my billet on the 22nd.

I had just been out for a gallop. "Alick," as our officers affectionately called our regimental surgeon, had been sitting on the doorstep surrounded by a group of Flemish children. He was engaged in giving them a lesson in English as I rode up. Wherever we went, the children seemed to recognize a friend in our regimental M.O.

I told him that I was glad we were going to the trenches at last and that we would form a staff mess which would consist of Major Marshall, the adjutant, Captain Darling, the signalling officer, Lieutenant Dansereau, and myself. That evening the officers of the 15th Battalion dined together in the Academy at Caestre, and it proved to be the last time we were all to dine together. We were all in good humour, but there was not much ceremony.

Our orders were that we were to move up nearer to the trenches and take up quarters at the city of Armentieres. Armentieres is about ten miles west of Lille, the famous fortress built by Vauban and besieged and taken at one time by the famous Duke of Marlborough. Previous to the war it was a great manufacturing centre. The line of opposing trenches was about a mile and a half east of Armentieres. We were to march as light as possible, our packs being carried on transport motor trucks. We spent all day getting ready for it as it was to be a hard march along a stone paved road.

Our first march to the trenches began on February 23rd, and it took some time for us to parade. For the first time my regiment did not march on the minute. We were ten minutes late in starting. Then I halted five minutes to let the transport catch up. Three hundred pairs of rubber boots had been issued to us the night before and we had to pile them on the waggons which caused delay.

Two miles up the road General Alderson stood waiting for us to go past. Each platoon was called to attention, and the officers saluted. The general was apparently highly pleased. Near the village of Fletre General Sir Horace Smith-Dorrien and his staffs were waiting for us. He marched with us on foot for a while, and complimented me on the appearance of the regiment on the march and wished us good luck.

At the village of Fletre General Pultney and General Turner, V.C., with their respective staffs, were waiting. We gave them the customary salute, and later on in the afternoon General Pultney sent word to me that one of my officers had saluted him with a stick in his hand, and that two of the men had failed to remove their pipes when called to attention.

We recognized General Pultney as having what we called "class" and we were delighted that that was all the criticism we had evoked.

The march came to an end about half past three. We soon found our billets. It was a stone block paved road all the way. The men had on new English boots with iron nails in the soles and the hard smooth stones made the walking very hard. It was the most trying march the regiment had. Putting the packs and great coats on the waggons had caused great confusion. The men on reaching town found their packs and coats all mixed up and it took several days to straighten them out. The men would never be allowed to part with their great coats and packs again if I could help it, unless they are going into action.

On going into billets, with the trenches only a mile and a half away, we learned some new wrinkles and it is a blessing we were now in double companies.

Our platoon commanders were ordered to go to the trenches that night to learn something. It was to be their baptism of fire. They came back to my orderly room at ten o'clock after going the rounds and dodging a lot of German bullets. I was to go in on the 26th with Colonel Levison-Gower of the Sherwood Foresters who had called and said he would take me around and show me what to do when my men were in the trenches.

Our orderly room was in a fine house. We had good cooking facilities and two women to look after the meals. Our orderlies had only to look after the kits. The number of the house was thirteen and we came here under gun fire on the 23rd. That meant bad luck to the Germans.

Armentieres was a factory town. They made linen chiefly and there are several large weaving mills. The people were very friendly and cheered us along the way. We met a lot of English soldiers, the Westminsters, the Yorks, the Durhams and Sherwoods. They had been fighting here since early in November and were rather "fed up" on the trenches as they describe it. The Toronto Regiment was up here and were full of ginger, they told us. Outside of being a little too eager to let off their ammunition, the Canadians were declared to be first class troops. We are at the point of a small salient that sweeps east in the German line towards Lille.

That famous city was only about seven thousand yards from our trenches, well under our cannon fire.

The next day I had lunch with Colonel Levison-Gower of the Sherwood Foresters. They were quartered in a magnificent *chateau* owned by a French cavalry officer who was married to the heiress of the place. She owned most of the factories. The town was shot full of holes, about one house out of every ten having been peppered with shell fire. The British had some big guns there. One half of my battalion was to go into trenches one night, and the other half went the next night. I warned the officers against any foolishness or bravado. I could hear the rattle of rifle and machine-gun fire and I tried to sleep. The billets we occupied were the finest we had lived in so far. I had a good coal fire in my room.

Some devilish battery commander kept pounding away all night. Every ten seconds his blighting guns would go off and rattle the windows. Major "Billy" Marshall slept in the next room, and his snore told me he was dreaming of Paardeburg, Poplar Plains and battles of South Africa. A few days before we left England his horse had slipped and rolled over on him, lacerating some of the ligaments of his hip and rendering him virtually unfit for duty. He could hardly walk or ride, and should have been put in hospital, but he pleaded so hard with MacKenzie and I to let him go, and forget that he had been hurt, that he was passed as fit for duty. He was a brave, keen soldier.

February 25th was my birthday and it was the first day that the regiment I had helped to organize twenty-four years before went into action. I hoped it would be a fortunate day and that none of my officers or men would be hurt. Trench work is bad, and gunshot wounds there are usually fatal as they are generally in the head. I spent an excellent day and in the evening the staff had a little dinner for me. I telephoned Brigade Headquarters and found out that up till noon none of my men had been hurt. They had been told off with the British soldiers and mixed up so they would learn the work.

While we were at dinner the first of the officers that had been in the trenches came in. This was Lieutenant Barwick and he reported no casualties in his section. He was as cool as a cucumber. He was followed by Captain McLaren and Lieutenant Bickle. Then Captain McGregor came in and reported for his company. In a few moments I got a note from Major Osborne saying his men were all right so that the first day was a fortunate one. I thanked God that it was so, and the officers were as cheerful as if they had been at a ball game and had won it. They said they had put several German snipers out of business. They drank my health in cocoa and we all hoped that my next birthday would be spent at home with all the officers and men with me safe and sound.

It is wonderful how careless of danger people become. In the afternoon while I was out riding the Huns started shelling the station and town. Half a dozen British Howitzers 9.2 inch guns started to reply. The German high explosive shells, or "*Hiex*" as they were called there, were falling five or six hundred yards off, still the children were playing in the street and a bunch of little girls were skipping with a rope. That night there were several outbursts of rifle fire, and it sounded very much as if an attack was taking place in the section of the trenches held by the Royal Montreal Regiment.

When we got up the next morning the sun was shining very brilliantly. A big British naval gun had opened fire on the German lines, and overhead two aeroplanes were sailing about directing the fire of the naval gun. The Germans had opened fire on the aeroplanes with anti-air craft guns, and their shells were bursting high in the air in white puffs like Japanese fireworks. We took our field glasses out to the square in front of our billet and could follow the course of the air craft quite plainly. After each one of our shells fell the plane would shoot a rocket as a signal. The German air craft shells fell hundreds of yards short. The aeroplanes soon rose to such a height that the German guns quit firing on them. The British naval planes were beautiful large craft. On the frontier we had already established air preponderancy and were also doing well now with our artillery.

About five o'clock Colonel Levison-Gower sent a guide to take me to the ruined *chateau* near the trenches where he had his headquarters. Captain Darling and Major Marshall and Surgeon Major MacKenzie accompanied me. We took our horses as the *chateau* was about two miles down the road. The road wound along like a serpent with about every second house on either side blown up with shell fire or the walls peppered with rifle bullets. The British guns were growling on either side. This is an old historic road. Many a time William the Silent, Count Alva, and the great Marlboro galloped along it. Lille, the great masterpiece of fortification designed by Vauban, is only a few kilometres further on. We were beginning to think and calculate now in kilometres. After a smart trot of about twenty minutes we came to a coal yard on the left side of the road. We had passed a number of batteries of heavy guns in position ready to open fire.

It was a beautiful evening. The moon was in its first quarter and there was every prospect of a bright night. At the wood yard we were told to stable our horses, and pretty soon we were struggling along the muddy paving stones on our way to the *chateau*. We had on one side passed a small cemetery that had been set aside for the British and Canadian soldiers shot in the trenches. I should have said that just before I left, word had come in that Private Ford of "H" Company had been shot in the thigh. This was our first casualty. A bullet struck a British soldier of the Westminsters in the shoulder and cut into Ford's thigh, failing to go through.

Ford was a fine brave man. He and another chum came over from the Edmonton Regiment just before we left Lark Hill. He asked to be allowed to join the 48th, and as he was a very likely chap, with a clean conduct sheet, I said, "come along." He was steward of the Edmonton Club and joined at the outbreak of the war. He was hit in the thigh, and the fact that he was wearing the kilt greatly facilitated the bleeding of his wound being stopped. He had two small arteries cut, but the first aid dressing which he carried was soon tied over the wound and the haemorrhage ceased.

It was still light when we got to the *chateau*. Colonel Levison-Gower welcomed us into what was originally the kitchen, where a beautiful range decorated with tiles made the room look very cheerful. Several of his officers were there having tea, and I was offered a cup which I accepted. We sat around waiting for darkness. It was going to be a moonlight night, just the night for sharpshooters, but we had some good sharpshooters of our own out in front of where we were going, and we felt that not even a hare could get through the lines. When it became dark Colonel Levison-Gower said "get ready," and began putting on his togs. He wore an old Burberry coat with the skirts cut off, heavy trench boots, a slouch British cap and armed himself with a long pole, in other words a stable broom handle. He gave me one and said, "This will help you to find a footing in the trenches."

We started out the front door of the shattered house, turned to the right past the driving shed where a sentry sharply challenged us. It was one of those moonlight nights with a bit of a haze making objects indistinct and exaggerating them. We started out across the fields towards the trenches. There was plenty of light to see our way across several ditches. The ground was perfectly flat and the outlines of several pollard willow stubs, with a bundle of small branches growing out of them, etched themselves on my memory.

"Ware wire," said the colonel, who walked ahead to show the way. I ducked a field telephone wire strung between trees.

"Ware wire," he said again, and I found we were making our way between barbed wire entanglements.

"These are the breastworks," he said, pointing to ghostly heaps that loomed on either side. "We line them every night, they furnish our support."

Several wet ditches were jumped by the aid of the broom handles we carried. The ditches in Flanders are exceedingly deep and the gunners find much trouble in negotiating them.

The colonel pointed out a line of shelter trenches his men held on the first advance. They held these trenches where they "dug themselves in" on the first night they won this ground. A little further on we came to small holes dug in the beet field.

"Here is where they did some digging that afternoon." "They are pretty shallow fire trenches, barely deep enough to give cover to a man." Pretty soon a shadow loomed up ahead of us. "This is our first line of trenches," he said.

The line of trenches proved to be a wall of mud, willow hurdles and sand bags; in reality two walls. I followed him down a short bit of zigzag ditch or communicating trenches and found myself in the trenches that will go down to history, the famous trenches of Flanders.

It would require the pen of a Dante to picture this inferno. Day and night, night and day the rifles were cracking like the sound of a big rifle match on the ranges at home. Two lines of parapets, for there are really very few trenches, wind sinuously over the country from the sea to the Alps. These parapets are about the height of a man, and run in zigzag fashion. Here and there where the wall is specially built a dugout is constructed that will hold four or five men. In these huts the men cook and sleep during the day.

At night they come out like moles digging or straightening their defences or else running saps towards the enemy. Here and there along the line about every hundred feet a machine gun position is built into the wall. These positions are not disclosed. The sharp "chop" of the Ross Rifle, the hoarser report of the Lee Enfield and the double cough "*To hoo*" of the German Mauser made it impossible for any conversation to go on except at very close range. Now and again an eighteen pounder would crack wickedly in our rear and its projectile went screaming overhead down to the rear of the German lines to keep the supports and reserves in their "funk holes."

Now and then a German bullet would strike the edge of the parapets in our front and ricochet with a wicked note overhead. The air was filled with a swishing sound as if thousands of swallows were passing overhead. Down the line of the trenches we went to the right, then back to the left. The new relief were going in and manning the parapets. Manning the parapets means standing in a recess built into the wall of the parapets on the side away from the enemy. At stated periods during the night the men man or line the parapets ready for an attack. "*Tut tut tut*," sung out a German Maxim and a shower of the bullets swished uncomfortably close. "*Bir-r-r-r*," replied a British Vickers that fires twice as fast, and the German subsided.

Death was sailing about in the air everywhere, but everybody went on with their "business as usual." The Canadians were cool under fire, just as cool as the British Tommy, and violent language and "swank" was very little in evidence. After inspecting the line we walked back across the turnip field in the fitful moonlight to the ruined *chateau*.

"How is it all going to end?" I asked Colonel Levison-Gower.

"We will have to break through when the time comes," he said, "and we can do it if they give us support."

The total losses in his corps since he came over in September has been over fifteen hundred. Very few of the original battalion remained. I forgot to say that in the trenches we met Captain Street, son of the late Judge Street of Toronto. He had been distinguishing himself as a very brave man. He had been caught out the day before in front of the trenches on the devil's strip with a scouting party as a fog lifted and two of his men were wounded. He had his own clothes ripped with the German bullets. He got his men in safe and doubtless will get his decoration. We returned to our quarters, had a bite and went to bed.

On the morning of the 28th word came from the trenches that Private Ferland of my regiment had been struck in the head and killed. Ferland transferred to the 48th at Valcartier. He had seen service in the American Army and Navy and wore a medal for bravery which I understood he had won in the Philippines. He was of French Canadian descent and was a very good soldier. When the time came to man the parapets in the morning he jumped up on the banquette and called to his comrades to come along and not be lazy. He was tall and his head was above the parapet and two bullets caught him, one in the eye, the other in the temple. He was stone dead when he fell. He belonged to Captain Alexander's Company and the captain felt very badly about him. They took the body out in the evening. He was a Roman Catholic and his nearest of kin lived in Quebec.

The next morning the Sherwoods had a casualty. A soldier was shot through the heart by a sniper. There was one consolation, my men claimed they got the men of two patrols of Germans. In one patrol there were six men, and the six went down on the first volley. One got up and tried to make his trench, but poor fellow they were too much for him. It seemed cruel and rather rough, but the Prussians are not sports, they snipe all the time and when a man falls they fire away at his body for hours to make sure he is not "foxing." This war is a game without an umpire or referee.

We buried Ferland at nine o'clock the next morning. Reverend Father Sylvester performed the service which was very simple. The section to which he belonged marched to the little graveyard. Bullets sang over our heads and pattered on the clay tiles of the barn as the simple Latin service of the old church was read. High in the easterly sky a German aeroplane hovered and our guns were making trouble for him.

I rode home and found the regiment, all that were out of the trenches, formed up on Victor Hugo Square ready for church service. Canon Scott, who had accompanied my regiment from Caestre, and who had managed to make his way up from the front in spite of many obstacles, preached a very fine sermon. Eight of my best shots formed the choir.

General Congrieve, V.C., was present and before the service began he instructed me to post a man with a strong field glass to observe if any German air craft approached. After the service he reviewed the regiment and complimented us very highly on our appearance. He said that I had every reason to be proud of the men, and that he had heard nothing but good words spoken of them since they went into the trenches with his men. He invited me to luncheon next day. Late that night, however, I received my marching orders for next day, which precluded the possibility of accepting his kind invitation. I was to go next day to a conference at the headquarters of the Seventh Division, the Guards and the Gordons whose trenches we are to take over shortly. We are to take their places and give them a chance to rest and refit.

Chapter 15

The Flare-Lit Trenches of Fromelles

Next day I started out on foot with an officer of each of my companies to go to the headquarters of the Seventh Division. We got a motor bus where the railways cross the Armentieres road. Our Brigadier and Staff were all there, and we rode out to a big farmhouse where the conference was held. As we went along the road we could hear the Maxims going like air riveters. The Germans were shelling Armentieres which has been shelled again and again. They threw two shells a couple of blocks away from where I was quartered. When the Germans start shelling the people take to their cellars. The Germans are great on killing children. Priests are also a specialty of theirs. At the last town where we were quartered they were being run out by the English, and they wanted the church tower for a machine gun position. They asked the *cure*, an old man, for the keys of the church tower and he refused to give them up to them. He was at once taken out and shot. They broke into the tower and cut a Scottish battalion up pretty badly with their machine guns, but a Scottish sergeant of the battalion made his way into the church, climbed the tower and surprising the Germans bayoneted them all single handed. He was decorated for this brave act and the shooting of the priest was thus avenged.

We considered it a very great honour for our regiments to relieve the Guards and Gordons. The people at home in Canada would thus understand that in spite of bad weather, sickness and other difficulties that made us leave over one hundred and forty men of the battalion in the hospitals in England, that our hard work, drill and discipline had not been in vain. We had learned a great many lessons and the men now drilled and moved like regulars. In fact, the British had no regiments there that were smarter, for to tell the truth they had found the trench work very trying. I desire to give every praise to my officers. They had their work up perfectly, and the men as a result gave me very little trouble. On parade the men stood like a rock. The captains and other officers had the knack of getting along with them which makes for the best of discipline and prompt obedience born of respect. There were many regiments there, good ones, but there was very little fault to be found with ours. No commanding officer was ever better supported by his officers, non-commissioned officers and men.

It was on March 1st, St. David's day, dear to the Welshmen, that I visited the headquarters of the Seventh Division and of the Guard's Brigade, whose trenches we were to take over. We met Colonel Fisher-Rowe of the Guards and had a cup of tea with him. He was a very kindly-mannered man and we took a liking to him. One of his officers, Lieutenant Barry, was to remain with my regiment and initiate us into the mysteries of the flame-lit trenches in front of Fromelles.

The regiment paraded on the morning of the 2nd and General Congrieve and Colonel Levison-Gower were on hand to bid us goodbye. It was a very pleasant march. The day was fine and cool and the men in splendid spirits. We reached Bac St. Maur in the afternoon and went into billets for the night. I was quartered at the Mayor's house. We now began to realize that in Flanders every cross road means a town or village. The men were quartered in a flax weaving mill. Every town in this country boasts a flax mill with numerous weaving and bleaching plants. Many of the factories before the war were owned by Germans. As the German-owned factories are never shelled they make splendid billets for the troops.

We spent one night in Bac St. Maur, and next day we marched to Sailly, taking over the billets held by the Guards. My quarters were in a large farm house. The companies were each quartered at a similar farm and telephone wires were soon laid by our signallers. We took over the living room of the farm house for our sleeping bags, and as straw was plentiful we made some trusses to soften the feel of the red tile with which the room was floored. It was chilly so I ordered a fire to be made in the grate. We had only just stretched out to enjoy the warmth when suddenly there came the report of a rifle followed by a fusillade, and bullets flew all over the place. We at first thought the Germans were upon us, but the scattering of the fire brands all over the room told us that some "blighter" had left some clips of live cartridges in the sweepings of the fire place. The stampede which had followed the first burst of fire died away in roars of laughter. No one was hurt although pieces of cartridge cases had been shot some distance.

While we were in these billets we experienced for the first time the splendid system that had been organized to keep the men of the allied armies clean. Soldiers from time immemorial have suffered from vermin but a new cure has been discovered by someone attached to our column which was soon used universally. The cure is gasoline. One or two applications destroy all living creatures or their ova. Arrangements had also been made so that the men could all have a hot bath once a week. A factory, usually a bleachery, was commandeered and about a hundred large tubs of hot water were provided. One after another the various companies and units were marched to these bath houses. Every man handed in his soiled shirt and underclothing on entering, and received a complete clean outfit after he had performed his ablutions. The only inconvenience attached to this system was that the underwear, shirts and socks were pooled and they sometimes got mixed, and our battalion being comprised chiefly of very large men sometimes had difficulty struggling into their clean underwear.

On Saturday evening, March 6th, we went into the trenches opposite Fromelles at La Cardonnerie Farm which had been the scene of a very warm action in the previous November.

Before we came to Flanders we had been told a great deal about the trenches in the Low Countries. We had seen pictures in the illustrated papers of deep ditches in which men were packed like sardines, so deep that we wondered how they used their rifles. After we arrived at the front our ideas were changed, and we came to the conclusion that the trenches we had seen depicted at home had been dug for the benefit of photographers, and were situated in some nearby park. Certainly the trenches in Flanders were not at all like the photographs we had seen. In addition, the trenches described in *Our Notes from the Front* were the trenches at the Aisne, where the country is altogether unlike the country in Flanders.

At the Aisne the soil is chalk and limestone and the country broken and rolling. In Flanders, on the other hand, the soil is sticky, yellow clay, and the land flat with the exception of an occasional sand dune like an inverted pudding dish, at intervals of about ten or fifteen miles apart. Hill 60 was one of these. All over this flat clay country there are countless ditches. The roads are elevated above the level of the fields, and along each road there is a deep ditch or two, while there is sure to be one along each hedge. Water is invariably found at a depth of about two feet. One can therefore quite comprehend how in such a country trenches dug in the form of ditches would be full of water in a very short time.

The trenches in Flanders are altogether unlike our conception of them. Trenches are an evolution, not an accident nor a design. This is how they happen. Our troops will be advancing or retiring as the case may be, and will have reached a point where progress is difficult, either by reason of the resistance of the enemy or the impossibility of the flanks coming up and conforming. Word comes from a higher authority that the men are to "dig in." Every man carries, attached to his waist belt on his back, a small entrenching tool, a "grubber" it is called. This tool is like a hoe, only the blade is pointed like a Canadian railroad shovel, and opposite the blade there is a chisel-shaped pick. The handle, about eighteen inches long, is carried in a sling along with the bayonet and enters the "grubber" at right angles.

Immediately the word comes to "dig in" the men get out their entrenching tools or "grubbers" and set to work. They stand at intervals of about a yard apart, make a half turn to the right, lay down their rifles at arm's length, and as they are taught to use the grubber in the prone position, when the ground is favourable they can dig themselves in in fifteen minutes. The trench is dug at an angle of about 90 degrees to the enemy so there will be a clear field of fire in front. Each man places the earth in front of him and digs a hole about two feet wide, six feet long and about eighteen inches deep. These are known as "hasty" or "shelter" trenches. They are the safest trenches to be in when high explosive shells or Mauser bullets are about. If a shell falls it will rarely get more than one man. A little straw in the bottom makes these shelter trenches not uncomfortable at night.

After a battalion has spent a night in the "dig ins," as they are called, it is usual, if no retreat or advance is ordered, for higher authority to send word for the trenches to be "consolidated." That means that more deliberate entrenchments are to be made. "Deliberate" entrenchments in the Low Countries mean parapets, not ditches. "Consolidating" invariably means building parapets. Before a man "digs in" he is supposed to move forward to a position where lying prone he can have a clear field of fire of about one hundred yards in front of him. It will thus be seen that the line of parapets will usually come just in the rear of his shelter trench.

At night the engineers send down waggon loads of sand-bags and hurdles. These hurdles are made by driving a number of sharp stakes about two inches in diameter into the ground, the stakes being about four feet high and eight inches apart. In and out between these stakes wire and elm or willow branches are woven basket fashion and the ends are strengthened by a warp or two of wire. When the hurdle is completed it forms a grill-like section of from four to ten feet in length, ready to be set up like a fence by driving the stakes into the ground. Similar hurdles were used at the time of Caesar, so they are not new in this war. In fact such hurdles were used by Julius Caesar in building his camp a few miles east of the Fournes ridge opposite the trenches which we occupied, for it was there he met the Nervli. These hurdles were set up on the side furtherest away from the enemy and the men, being provided with picks and shovels by the engineers, build parapets of earth against them about four feet high and four feet through at the top. The hurdle is fastened into the parapet with stakes and wire, and on top of these parapets are placed three or four rows of sand-bags filled with earth.

At intervals among the sand bags steel plates about half an inch thick are inserted. These plates have a hole in them for the rifle to go through, and sharpshooters "man" these port holes night and day. Immediately behind these parapets zigzag trenches about four feet deep are dug. These are called "fire" trenches. When the enemy shell us we get into these deep trenches. When they come to an attack we "man" the parapets. Behind the parapets at intervals are located the "dug outs" where the men sleep and hide in the day time. These are built to accommodate about four men each. They are eighteen inches high, dug into the ground about one foot, then a row of sandbags make a bit of wall. The roofs are sheets of corrugated iron with three or four rows of sandbags piled about four feet high. On top of the earth and sandbags there is generally placed a row of broken brick to cause any shell striking the roof to explode before it penetrates. Behind the parapets are places where the men cook and attend to their wants.

Behind the first row of parapets about two or three hundred yards is a second line of parapets or breast-works with fire trenches. This constitutes the second line or supporting trenches. Behind these again about one thousand yards, with plenty of barbed wire entanglements and a clear field of fire, will be built a line of small forts or redoubts. In the parapets at various intervals are located machine-gun positions hidden so that the enemy's aviators cannot see them.

Two lines of parapets such as I have described with but few variations extend from the North Sea near Nieuport to the Alps, for the Germans build their trenches exactly like ours. Sometimes they run short of sandbags, and at one place where we were they were using

Signallers in Flanders

blue drill, such as engineer's overalls are made of, for sand bags.

The distance between these two lines of trenches varies; sometimes it is one hundred yards, sometimes two or three hundred, but never more than four hundred yards. This "devil strip," as it is called, is night and day subject to fire from sharpshooters from both sides.

All night long the Germans shoot "flares" into the air. These flares are like rockets filled with magnesium and they show a very brilliant light, so brilliant that objects on the darkest night are brought into prominent relief a mile behind the line of our trenches.

The Germans are prodigal in their expenditure of these flares. We had to husband our supply, but if the lights began to die down a few rounds of rapid fire from our trenches would soon cause them to send hundreds of their flares into the air. The Germans are rather given to "nerves," and while they were cooling down our men read the papers by the light of their flares.

On the evening of the sixth we went into the trenches at La Cardonnerie Farm, which being translated means thistle farm. The trenches were very wet and muddy and my headquarters were located in a ruined farm house about five hundred yards from the trenches. There was a fine row of tall elm trees in front of the house, which offered a splendid target for the German gunners.

We took over the trenches from Colonel Meighen of the Montreal Regiment who had gone into them three days before. In running wires to the various sections Lieutenant Dansereau and Captain Cory had an exciting time. They had to drop flat in the mud several times while the German flares and bullets flew overhead. The left section was taken by Captain Alexander, the right by Captain McLaren and the centre by Major Osborne. The left section was about eighty yards away from the enemy and subject to constant bombing and enfilade fire. The River Layes crossed our line of trenches. What we would call a creek in Canada is called a river in Flanders. Five lines of wire connected us with the various sections of the front. Captain McGregor's Company was in reserve, hidden away in dugouts. No finer officer ever drew the breath of life than Captain McGregor. Always cheerful and loyal, an experienced soldier of the King, he did credit to his name. There were many McGregors in the army but none braver, more skilful or careful of their men than Captain Archie McGregor, veteran of Paardeburg.

The duties of a commanding officer, and also of company officers while their units are in the trenches, are so strenuous as to leave very little leisure. A great many reports have to be sent to headquarters during the night, and at least once an hour the signallers in the trenches have to report that they are awake. Every burst of rifle fire, every bomb explosion, has to be reported, and any unusual happenings explained. It soon becomes the usual thing to throw one's self down on an old mattress, tuck a blanket over you and take forty winks.

It did not take us very long to get into the swing of things and become quite at home. It is a law of the trenches that at night the men must sleep on their arms, that is to say, they must sleep, if they sleep at all, in their greatcoats, clothing and boots, with equipment and ammunition buckled on and rifle in hand, so as to be ready to "stand to" at a moment's warning. To "stand to" means to fall in behind the parapets ready to repel or take part in an attack. In the trenches the men "stand to" at least half an hour before daylight and remain in readiness to man their parapets until half an hour after dawn. Then they are ordered to "stand down."

The first duty of a soldier in a well ordered regiment after he "stands down" is to take out his oil-bottle and cleaning apparatus and clean his rifle. Then he takes off his *puttees*, boots and socks, rubs his feet to restore circulation, and if he has an extra pair of socks he puts them on, or if not he changes the ones he is wearing from one foot to the other, puts on his boots and *puttees* again. Cotton socks are very uncomfortable, for when a man stands all day and sleeps at night in his boots, if the socks are made of hard thread, the thread will leave a mark in the feet. Unless the men remove their *puttees*, boots and socks once a day they are liable to have "frost bite" "cobble feet" or varicose veins. These troubles soon render them fit subjects for the hospital.

After the rifle and feet are attended to the men shave. Our men always shaved every day, and were very proud of their clean appearance in spite of the mud. One man was brought before me shortly after we went into the trenches for neglecting to shave. He explained that he had served in one of the South African wars and that on service there he was supposed to wear a beard. I fined him for neglecting to observe the King's Regulations and Orders, and his comrades who had warned him against trying to "put anything over" on the commanding officer gave him the laugh. He asked to see me and expressed such regret that I forgave him. He was a splendid soldier and his example made a rule for the others.

Perhaps it will be just as well here to explain the remainder of the daily routine and how the men are fed and cared for. Sometime during the night the company waggons, which are kept in billets at the quartermaster's stores, are loaded with food for the men in the trenches. This food, also charcoal, for fuel, barbed wire and other supplies are placed in sand bags, in weights that one man can carry. A fatigue party from each platoon meets the waggons at a convenient spot, and carries their respective sacks into the trenches held by their platoons. A non-commissioned officer from each company remains always in the quartermaster's tent to supervise the preparing of supplies for his company. He sees that the company cooks prepare steaks, soups and other food to be sent into the trenches. He is responsible to his company commander that his company gets its proper share.

The rationing usually begins about eight o'clock, and if you listen you can hear the rumble of the ration waggons in the German lines as clearly as in our own. At this hour there was generally a truce to sniping, but as soon as either side finishes rationing a few rounds of rapid fire warns the other to hurry up and get down to the business of killing.

When the water in the vicinity of the trenches is bad, water waggons are brought down along with the ration waggons, and the men's canteens and a number of dixies or camp kettles are filled with water and sent into the trenches.

Every man, besides carrying a "First Aid" bandage in the flap of his coat, carries a day's "iron" rations in his haversack. An "iron" ration consists of two or three hard-tack biscuits, a package containing tea and sugar, and a tin of what is currently known as "Macconnachie's Rations." This consists of a tin containing about a pound of what would generally be called thick Irish Stew, made of meat, potatoes, green peas, carrots and some condiments. Thank goodness it contains no brussels sprouts. Great Britain went brussels sprout mad about the time we got over there. Wherever we went, on the trains, in the restaurants we had indigestible brussels sprouts.

In the trenches the men make charcoal fires, boil water, make tea and fry their ham or bacon and eggs. Ye gods what eggs they ate. All the hens in Flanders seemed to be busy night and day laying eggs for the Canadian soldiers at five cents an egg.

This is a standard feeding routine for the men in the trenches. The men and officers get the same rations. Often the men fare much better than the officers for they get parcels of food from friends in Great Britain and Canada. The officers are supposed to be millionaires and of course are expected to live like *nabobs*. But they do not have anything better than the men.

After the men have cleaned up they gather about the charcoal fire with two or three chums that mess together. Bacon or ham of the best quality is soon sizzling in the lid of a dixie. Frequently some cold potatoes are provided which are sliced in with the ham and the meat ration is ready. There is always plenty of good white bread, which arrived the day before fresh from England. There is tinned butter from Australia, and hot tea with plenty of sugar in it. After the meat they have dessert. Usually a fine tin of jam with more bread and butter. If jam does not suit, or they grow tired of jam, they have honey. What a breakfast for a hungry man. The noon day meal will consist of thick soup, steak or mutton chops grilled on charcoal, potatoes dug from nearby pits in the deserted farms, bread, butter, tea and jam or honey. For supper they had cold meat, cheese, bread and butter, jam and tea. The men seldom grumbled at their food as everything was of the best quality, and they had plenty of work and fresh air to give them good appetites, and with such excellent fare they gain in strength and weight. Many a weak, hollow-chested "mother's boy" has developed in a few months into a rosy-cheeked, bread-shouldered athlete, weighing twelve or fourteen stone.

It was a wonderful sight at night to watch the trenches at Fromelles. As far as the eye could see from the North Sea, away past Bethune and death-stricken La Bassee, streamed the meteor flares like a great Milky Way, the flares crossing and recrossing each other. In front of us the German Mausers sound with their constant "*to-ho*," "*to-ho*," for the Mauser has a double report. On the right the wicked bark of the English Lee-Enfield rifles, and along our front and to our left the "*chop, chop*" of the Ross rifle of the Canadian Division. The Ross has a sound at a distance, for all the world like a lot of men chopping wood in a hardwood forest. No wonder the Germans knew when the Canadians came opposite their sector. Whenever they heard the Ross they generally got an attack of nerves and would fire wildly into the air on the slightest excuse.

I visited the line of the trenches passing from flank to flank the second night we were in them and laid plans with our officers to strengthen the position so as to make it almost impregnable. The first man to be killed in these trenches was Private Stanley, a Toronto man, who was shot through the head while standing behind the parapet at night. He fell dead in the arms of his son. We buried him the next evening at the Canadian Cemetery at La Cardonnerie Farm by the fitful gleam of an electric torch while the bullets and shells whistled overhead.

The Germans were very vicious when we went into the trenches for the first time, but we adjusted our fire so as to enfilade their trenches, that is to say, instead of firing at the trenches opposite we aimed to the right or the left so our bullets dropped behind their parapets. I went along the trenches with a photograph of their position taken from an aeroplane and pointed out to the section commanders the targets and range so as to get in behind the German lines. Sand bags and port holes were adjusted to this new form of fire and orders were issued to open enfilade fire after nine at night, sniping briskly. Some of our men suggested that we must have hit a German General because suddenly the whole German line burst into a sheet of flame and they continued to fire their rifles for all they were worth for about fifteen minutes. After that night the Germans opposite kept very quiet when we were in the trenches. A few days later we heard that General Von Kluck had been wounded opposite our lines. We wondered if we had hit him.

The friends of the regiment at home were kind enough to present our battalion with Khaki Tam O' Shanters which we used in the trenches. They were a splendid headdress and we had very few casualties during our various turns of duty in the front line, which good fortune we ascribed to this headdress. General Sir Horace Smith-Dorrien was very much taken with the "tam" as a trench cap.

On the morning of March 8th, while Major MacKenzie and I were having coffee, the Germans began shelling our quarters. We were in an old brick house on the Rue Pettion and our breakfast was rudely disturbed by several loud reports. One of the orderlies came in to say that German shells were falling in the field in front of the house. We went out to see what was happening. The Germans were firing salvos of four shells at a time and "searching" for my humble quarters. First four shells fell about fifty yards apart about five hundred yards away to the right looking to our rear. Then four more came closer. Salvo followed salvo but a number of the shells failed to explode.

After they had raked out our front yard we heard four burst behind our quarters and we knew that the next bracket would get our happy home. It did. Four struck the barn and the quarters occupied by Captain McGregor and his staff fifty feet away from where we stood. We feared that our cows were gone, done to death by miserable Hun gunners. When we took over these quarters the Scots Guards were good enough to turn over three cows in good milking trim to our headquarters. These three cows were all that were left on the farm of a fine herd of brown Swiss cattle. The rest of the herd were scattered about the fields with their feet sticking up in the air, and it was our unpleasant duty to later on bury them darkly at dead of night. We forgot our three milkers for the moment, however, as we heard the whistling of more shells and orders were given for everybody to duck and get under cover.

Two shells struck the house and tore about two inches off the tile ridge at intervals of about ten feet apart. They fell in the ditch in front of the house but failed to explode. Four more fell to the right, and then the gunners began to rake back and forward, dropping in all about fifty shells within a radius of five hundred yards. Then they took up another target and we had leisure to examine the damage. Our shack had escaped except for a few broken tiles, the next building south occupied by Captain McGregor had one room blown up, that in which he had his cot. Fortunately he was out when the German visitors arrived. The shell, a four inch high explosive, tore a couple of sandbags out of the back window, and as it apparently had a "delay action" fuse it burst fairly in the middle of the room. There was nothing left of Captain McGregor's cot but a pile of woollen shreds. His trunk and the clothing hanging on the wall were ripped to pieces.

Captain Perry was having a bath in an old fashioned wash tub in the next room when the explosion took place. Nothing happened to him as he bore a charmed life.

Some of the shells that fell into the ditch were dug up by Sergeant Lewis who was in charge of our pioneers. They were four inch high explosives.

Chapter 16

With General Sir Douglas Haig

When we left the trenches at Fromelles for the first time we took up billets on the Rue Du Quesne. This street was named after a one-time General and Governor of Canada during the French regime. His name is still perpetuated in the great steel works at Pittsburg, U.S.A., along with that of Lord Pitt and Braddock, for it was before Fort Duquesne that General Braddock fell in 1755. Braddock was one of those unfortunate British Generals who were sent out to command colonials. He would not take the advice of his colonial officers and paid the penalty of his unpreparedness with his life. A comparison of Indian warfare of one hundred and fifty years ago with the war of today will convince anyone that the Red Indians on the warpath had nothing on the Germans. They burned houses and killed innocent women and children.

For these atrocities they gained unenviable notoriety. The Germans do the same things. Hardly a farm house where we were billeted that did not have the graves of the peaceful occupants in the gardens close by. Men, women and children were destroyed by shell and other implements of war. At Armentieres we were shown Belgian children whose hands had been hacked off, and at the farms we saw old men maimed and with withered arms and legs still bearing the marks of the cords which bound them to trees and posts.

"Frightfulness" was part of the German war religion. When their artillery or sharpshooters were bested in the trenches, like a lot of mad dogs they turned their guns on the farm houses at their extreme range hoping to kill or destroy somebody. The poor peasants suffer. The old men, boys, women and children who try their best to till the soil are caught unawares by the deadly shrapnel and are killed. The courage of these people is wonderful. I have seen a young girl driving a single horse in front of a hand-made wooden harrow all afternoon with the shells falling within two hundred yards of her. The dastardly German gunners were trying to kill her and her horse but an all-wise Providence destroyed the aim of the cowards and she escaped unhurt.

These doctrines of "frightfulness" are laid down by two of the foremost German writers on the Art of War. Clausewitz, who is always quoted in the war schools dealing with the question, says;

> Philanthropists may think it possible that the disarmament or subjection of the enemy can be effected by some artificial means without causing too many wounds and that this is the true aim of military science. Pretty as this looks we must refute this error, for in such dangerous matters as war, errors arising from good nature are the worst of all. As the employment of physical force to its fullest extent in no wise excludes the co-operation of intelligence, it follows that he who makes use of this force ruthlessly and without sparing blood must obtain an ascendancy if the enemy does not do likewise. By so doing he frames a law for the other and thus both strain every nerve without finding any other limitation but their own natural counterpoise.

Von Der Goltz, the tutor of the Turks and the author of a German textbook on war, *The Nation in Arms,* says;

> If from humanitarian principles a nation decided not to resort to extremities, but to employ its strength up to a given point only, it would soon find itself swept onward against its will. No enemy would consider itself bound to observe a similar limitation. So far from this being the case each would immediately avail himself of the voluntary moderation of the other to outstrip him at once in activity.

In other words, according to the German conception, war is a game without an umpire or a referee. The boast of civilization that it has ameliorated the conditions of war, and of chivalry that the old, the women and children shall be protected in the zone of military activity, have ceased to be of any value.

We had comfortable quarters on the Rue Du Quesne but we were well under shell and rifle fire. Every night the Mauser bullets rattled on the roof and during the day the German gunners shelled the houses along the road. Rifle bullets flew around very freely at night and we fancied at first that snipers were busy within our lines. Sentries were posted on the roofs of barns and outhouses to watch for these pests. Several men of other regiments had been hit at nights on the roads, so orders were given to the peasants to clear out of the front line and stay in the houses at nights. Sentries, who were always in the war zone posted double, were warned to be more vigilant. While here Corporal Y—— of the headquarters staff distinguished himself by hitting a German artillery observer at a range of thirteen hundred yards. Y—— and several others had climbed to a barn roof to view the country with powerful telescopes to see if the Germans had any snipers in barns or trees.

A careful reconnaissance of their lines disclosed an officer in artillery uniform up a willow tree. Y——, who was a dead shot, took his Ross, gave two degrees of wind and we all guessed the elevation as fourteen hundred yards. He fired and our glasses were all levelled on the German, who we knew had heard the bullet whiz past, for he looked up, so Y—— cut the range down to twelve hundred yards and fired again, and this time the German looked down, so we knew his aim was too low. We then saw him deliberately take aim at our trenches and fire. Y—— then cut the bracket in two and put his elevation at thirteen hundred yards. This time the Hun toppled over out of the tree, head first, and a cheer went up. He would snipe or observe no more.

We were now in General Haig's command, and rumours were going around that there would be something doing before very long. We were very eager to get into the big drive which was expected in the spring.

The second time we went into the trenches the men were warned to be exceedingly careful of themselves, but to enfilade the German lines with steady sniping so as to keep the fire down.

Every night the companies had to patrol in front of our trenches and examine the wires. This is a very dangerous pastime and everybody wanted to volunteer for the service so I ordered that the men should be chosen by roster, that is, according to their turn. Sergeant Jones got out one night in a turnip patch in front of our lines. There was a German sniper in the same patch so they began to stalk each other. Jones got his man first, but as the German keeled over he fired and the bullet tore some fingers off Jones' hand and gave him a severe flesh wound in the chest. We got Jones in and bound him up, and brought him to my headquarters where a motor ambulance came and took him away. He was suffering a lot of pain but was game. His wounds were not dangerous.

There are certain laws of the trenches that must be obeyed. First, if you lose your trenches you are told in general orders that you must take them back at once with the bayonet. You must not look for anyone else to do that trick for you. Another is that if a man is wounded the stretcher bearers must bind his wound with a first aid bandage, which each soldier carries in the flap of his coat, after the wound has been cauterized first with tincture of iodine, which is supplied to the officers and bearers in bottles. The man is then kept in the trench till evening when he is taken out on a stretcher. If shot through the lower part of the body a man is kept quiet where he falls for a couple of hours so that nature will herself repair internal bleeding. To at once move a man who is shot through the body is to spoil his chance of recovery.

Our sharpshooters are told to shoot constantly at the enemy's port holes or at any moving figure along the enemy's line. When we see a periscope shoved over the enemy's parapet it is the custom for our sharpshooters to aim at it, and after lowering the aim to fire about six inches from the top of the German parapet. As their parapets are thin we invariably find we have scored a hit. Sometimes duels are indulged in between the German snipers and our sharpshooters. One day a duel of this kind took place between Company Sergeant-Major De Hart and the German who manned the porthole opposite. They fired shot for shot. Our sergeant fired at the German's plate, and he answered back on ours. Shot after shot was exchanged. Alongside of the porthole we had a man watching with a telescope through another porthole. On the tenth shot De Hart scored. His shot went through and the Germans closed up the porthole and went out of business for the day.

One afternoon Lieutenant Williams-Taylor of Montreal, a very brave, bright, young officer, came to see me. He was on the headquarters staff and I had promised to show him around. Staff officers seldom want to look over the trenches but he did. I took him along with me and had to caution him several times as he is tall and the parapets in places were low. We went the whole line of the trenches. When we came to Captain McLaren's section one of our men was firing and I asked him what was the matter. He said he was firing at a German who was digging in a sap-head at the salient opposite, about four hundred yards off. Our man was firing and missing, and every time he fired the German waved a miss, as they do on the rifle butts with his shovel. Now sapping is a most dangerous form of employment. It is dangerous for us and it is our business to make it dangerous for the enemy who is running the sap. What is a sap? Well, this kind of a sap was a connecting trench which the Germans were running out from their line so they could get closer to our line in order to start another line of trenches, or else get close up with a lot of men to attack us.

A sapper works on a trench of this kind differently to the way he works on an ordinary trench. He digs and picks ahead of him and throws the loose earth on a blanket between his feet. This earth is carried away in sand bags and put somewhere else, and there is nothing to show that sapping is going on in your front unless an aeroplane detects it. This sap was being run towards us along an irrigation ditch, and as the German sapper could not see us for trees he did not know that there was a point in our line from which we could see him. He was something of a humorist and thought he was having a lot of fun at our expense. Several shots from our men had failed to stop him. I tried two shots but he still kept on waving the shovel. I gave the rifle to Lieutenant Taylor at his request and pointed out the target. At his first shot the German failed to signal a miss. The men congratulated Taylor on scoring a hit, but he modestly remarked that it was a chance shot and he did not think he had scored. From that time on Lt. Williams-Taylor was a constant visitor in the trenches. He was in the hottest part of the action at St. Julien, rifle in hand, fighting like a hero.

In the first trenches we occupied the line consisted of two rows of parapets. The front one was called the parapet, the rear the *parado*. The latter was to protect the men from the "kick back" of the German high explosive shells. This form of entrenchment has the disadvantage that if the enemy gets over your front parapet he has a rear parapet which he can use against you and you have great difficulty in getting him out. Where we were later the line consisted of a series of small redoubts or forts connected up with a parapet or curtain. The redoubts were closed at the back and in them were built the dugouts in which the defenders sleep. The redoubts were very strongly held, and if the Germans got over the single parapets they could be driven back with fire from the redoubts and supporting fire trenches.

For some time we had been waiting patiently for the big advance which had been promised as soon as the ground got hard enough for troops to manoeuvre over the fields. In the fall and winter in Flanders the brown clay of the field is so sticky and soft that troops cannot manoeuvre except on the roads. That is why in former wars in the low countries the troops went into trenches during the winter. The weather had been warm and sunny for some days and the creeks, which they designate there with the euphonious titles of rivers, had fallen a foot or two. There was still plenty of water in the country for the Flemings are great lovers of water. Drains are not used there to carry off water at all. They are used to contain water.

Every farm has a series of big ditches, three to six feet wide and about five feet deep, running across it. The water is drained off the land with tile into these ditches, but on the other hand these ditches provide with the aforesaid tile a form of sub-irrigation inasmuch as the water in the dry season flows back into the sub-soil through these same tile. The ditches play a big part in the economy of the farms. The farmyard buildings are built close alongside the paved roads. The roads are paved with stone blocks about 8"×16". The Flemish farmer does his road work once in a hundred years when he turns these blocks over and gives them a fresh surface. A gateway, generally arched, leads into a square around which the farm buildings stand.

Next the road will be the dwelling houses all under one roof two storeys high. One part,—the master's,—will have its parlour and parlour bedroom. Then there will be a kitchen, then other rooms for the help, then a dairy. On the other side of the square the pigs and horses have quarters. Opposite on the right from the gate there will be cow stables, then the back of the square will be the barn. The roofs are all connected up. Around the inside of the court yard next the buildings will run a brick sidewalk about six feet wide, and the square in the centre contains a brick walled pit into which the refuse of the stables and houses is thrown. One corner of this midden is bricked off to form a drainage pit. Of all the smells! Enough said.

One of the most interesting features of the farm is the dairy. Each farm boasts of one, and sometimes as many as three dogs. These dogs are never allowed to roam at will as in England or Canada. They are a fine robust breed, like small mastiffs with pointed wolfish ears. On the outside of each farmhouse one of the most prominent features is a big upright wheel like a water wheel, fully fourteen feet in diameter. All day long the dogs run in this wheel driving the machinery for the dairy. After one dog gets tired he is taken out, and if the farm is a large one another dog is put in. The Flemish dogs certainly have to work for their living and make up for the lazy life of their brethren elsewhere. Many of these dogs have long bodies and run to what we would call the dachshund type. I can quite understand how in trying to catch

The Trenches in Winter

his tail while working the wheel the process of evolution has brought about the long body of the dachshund.

According to my recollections of Caesar they had hedges and ditches, beautifully cultivated fields and beer and wine in Flanders two thousand years old. No doubt they had those dog wheels then also. But that does not end the ditch question. Around each group of farm buildings there is what we would call a moat, the biggest ditch on the farm. This moat will be from five to twenty feet deep and fully twenty feet wide. There will be a bridge at the front and back. When the front and back gates are closed no one can get at the Flemish chickens. Now what use are these high-smelling pits and ditches. The Flemings have a use for them. They pump out the contents into great big *puncheons* on their three-wheeled carts, and they spread this liquid, rich in nitrates, potash and other fertilizing materials over their growing crops. That is why if a man or a horse gets cut in Flanders he has to go and be inoculated against lock-jaw. Wounds do not heal readily here, the soil and air are too rich in bacteria. If a wound is not sterilized at once with iodine a man generally gets gangrene and dies of it.

The farmers in Canada will no doubt be interested in the kind of stock on these farms. Well, first the horses. They have a magnificent breed of heavy horses called the heavy Fleming or Belgian, which is like a great Percheron with a flat bone and a foot or so sawed off its legs. They are like our Canadian general purpose breed, but much heavier. I have seen horses on almost every farm where my men were billeted that would weigh from 1,600 to 2,000 pounds. These horses are clean-limbed, close-coupled and wonderfully docile and obedient. They answer to the word "Gee," which seems to be an international phrase. A "jerk-line" on the collar does the rest. Most of the best horses are brought from Belgium. A thoroughbred three-year-old mare will cost three hundred dollars.

The cows on the farms are a fine brown breed, not quite as large as the Holsteins, but they are prolific and splendid milkers. They are not allowed to roam the fields. They are much like the brown Swiss breed or red Devon, such as can be found in Devonshire. What struck me most was their splendid vigour. They are not placid and anaemic such as our average dairy cows, but full of life and action.

The hogs are a large white razor back with long ears that droop over their noses. They give very little trouble and live on comparatively nothing. I have never seen them fed. The farmers say they let them root for themselves until they are getting them ready for market.

The hens are a very fine breed, akin to our Wyandotte in shape, but of various colours. They are great egg producers and kept the soldiers going at sixty cents a dozen. The Fleming, with all his splendid farm land, still makes his own implements. Homemade wooden, iron shod ploughs and wooden harrows are the rule. The implement manufacturers are not encouraged.

Chapter 17

The Battle of Neuve Chapelle

On the morning of the 8th of March, being Monday, the Germans began the week early by heaving some more shells in the direction of the ruin that guarded our quarters. Some one of our men during the night had trundled a Flemish cart that was in the way in the farm-yard, out into the field about two hundred yards away. The vigilant Germans' aircraft took it for a field gun, and notifying their batteries they proceeded to shell it with shrapnel and high explosive shells. The cart, however, stood it well. After they quit shelling some of us ventured over to see what damage had been done. Beyond peppering the woodwork the dummy gun was intact. I picked up the fuse of one of the shrapnel shells and found that the range had been set at 3,400 metres. The shell in its flight had clipped a small limb off one of the tall sentinel elms in front of our dugouts. With a compass we learned the direction of the German battery on the map, which was located behind a hedge at the cross roads east of Fromelles. A telephone message to our guns and a half dozen shells from our five-inch guns, and this particular German battery troubled us no more.

After the shelling the adjutant of the Royal Scots Battalion on our right came over to see me to talk over the battle which we knew was now due. I had been told of this by General Turner, V.C., the day before. We knew that the big advance was about to begin, and a study of the map told us that the first blow would likely be struck at Neuve Chapelle, with an idea of forcing our line forward several miles so we would gain the command of the high ground back of Aubers, Herlies and Fromelles, a region of coal mines. A branch line of railway ran from La Bassee to Fromelles and supplied the German batteries on our front with ammunition and no doubt took coal back. On the east side of the ridge ran the canal from La Bassee to Lille, also the two lines of railway between the same places. With our footing secure on the Aubers Ridge the gates of Lille and La Bassee would be at our mercy. Then with a mobile field army there would be nothing to stop us till we got to Ghent or Brussels.

This was the place to drive the wedge that would cut the German line in two, and once we had Lille we would endanger the whole German lines of communication north and south. It used to be a favourite amusement among the officers of our staff in the evenings to take the map of Western Europe, which we kept hanging on the wall, and plan campaigns to drive the Germans out of Flanders. Invariably two lines of advance would be chosen. The first *via* Lille and Ghent, to Antwerp, along the high ground between the River Scheldt and the Lys. The second route would invariably begin at the Somme and run along the plateau between the Sambre and Meuse *via* way of Le Cateau, Mons, Charleroi to Namur.

All this is historical ground, the Low Countries of history. Over this ground fought Caesar, Charlemagne, William the Silent, Marlborough, Napoleon and all the great captains of history. We used to calculate the men, the marches and the guns required. We would plan how we would form a great corps army behind the trenches in preparation for a grand advance. The attack would be delivered against two different points. A feint against one position that would bring the German corps reserves, that were always available in some central point, to the assistance of their comrades. This corps army we knew always come on the third day of a fight. We would have it come to the wrong place. Then a fierce storm of artillery fire would be delivered at the point where the real gap in the line was to be made; a drive through it with the infantry, with plenty of supports; such were Wellington's methods.

Then a "steam roller" advance for the objective, surrounding and disregarding fortified villages and redoubts, that would send the Germans scattering right and left for the Rhine. We realized that our task as part of the trench army would be a difficult one, but we had every confidence that the trench army could open the gate for a field army at any point in the line required. But a trench army in so doing would lose one third of its effectives, and putting a regiment in the trenches for a long tour of trench work destroys its initiative as far as field manoeuvring is concerned. All these things were planned and marches calculated. It was figured out where the Germans might make a stand, generally where some famous battle had been fought in the past, how they would be overwhelmed with fresh divisions on their flanks, brought up in motor trucks and their troops blown out of the earth with hundreds of "four point five" and "six-inch" field howitzers which were proving to be such excellent guns for our troops.

That is how we planned to drive the enemy out of Flanders. Alas, most of those young ardent soldiers who were so well trained by our military colleges to carry on the staff work of such an army of invasion were doomed to give up their lives in the sodden and muddy trenches. We had confidence that the day would come soon when a big field army would be ready behind us, and it would be only a case of "*whoop*" and "*haloo*" and the German fox would be off full tear for the cover of the Rhine and its fortress strongholds.

For days we had been gaining superiority in various ways over the enemy. Our riflemen dominated theirs. When we took over the trenches first, if we fired one shot they answered with ten. Now they did not answer at all. When our guns fired on their guns for every shell we handed to them they religiously gave us five back. Now they kept still and took their gruel. They had given us trouble with their trench mortars. They had wounded several of my men with the bombs, but they tried to move their mortar into a new position one day and we spotted it. The artillery observing officer in our trenches, young Lieutenant Ryerson, called up the guns and the second shell sent their mortar to smithereens. A great artillery officer was young Lieut. Ryerson, fit to command any battery.

For a long time the German aeroplanes flew over us every morning at sunrise, but now we had a dozen aeroplanes to their one and theirs were rather shy. Our guns had ranged up and down the whole front and we had all begun to get confident and to think that it was only a matter of a few days until we would be on the high road to Brussels.

On top of all this came a very inspiring address from General Sir Douglas Haig, commanding our army. He pointed out that the time had come for a fresh great effort. He also informed us that we were stronger than the enemy, all of which gave us more confidence.

I was told privately that the drive was to take place on our right, and as soon as the brigade on our right had cleared out the Germans on their front that we were to echelon and follow suit and charge.

On our right the Germans were four hundred yards away across the open. I went down and examined the lines carefully with Captain Daniels, and found that there were two places where a lot of men could be taken out of our trenches and led half way across to the German lines on "dead" ground, that is ground on which they would be hidden. Lieutenant Schonberger and Captain Warren made a sketch of this ground. I talked the matter over with the captains and they were very much cheered up over the prospect of a fight. Captains MacLaren and Daniels immediately began fixing up exits from their trenches. Steps were cut in the parapets, and in other places openings were made. The opening in the parapets that were used for "listening" posts and for the patrols to go in and out were widened.

What is a listening post? A listening post is made in this way: A gap which is carefully hidden with sandbags is cut in the parapets. Then a sap is run out several hundred feet in zigzag fashion, which terminates in a rifle pit, about five feet deep that will accommodate about four men. At night two sentries sit in this pit and listen to the sounds in the enemy's lines. Sometimes if the rifle pit is wet a couple of barrels are put in and the sentries stand in the barrels. They notify the trenches of any unusual movement or sounds made by the enemy.

In the evening we left the trenches and went into divisional reserve at Rue Du Quesne. Let me give you some idea of the lay of the country. There is a road about every kilometre and they run roughly northwest and northeast.

Running southwest and almost parallel with the trenches was Rue Pettion, a short road that terminated at the Fromelles road near our headquarters. The next street, a little over a mile back, is Rue Du Bois, north of the Fromelles Road, south of the Fromelles Road it is called the Rue De Tilleloy. At the corner there was a shrine which had suffered from shell fire and which Canon Scott had immortalized in a poem, the best he has written and the best I have read since the war began. The next street back is the Rue Du Quesne. Right through the centre of our position ran the Fromelles Road. A kilometre southwest, the trench line is crossed by the road to Aubers called the Rue D'Enfer, or in our language, the Road to Hell. If this road is paved with good intentions I have never seen any of them. It is strongly held by the Germans. The "intentions" take the form of "crump" holes excavated by German shells in the pavement.

The country on our side is perfectly flat and full of hedges and ditches. Every hedge concealed a battery of guns of all kinds and sizes. On the German side, half a mile back from their trenches, the ground slopes up. The villages of Aubers and Fromelle are on the western slope and the ridge behind is our true objective. On the ridge we could see the church steeples of Herlies to the right and Fournes to the left, while here and there peep the derricks, or as we in America call them the "breakers" of coal pits. Beyond the ridge the land slopes to the Scheldt. It was on the eastern slope of this ridge that Caesar fought his greatest battles. There the Nervli charged across the stream in thousands and fought until hardly a man of them was left, fought until their dead were piled up breast high, fought till Caesar had to take a buckler and spear from a fallen soldier to defend himself.

On all sides, from the horizon downward, rows of tall elm trees cast their gaunt leafless branches in the air. Between them were a sea of hedges and green brown boles of pollard willows. Elms generally grew along the roadways and the limbs for fifty feet up are trimmed off annually and tied up into faggots. The willows grew along the ditches. They are trimmed off about twelve or fourteen feet above the ground and the new branches that sprout out from their trunks provide faggots for firewood as well as withes for the manufacture of chairs, baskets and hampers. The faggots are sometimes placed in earthen pits and burned into charcoal, providing an excellent fuel for the interesting Dutch stoves found in the kitchens in this country.

For several days our guns had been registering on the enemy. That is to say, our artillery observing officers would go into the trenches with a telephone connected up with their batteries. Then the battery fires a shot at the enemy's parapets, generally well over. He reports the hit right or left, and then the range is reduced until the object is hit. That range direction and elevation is recorded in a register at the gun. The man who sets the gun does not see the object he is firing at at all, but he knows when his gun is trained in a certain line at a certain elevation he will hit that part of the enemy's parapet. We had all kinds of guns ready for the fray. The Canadian sixty pounders under Major McGee a few days before had smashed up the brown tower of Fromelles. This tower had been used by the Germans for an artillery observing station, and for several months the British had been firing at it without success.

In about three shots McGee's guns got the tower and a half dozen shells reduced it to a hopeless ruin so that it was of no use to anyone. The church tower of Aubers followed suit. When the British Tommies heard the "birr" of the five-inch Canadian shells they all asked whose they were. The Scots thought they had come from Scotland. When they saw Aubers tower disappear in a cloud of dust they inquired again, "What bally gunners are those?" When told they were the Canadians, they said, "Bravo, Canadians, you are some class," and cheered heartily. This gave our gunners a reputation that lasted for the rest of the war.

Besides our five-inch guns we had our eighteen pounder batteries lined up and down behind us, also horse artillery guns from India and an armoured train manned by the navy. They had long six-inch guns that threw a terrible projectile. We had also some new fifteen-inch howitzers that had been brought over from England. "Grandmas" they called these guns because they were short and stout. "Grandma" when fired only gave a low grunt, but when her shell broke four or five miles off, it burst with a "*Car-u-m-p*" that rattled the windows and shook the earth down in our dugouts.

I had a very interesting time one day riding to a conference at the headquarters of General Sir H.S. Rawlinson, Bt. I came cantering along a road and a sudden turn brought us to a railway crossing. The naval guns were on an armoured train, the Churchill battery on either side of this crossing, and the gunners seemed to have wakened up for they began firing when we were about five hundred yards off. I was riding a powerful "Cayuse" or western horse, which Captain "Rudd" Marshall, with rare good judgment, had selected for me at Valcartier. He turned out to be a splendid charger.

Although low set he carried me easily. He was as wise as an owl and as sure-footed as a cat. It took a good deal of courage on his part to face the naval battery firing for all it was worth, the flames from the black fiery muzzles of the guns almost scorching his hide, but he did it without flinching, although the jar of the guns almost shook him off his feet several times. I can quite realize the task of the Noble Six Hundred had in charging the Russian batteries at Balaclava. I have since seen a moving picture of this battery in action and recognized the raised gate of the railway crossing through which we rode, in the centre of the picture, and I wondered if the battery was "demonstrating" for the benefit of the moving picture photographer when we were passing through.

In my rides about the country when the battalion was in billets, I several times ran across "Archibald the Archer," which is the name given to an anti-air craft gun which is mounted on a motor truck and is used against the German aeroplanes. "Archibald" is capable of firing to a great height and very rapidly. He can also move about the country quite readily. When he starts after a Hun *avatick* there is something going on in the sky. I have watched the Germans outwitting him.

Now the aeroplane would dip and glide and circle as the "Archibald" shells broke about him. Watching with a powerful glass one could see the airship tremble with the explosion of the shell in its vicinity. "Archibald" does not always get the German observers, but he hastens to make it so hot for them that they cannot observe. Observation cannot be carried on with much accuracy above five thousand feet, and the ordinary rifle can fire that high. Who named the anti-air craft gun "Archibald" no one knows, but the Belgians are credited with the naming.

The Belgians are great archers, the sport still surviving in that country. At every village you will find a tall mast which you at first think belongs to a wireless station. On examination, however, it will prove to be an archery pole. At the top of a tall pole the target is drawn up by a rope and pulley, and on holidays the local sports indulge in shooting at the mark with a long bow. In every farm house you will find the long bow and a bunch of arrows.

The programme for the big battle ran something like this: Everything being in readiness several divisions were to be brought up behind the trenches at Neuve Chapelle during the night of the ninth and tenth. Next morning at 7.30 the ball was to open. It was to be a case of "nibbling" as General Joffre calls it. Our guns were to form two zones of fire. The big guns were to smash the first line of trenches for a mile into fragments, while the second line of lighter guns were to rain shrapnel on the ground over which supports might come so that the first line would be isolated. When the first line was sufficiently hammered the infantry was to rip the German parapets with rapid rifle fire, then a charge with the bayonets across the devil's strip, and once inside the first lines of parapets bomb throwing parties were to be told off right and left to clear the trenches.

These bombing parties consisted of three or four men with bayonets to lead, and behind them two or three bomb throwers to throw bombs at the enemy ahead of the bayonet men. The leading bayonet men carried a flag which they were to plant in the parapets as they passed along so that the supporting infantry would know not to fire on them. The first line of trenches was to be consolidated the first day. On the second day the second line was to be assaulted and on the third day the third line. In a similar manner everybody knew there was stiff work ahead. That evening my battalion was relieved in the trenches by the Royal Montreal Regiment. When we got back to our quarters we received orders to "sleep on our arms" that night. That meant in our clothes, with our belts and ammunition strapped on, ready to march at a moment's notice. There was a good bed, but it was sleep in your boots for me. The fact that a blighter of a sniper kept firing off three or four rounds of rapid fire at my headquarters every few minutes, his bullets rattling on the brick wall close to my window, was not very conducive to sleep or good temper. I vowed that I would make it pretty hot for snipers, and agreed with myself there and then to pay a reward of fifty dollars for every sniper captured dead or alive inside our lines.

The German sniper is really a lineal descendant of the impenitent thief. When I say a sniper I do not mean a sharpshooter who fires into our lines from the German lines. I mean one of those horrible creatures that goes about clad in a stolen uniform or the clothes of a Flemish farmer during the day, and at night takes a Leuger automatic pistol and haunts the billets and roads in hope of killing some lone British or Canadian soldier or sentry, whose duty calls him abroad during the night and relieving the dead body of any money or valuables that may be on it. Truly this war developed into a form of warfare akin to that between the whites and the North American Indians.

We suspect a few of the habitants of being snipers and not without some reason. Several of these farmers and small saloon keepers would like to see the Germans win the war so that they could "cash in" on the German requisitions they hold. It happened in this way: When the "Boches," as they call the Germans, overran the country last August and September, they took all the wine from the saloon keepers and brewers, and the best horses, cattle and hogs from the farmers. They paid for these articles with requisitions or orders on the German Government, payable after the war if Germany won. We were constantly coming up against these people that were devastated by the Germans, and when we remarked that the British or French Government would pay the "requisitions" after the war they inform us that they hold requisitions for 5,000 or 10,000 *francs* given them by the Germans for their property.

At one place where I was quartered the proprietor had lost 40,000 *francs* worth of stock and wine. He was rather "frosty" to the British. That is why we suspected some of being snipers, and there are some cases on record where they were caught red-handed in the act. Our experience had taught us to put a dead line of sentries several miles behind the line of trenches, and our vigilance was rewarded because the Germans throughout were unable to locate our batteries and were at sea as to what was taking place behind our lines. On the other hand our scouts were so bold that they often crept forward at night in spite of the constant firing of flare lights or rockets by the enemy and had looked right into the German trenches. Conversations were of constant occurrence. "How is your bloody Ross Rifle?" a hoarse German voice would enquire. "Stick your nose up and see" would go back the prompt reply.

March 10th was the day set for the beginning of the battle which will go down in history as the battle of Neuve Chapelle. The village of Neuve Chapelle was just like every other Franco-Fleming village on the firing line, a huddle of houses partly unroofed by shell fire, deserted by the populace, and shunned by the soldiers. It had been at one time a smart village of two-storey brick houses with red tiled roofs. It possessed the typical church and graveyard such as are found in these villages. Almost every second house was a wine or beer saloon called an *estament.* There were butcher shops, millinery shops and shops where they mended shoes. But the British rush, which in October had driven back the German lines beyond Armentieres, Aubers and Fromelles, had left the Germans in possession of Neuve Chapelle. They had a lot of stout-hearted rogues holding on there who would not let go, so Neuve Chapelle formed the apex of a salient in the British trenches which weakened our line north so much that later on we had to give up good ground south of Lille in order to straighten and consolidate along the line of the River Layes for the hard winter campaign.

Late in December someone in the War Office thought that we had given up too much ground about Fromelles and Armentieres, so an attack was ordered which resulted in nothing beyond the killing of a great many Highlanders, Gordons, Black Watch, Argyles, and virtually destroying a Brigade of Guards. But nothing came of all this, and it is, as I suppose as Rudyard Kipling would say, "*another story.*" Yes, and a "top hole" one at that, but it does not come within my province to tell it.

Now we were going to drive the Germans out of this salient and begin the spring cleaning up. When we speak of towns and villages, please do not get any idea of distance as in Canada or America in your heads. There is a town or village in Flanders at every cross road. The "town siter" has not been abroad here selling lots for miles about every hamlet, so the result is that a town of three or four thousand people will happen at every cross road, all within a diameter of a quarter of a mile. As for the roads and streets, they follow the game trails haunted by the cave dwellers and trogdolites a thousand centuries ago. They wind in every direction and are all good. The main roads are covered with heavy square stones, blocks. Once in a hundred years the Flemish farmer does his road work by turning these blocks over. They are called *pavè* roads. All the other roads are covered with macadam made out of black whinstone that is as hard as iron. This will explain why the towns of Armentieres, Fleurbaix, Neuve Chapelle, Aubers, Estaires and Bac St. Maur are all within a radius of five miles of each other. Aubers is a short mile from Neuve Chapelle, while Fromelles is only a mile or so from Aubers. The whole British line from Ypres to La Bassee is not as far as from Toronto to Hamilton, not forty miles.

Our brigade had two battalions in the trenches, the Royal Montreal Regiment under Lieut.-Colonel Meighen and the Canadian Scottish under Lieut.-Colonel Leckie. The Royal Highlanders of Canada were on the left of our brigade and we were on the right, and our two battalions were available as reserves for the British troops on our right that were going into action. There was one British Brigade between us and the section of the line that was to attack. We were not to move till this brigade moved. Reveille was sounded early and the battalion fell in by companies shortly after seven. We were ordered to march down to the Rue De Bois and get out of sight among some farm houses and keep out of sight, which we did. Some of the companies crossed the fields scouting along the ditches and hedges. A company marched by the road Croix Blanche. We found billets at farm houses a few hundred yards east of the corner of the Rue De Bois and the Fromelles road.

Across the road from where I was quartered there was a big straw stack which the artillery were using for observation purposes. Behind it Captain Pope of the Third Brigade Staff had established a telephone office in a couple of wheat sheaves of last year's crop. A cup of bad black coffee and a hardboiled egg provided me with breakfast. The men made tea and had plenty of food with them. In an emergency of this kind I saw that they had two day's rations in their haversacks. They also carried a hundred and fifty rounds of ammunition in their pouches and two *bandoliers*, each of fifty rounds, slung over their shoulders. They would not be short of grub or ammunition if it could be helped. After I had finished the coffee I surveyed the barn and found a spot where a hole through the straw thatch gave a good view of what was going on.

I had a very powerful pair of field binoculars with which I could count the chickens in a barnyard five miles off. The battle was about to begin. A few of our guns were giving the morning "straffing" as usual. The sun was up and it was a bright clear day. I could see the British lines marked by brown sandbags, now hidden by hedges, again showing across the Rue D'Enfer, but hidden by the houses and church at the corner called Fauquissart. Beyond that again to my right rear the line crossed the Rue Du Tilleloy and swept on to Neuve Chapelle. A clump of tall elms here interfered with the view. I could also see the German trenches. They were crowned with rows of white sandbags, interspersed with blue bundles that looked like army blankets or blue bed sticks filled with earth. There was not much stirring for the moment.

Suddenly the guns woke up behind our line. The Canadian eighteens and five inchers took up the chorus. Back came half a dozen German forty pounder shells bursting in the field on my right. They were miles away from our guns. One by one the British batteries joined in the chorus until in less than five minutes over three hundred cannon of every description were pouring death and destruction on the German trenches. At first I could see our shells bursting with volumes of green and yellow smoke and blowing up the German parapets. I could see sandbags flying fifty feet in the air and what looked like men as well. Debris flew in every direction, and in a few minutes I could see neither sandbags nor parapets. Nothing but the yellow smoke of lyddite and behind this in the air a ring of fire where the shrapnel were bursting and showering their leaden curtain to keep the enemy's supports from coming up.

I could see that there was much excitement along the British parapets. Men clustered together like bees, and in some places I could see soldiers climbing up on top of the parapet, waving their rifles and caps in the air. They were telling the Huns what they were going to do to them. They were too far away for me to hear what their language was, but they were evidently enjoying the punishing the Germans were getting. At 8.30 o'clock the roar of the guns died away suddenly, only to be followed by the most intense musketry fire. It was something like the distant sound of Niagara Falls. I never heard anything really like it. This continued for about ten minutes, then died away.

A light yellow cloud had settled down over the place where the German parapets once were. I could not see through the smoke, as the more powerful a glass is the more it exaggerates the fog or smoke.

I could hear the loud, sharp detonations of grenades, and I fancied cheers, more detonations and cheers and cries. All this was occurring within less than a mile of where I was standing. From the detonations I judged we were bombing their trenches. The noise died away and our artillery woke up again and began shelling leisurely in the rear of the first line of German entrenchments. Evidently we had won easily. I hurried down and over to where Captain Pope and several of my officers were grouped about the telephone. "They have carried the first line of trenches easily" was the answer he gave to my query as to what had happened. "They are going after the second line of trenches right away."

I returned to my observation post and once more the guns were hard at it. It was now a little after nine o'clock and the haze that hung around the German positions made observation difficult. The guns redoubled their efforts, and at about ten o'clock they stopped and again the rifle fire followed, if anything, more intense than before. The detonation of bombs, the rifle fire and cries of the combatants came to my ears distinctly now that our own guns on both sides and behind us were silent. Again I travelled over to the telephone station wondering if they had forgotten us, or if we were going to have a hand in the game. "The second line is taken" came over the wire at 10.30 o'clock. "They are going to attack the third line." So they were going to force through and make a one-day job of it after all. That would surely bring us into the fight by the afternoon or the next day. So my young men would be pleased.

I had had a lot of pacifying to do among my officers over the question of "When are we going to get into this thing?" Major Osborne always had an idea that everybody from General French down was trying to keep the Canadians from starting a grand parade to Berlin. Lieut. "Fred" Macdonald's question to me would always be, "How long are they going to keep us at this rotten trench business?" "It's about time we got into a mix-up. Look at the Princess Pats what they have done! They must be afraid to use us," etc., etc. I would gently chide him and say that we were on the lap of the gods, in other words sitting on our general's knees, and Mac would look as if I were a partner in a deep laid conspiracy to keep the regiment from being covered with glory.

When we last went into the trenches Captains Alexander and Cory had to take the line nearest the Germans. They were only eighty yards away and the parapets were as thin as bargain day wall paper.

First Aid in the Trenches

Lots had been cast, and McGregor had won the reserved position and Alexander the hot corner. I ventured to remark to Alexander that I was sorry that his luck had put him in a dangerous place, and that he should have his turn next in reserve. I did not get far with this speech when he snapped back quietly and firmly, "The post of danger is the post of honour." As for Cory and Jones, I had to threaten them with a court-martial if they did not stop hopping on the parapets in full view of the Germans both day and night.

They were all feeling happy today, even grim Captain MacLaren was wearing a broad smile. As for McKessock, well his ancestors followed Bruce from Kilmarnock to Ireland. There is no need for further comment. He had the machine guns well cleaned and the cartridges in the belts polished like front door knobs so they wouldn't jam.

After hearing that the third line was to be attacked I hurried back to my post. The artillery had stopped firing for a while to let the haze and smoke clear away so they could observe, but it still hung heavy over the German lines.

Shortly after eleven o'clock the artillery started in again. Most of the Canadian guns seemed to be firing at Aubers, and if there were any Germans in that town they must have suffered. For nearly an hour the bombardment of the third line continued. Then followed a longer interval of rifle fire and then the bombs; shouting and rifle fire died away shortly after one o'clock. At about half past one I could see khaki figures in kilts in the outskirts of Aubers. They seemed to be strolling around looking for something to do. When I went to the telephone I learned that the third and last line of the German trenches had been taken and the battle had been won. What a place to win a victory over the same Germans that for two thousand years have been crossing the Rhine and invading Flanders, only to be defeated and driven back again as the Germans of today will be driven back. History will surely repeat itself. What is the use of these invasions, these fierce raids by the Germans? Nothing but the loss of thousands upon thousands of lives. Every acre of the ground we were fighting on has been watered with the blood of German and Fleming long ago. We were only repeating the centuries' old feud.

All afternoon we waited patiently, expecting that in the pursuit that would follow our battalions would be echeloned through the gap made, but not a word came. We returned at night to our billets and were warned again to be on the *Qui vive*.

Thursday, March 11th, was slightly hazy and we were kept in readiness all day, but no new developments followed. Something must have happened, lack of ammunition, or something of that kind. My officers were worrying me all day wondering if the grand advance had gone on and we were left behind. I could give no explanation. It is a soldier's duty to wait and do as he is told. The impression prevailed for the moment that the terrible tales they told about us in England had followed us to Flanders and that General French was afraid to trust the First Canadian Division. In the evening we were notified that hot baths would be ready for the men and a change of clothing at Sailly next day. That meant that we would not take part in any advance, at least for the moment.

On March 12th, in the morning, accompanied by Dr. MacKenzie and Lieutenant Dansereau, I set out for Estaires. We were told before we left that the Canadian troops would not be required that day. The battle orders given to me confidentially by Colonel Hughes burnt holes in my pocket, but we would not need them yet. On the way we found a lot of cannonading going on, and as we came to Estaires we met long lines of ambulances coming in from the front with the wounded. There were Guardsmen, Indian troops and Highlanders. At first we thought they were the wounded picked up on the battle field on the 10th of March. In Estaires from some of the slightly wounded we learned the vastly important information that another big attack was on and that the British troops were making very little headway, and were having terrible losses. The artillery were not doing much, and the infantry were getting the worst of it. The German corps army had been brought up.

From a wounded Highland sergeant we learned that on the 10th the three lines of German trenches had been carried as stated. The British troops were in the environs of Aubers and along the Rue D'Enfer. The Germans were apparently in full retreat and our losses were only about five *per cent*, of the men engaged. The troops in the first line, victorious, were eager to go on, but they were halted on the western outskirts of Aubers all afternoon and then told to dig themselves in. Next day they were for some reason ordered back to the third line of German trenches and told to prepare these trenches, strengthening and consolidating the lines and to prepare for a German attack which did not come. Today being the third day they were ordered to carry Aubers, the Rue D'Enfer and the ground extending to the Wood of Biez. In these places a terrible resistance had been encountered. The Germans Corps Reserves, several divisions of them, had arrived. They had fortified Aubers by using the lower or basement storeys of houses for machine gun emplacements, and a large redoubt with wire had been constructed in the woods.

The commanding officers of both the battalions of the Gordons had been killed, also Colonel Fisher-Rowe of the Guards, who had turned the trenches at Fromelles over to us, was killed leading his battalion in a charge. The Gordons had lost sixteen officers from each battalion, killed and wounded, and about half their men. The Guards Brigade had lost about the same. Again and again the unconquerable British infantry this day charged across the open to carry ground that was virtually theirs two days before, but the Bois de Biez and the Rue D'Enfer bristled with machine guns that mowed them down in hundreds. Guards, Ghurkas, Highlanders, Pathans charged again and again till at last towards evening the attack was called off. The German counter attack had taken the form of a pure defensive and we had sacrificed ten or twelve thousand troops trying to retrieve what we lost through lack of support two days before.

There was no truth in the stories subsequently circulated that our guns fired in mistake on the British troops. A few Indian guns that had been worn out with constant firing since the Battle of Mons fired stray shells but that is likely to happen at any time. An error of a line or two on the indicating ring of the fuse when set will cause the shell to burst short.

The Battle of Neuve Chapelle was a great victory for the British, but we did not gather much of the fruits of victory. Everybody felt that something had gone wrong, but what it was only history will disclose. Our younger officers were beginning to think that the old Wellington tradition of "support promptly" had been forgotten in the army of Flanders.

Over eight hundred German prisoners fell into our hands. They were mostly Bavarians and Saxons. They were in the bombed trenches and had had a very hard time from our shell fire. Their clothing, hands and faces were stained yellow from the lyddite fumes. I saw these men at a factory at Estaires where they were held. A number of them spoke English. I also saw them on the street as they were being conducted by a French reserve officer and guarded by French reserve troops. They were a mixture of young boys and middle-aged men, well fed and well clothed, and it did not appear as if it was costing the German Government much effort to look after them. Like all Germans they had let their beards grow which made them look like "Weary Willies." From an intellectual standpoint they did not seem to be overburdened with brains. "Blond beasts" they would be nicknamed in the London music halls. We used to wonder why the German helmets would not fit us, they were so small. After seeing these men we knew. A number six to six and one-half hat would fit any of these chaps.

Chapter 18

Billets and Bivouacs

A terrible disaster happened the regiment on March 23rd. Our adjutant, Captain R. Clifford Darling, was wounded. This is how it happened: An artillery lieutenant was with us constantly in the trenches as observing officer. Sometimes it was Lieutenant Lancaster, son of an old colleague of mine, E.A. Lancaster, Member of Parliament for Welland, Canada. Sometimes it was Lieutenant Ryerson, son of Surgeon-General Ryerson, another friend of many years standing. This morning a young English artillery officer came along and said he wanted to be shown the German trenches and anything else that could be seen from our section. It was about noon, and Captain Darling insisted upon going down to the trenches with him.

As I wanted to go over the trenches myself and see how some work was progressing on our right sector, I asked the adjutant to stay at headquarters till I returned. We got as far as the corner of the Rue Pettion and the Fromelles Road when we proceeded to climb up on the roof of a ruined house to have a look at the trenches. I had with me a panoramic sketch of the trenches which had been made by an English officer at Christmas during the time the British and Germans fraternized, for this was one of the places where there had been a truce for a few hours and Briton and Hun forgot their grudges. The various villages and farms were pointed out. Aubers and Fromelles, with their ruined towers, the Bois du Biez, Aubers Ridge and other objects on the landscape. In front of us there was a partially erected factory of some kind. We suspected that its blinking, unglazed windows harboured machine guns, and I fervently urged him to try out his guns on this building as soon as he got them in position.

After we had feasted our eyes on the German lines we climbed down, and no sooner had we reached the ground than we were met by Captain Darling, who said he had a message for Captain Perry, who was in a small redoubt on our extreme left, and whose telephone wire had been cut some time before by a German bullet. We all walked down a zigzag communication trench which led to the centre of our trenches. As we walked along I warned Darling to be very careful and not to take the short cut back to our quarters, but to join me at the communication trench and we would come out together. We turned to the right and I showed the visitor over our right section. While I was doing so a message came to me over the wires from brigade headquarters, asking me to go there for a consultation with General Turner. I turned back and started for brigade headquarters, which were about a mile back of the line. When I got there Colonel Garnet Hughes informed me he had heard by 'phone that Captain Darling had been wounded while he was on his way out from the trenches.

After receiving my orders from headquarters I hurried to my own quarters to see what had happened to our adjutant. I met Major MacKenzie, our medical officer, as soon as I entered the house, and he was very much cut up over Darling. The three of us, with Captain Dansereau, had messed together under shell and rifle fire so long that we had become very much attached. Darling was an ideal adjutant, a fearless rider and a splendid comrade. He coupled with a graduate's course at the Royal Military College, a thorough training as an accountant and business manager. The "Red Watch" was sad that day, for he was universally admired by everybody. He had been returning after delivering a message to Captain Perry that he was to get ready to go to Ypres to assist the British forces there in some mining operations at Hill 60. On his way back he met several officers who insisted on taking the short cut. They had to run across a short space of about fifty feet to get into a ditch which saved a walk through the trenches of several hundred yards.

In a moment of weakness, having learned that I had been called from the trenches and would not be waiting for him at the communication trench, he gave in and took the short cut. The Germans, who were always on the alert at this point, and only about one hundred yards away, let drive a volley, and a bullet caught him in the back under the right shoulder blade. As he was stooping it penetrated his body and came out above the right collar bone. The wound was a clean one and bled very little. The bullet had not pierced his lung. He was resting quietly when I saw him. He had very little pain, was quite cheerful and told me he would be back to duty in a few weeks. He had left a youthful bride behind him in London and was anxious to join her, so I gave orders that he was to be sent as quickly as possible to England. General Turner seconded me in this, but he was kept in France a week after he was wounded, the reason given being that they wanted to make sure that the bullet had not penetrated the lung cavity.

I immediately offered the vacant adjutancy to Captain Warren, but he declined it, saying that he now had the cares of a company on his shoulders and was taking a great deal of enjoyment out of it. I sympathized with him, for I knew his men would miss him very much for he was an ideal company officer. Captain Dansereau, who had been my scoutmaster and signalling officer, and who had learned all the topography of that part of France on his hands and knees at night, laying wires and hunting broken ones, consented to take over the job. We took on Lieutenant Hamilton Shoenberger as signalling officer. "Shon," as he was affectionately called by his comrades, and Dansereau were graduates of the Royal Military College. Captain McLaren raised a storm when I asked for Shoenberger, but when I pointed out that Darling expected to be back in a month or so he consented.

The men took all the fun there was in life out of things when they were back in billets. They fed, slept and played football, and had a good time generally while they were resting. Beyond furnishing fatigues for the engineers, a few hours' physical drill or a march, they had very little work to do.

The motto of the Canadian Engineers is, "*We never sleep.*" They were very keen and ardent and were constantly working to strengthen the trenches. Major Wright of Hull, who was at the head of our section, was a very big man, about six feet four in his stockings, with a width of chest and shoulder that is found nowhere in the world so plentifully as in the valley of the Ottawa River and in Canada's Glengarry County. His towering form would loom up everywhere in the trenches at night, and along with him generally came young Pepler, another intrepid youngster, who was never quite at home unless he was in the most dangerous spot in the trenches, or out in front examining the German wire at close range. Wright was a born leader of men, and another of his staff whose light burned brightly was Captain Thomas Irving of Toronto. The exact opposite of Wright, they reminded me always of the two great warriors in Sienkiewicz's *With Fire and Sword.* All the engineers were men of technical training and much experience. They were right at home in Flanders, and deserved the tributes that we heard tendered them by the British General Staff.

Their confidence in the practical experience of the Canadians was demonstrated by their sending to us for a practical mining man to direct the big mining operations south of Ypres.

One of the happiest features of billet life was the receiving and writing of letters to friends at home. Pen and ink were plentiful, so was paper, and most of the spare time of the men was spent in writing letters to friends. All these letters had to be censored, and the censor was not Lord Kitchener, as some people seem to think, nor Sir John French, as the London papers would have it, but the colonel of each regiment. He is the heartless man who has to wade through reams of love letters, and he never even drops a tear when he finds one of his young men corresponding with two or more young ladies at home, and assuring each of them in the most fervent and fond language that he loves but her and her alone. Sometimes the commanding officer is so busy that the labour of censoring the letters is turned over to a junior subaltern who may happen to be handy.

The letters are brought in to headquarters and left unsealed. They are supposed to be read by the colonel, closed and his name written across the front page vouching for the contents. On one occasion one of my platoon commanders brought into the orderly room a very large bundle of letters. His men had been very busy with their pens that morning, and he made some remark to that effect to me. At the moment I was very busy writing letters to irate mothers who would write to me whenever their sons neglected to provide a weekly batch of correspondence, so I told the young officer to take my stamp and censor the letters himself. When he had gone about half way through the correspondence, he gave an exclamation, jumping half way out of his chair. "What's the matter?" I asked in alarm, wondering if he had caught one of his men in treasonable correspondence with the enemy.

"The matter," he said in a tone of rage, "Why, one of the men in my platoon is writing love letters to my best girl in Toronto."

I advised him to let the letter go through and leave the settlement of the matter until after the war. Such a situation would in ordinary times have provided a theme for a three-volume love story.

After the battle of Neuve Chapelle, the Seventh Division, comprising the Gordon and Guards Brigade, moved to our right. They were badly battered but still in the ring. The first night they were in the trenches on our right they would occasionally open up with their Maxims, and the scare they would give the Germans was a sight worth seeing. The German flares would go up, and the Huns "stood to" and blazed away like mad. Out of some 800 men in the second battalion of the Gordons only about 350 came out uninjured from Neuve Chapelle. Only about thirty of the original battalion that fought on the retreat from Mons remained in the ranks. In the afternoon the day after they came alongside of us, my adjutant, Dansereau, and I paid them a visit. There were only six officers left in their mess, but they were cheerful nevertheless.

After another turn in the trenches we were moved back to Estaires and placed in billets. We were given to understand that we would soon be given a chance at the Rue D'Enfer, and so we began to train for it. Dummy trenches were fitted up and our bombing parties practised daily. The men were turned loose with their entrenching tools and practised "digging in" every day.

While here another serious casualty occurred. On the evening of Saturday, March 27th, Sergeant Rose and Piper Miller were returning with several comrades from Estaires. They were passing one of our billets when a sentry challenged them. Miller was playing the pipes, and there was a high wind blowing at the time and they did not hear the challenge. The night was dark and the sentry who misunderstood his orders fired and brought down both men with one shot. Rose was shot through the hips and Miller across the back. They were both very severely wounded and the sentry was at once imprisoned. Rose was a very fine young man, having risen rapidly from the ranks to be quartermaster sergeant. He was an ideal soldier.

Miller was a splendid piper, a Lowland Scotchman with a Glasgow accent that convulsed everyone who heard him. He took great delight in using the dialect of Bobby Burns in its purest form, and could get his tongue around "*It's a braw bricht moonlit nicht the nicht*" like Harry Lauder. Dr. MacKenzie was quickly brought and did what he could to alleviate the sufferings of the two men. Rose received a wound large enough to insert your two fingers into it but did not bleed very badly. Miller had his ribs smashed at the back and bled internally. He had to lie on his face and groaned a good deal. Rose, like all the Canadians that I have seen wounded, never uttered a sound.

On March 31st General Turner took Colonel Loomis and me along with him to Laventie to reconnoitre the ground about the Rue D'Enfer. I was again told in confidence that the Canadian Division was expected to frame up an attack on this justly named road. We rode to Laventie and walked down to what was left of the village of Fauquissart. Laventie was deserted except for the troops, but the village with the euphonious name, which stood at one time at the corner of the Rue D'Enfer and the Rue de Bois, was nothing but a heap of bricks.

When we approached, the Germans were busy throwing coal boxes at the church tower, or what was left of it. They generally like to leave a bit of a church tower or gable standing, for as nearly as I could follow their gunnery they used these points to "clock on," that is to say, a ruined steeple will be the centre of the clock. The observer will then direct the guns something like this, "Aubers Church, one o'clock, five hundred yards." The above directions would mean to fire from the church tower as the centre, five hundred yards towards one o'clock from the tower. Our gunners use a different system.

We got into the village without any casualties, and I climbed into a ruined house and had a look through the tiles of the roof at the German lines and made a panoramic sketch. Then we went down into the trenches and met the "Yorks." They told us that we were to do the attacking and they were to do the looking on and cheering. They appeared to be pleased that it was not the other way on.

On the way out General Turner, V.C., had a narrow escape. He missed a communicating trench and started with Colonel Loomis across an open spot about two hundred yards from the German lines. He was spotted and several volleys sent after him. The general is a very brave man, and I was always afraid he would be hit. We went back and arranged for working parties to make more supporting trenches to hold troops for the assault.

I made Lieutenant Dansereau my acting adjutant. He was my scout master and signalling officer, and when I went into the trenches either he or one of the other young rascals would step up smartly and start a conversation when I was passing a dangerous spot. I noticed that these escorts always got between me and the German lines so that if a bullet came they would get it first. This touched me very deeply but I made them stop it. No commanding officer was ever served more devotedly by his officers than I have been. My acting adjutant was Scotch on his distaff side, a descendant of Colonel Mackay, who climbed the Heights of Abraham with the immortal Wolfe. His father was one of the ablest men in the public life of the Province of Quebec.

Young Dansereau knew no fear and would as soon go out in daylight and cut the Germans' wires as eat his breakfast. He was a graduate of the Royal Military College and a splendid soldier and engineer.

I had offered the position to Captain Trumbull Warren, but he declined it, as he was second in command with Major Osborne and he said he wanted "company" experience, how to handle men and to get to know them and learn how the military machine was worked. The real reason he stayed with his company was because he was so devoted to his men. He had formed ties which he did not like to break. Every man in the company thought he was the greatest company officer in the division, and I thought so too.

Chapter 19

With General Sir Horace Smith-Dorrien

The battalion paraded early on April 7th and once more we were on the march. We were working north and were to go into billets near Cassel. The intended attack on the Rue D'Enfer never took place. It was only an April fool joke.

We did the twenty mile march to Cassel in heavy marching order in good style and got into our new quarters at four in the afternoon. We were to have a week's rest there. Then we were to take over a piece of trench east of Ypres from the French so that the British line would extend between the Belgians and the French. As it stood, we were in the French line. Our billets at Cassel were excellent. We were in the Second Army under Sir Horace Smith-Dorrien.[1]

The battalion paraded on April 10th at 9.15 and marched off to Cassel to be reviewed by General Sir Horace Smith-Dorrien. The city of Cassel is situated on one of two sugar loaf hills that rise about a thousand feet above the adjoining plain. There is a wall around the city and it is now strongly garrisoned by French troops. From the summit of the castle you can, on a clear day, see Dixmude, Calais and the sea. You can also view Ypres, Armentieres and many other towns and villages. The city was not taken by the Germans in their rush last fall. The hills around Cassel are rich in historical associations, dating back to the Roman period. There is still shown the remains of one of Caesar's Camps, and underneath its walls William the Silent of Orange fought one of his most notable battles.

For review our brigade was drawn up in a field below the city

1. *Smith-Dorrien* by Horace Smith-Dorrien, also published by Leonaur.

walls. This field was in the form of an amphitheatre and the troops looked splendid in the bright spring sunshine.

General Sir Horace Smith-Dorrien did not keep us waiting long. We presented arms, and he went over each platoon most carefully. While he was inspecting one battalion, the others rolled in the grass or enjoyed themselves by tossing bits of turf at the tame pheasants that gazed on the soldiers in wonder from the hedges surrounding the enclosure. The general reviewed the 48th and expressed much admiration for the fine physique and soldierly bearing of the men. He said it was a pity that such fine men should be taken from their homes and sent to war, but he was sure they would give a good account of themselves.

When the review was over the general called the officers and non-commissioned officers together and told them that he had never seen a steadier or finer body of troops; that we would soon have some stiff work to do and he knew we would do it, but that he considered the war would be over in a year. He told us that when the Canadians came to France they had been preceded by rumours that questioned their drill and discipline, and that the British doubted their soldierly qualities. They were, however, much surprised to find that the Canadians were most excellent soldiers, that they were as highly trained as any British soldier who had come to France, that their discipline could not be questioned, and that their behaviour in the trenches had been splendid. The British generals at first thought the Canadian technical troops, such as the artillery and the engineers, might lack skill. They found that the artillery knew their business as well as the best British artillery, that the engineers were superior in many ways and that now every corps commander wanted the Canadians.

General Smith-Dorrien, at the conclusion of the review, called the men together and addressed them in a similar strain, and then we were ordered to march our battalions off to their billets.

It was a great pleasure to hear a few words of commendation from such a great soldier as General Smith-Dorrien, for the first Canadian Division had been greatly lied about and maligned in England. Every offence on the calendar had been charged against it, and one would have thought, instead of being composed as it was of young, well educated and well-behaved men, it was the off-scourings of the Canadian prisons and jails.

If we were well drilled we owed it all to ourselves. We went to England filled with high hopes that we were to be associated with

British Regulars and to have the best of British instruction. We were disappointed from the first. No British troops were associated with us. We had to work out our own salvation.

But the Canadian officers were a self-reliant lot, so the drill manuals were conned carefully and the men were exercised in a sound system that made the companies great self-confident fighting machines. Every officer was on his metal and worked hard to bring his men to perfection in spite of mud and rain and all sorts of difficulties worse than we ever encountered in Flanders.

Comparisons are odious, but experience has shown that the Canadian officer, on the whole, is equal to any officer in the British army. His Majesty graciously ordered that we were to be classed as "regular Imperial officers." We had to line up to that standard.

The present war is altogether unlike previous experiences in the British army. "Forget South Africa" became a byword. The numbers are so great and the ground so restricted that new conditions have arisen. The Canadians quickly assimilated the new conditions.

On the morning of April 15th the battalion paraded at its billets at Ryveld and marched to Beauvoorde. This hamlet consisted of a couple of stores and a saloon. The men were quartered on farms. On one side of the road is Belgium, the other side is France. I was quartered in the *estament* or saloon, and the landlady told me that in the room in which I slept a German Prince Este had slept the night before he was killed by the British near Caestre. This was very cheerful news, and I am thankful I did not have his luck.

The night before we marched we chopped down a tree at my headquarters and had a bonfire and singsong. The Germans east of Ypres must have thought Cassel was on fire. The tree was an old dead one and burnt beautifully, but next day the owner put in a demand for one hundred *francs*. I agreed to settle for twenty *francs* cash, or a requisition for one hundred *francs*. The shrewd old Fleming chose the gold. We had the worth of the money.

Early the next morning the battalion paraded again and marched to Abeele, where thirty-eight motor busses that had been brought over from England carried the men with their kits to the eastern outlet of Poperinghe, where we alighted and marched down the famous road to Ypres along which thousands of Canadians marched never to return.

We crossed a stone bridge over the Yperlee Canal, passed by a large basin for ships with docks and warehouses, and found our billets

Trenches at Neuve Chapelle

in the north section of the city. My billet was at an old gas works by the railway and the house, which was a modern brick, had previously been shelled, as a large hole through the wall and floor of the parlour showed. The chimney of the old gas plant made an excellent mark. The man of the house, his wife and nine children, were living in the house. I took the front dining room as an office, put the telephones up in the back parlour and took down the half inch steel plates that were over the windows to keep out the shrapnel and let in the light of day.

It is wonderful what fatalists we become in the trenches. This war is not like any other modern war. In previous wars if a man was under fire once a month he was doing well. Here on the western front of Flanders in the British section if he gets out of rifle and shell fire one day in a month he is doing well.

The effect upon the men is very evident. They sobered up as it were. They were very happy and cheerful, but every man that goes in the trenches soon makes his peace, with past, present and future. The Protestants attend service every time they get a chance. There was a great service in Estaires before we left for Cassel and every man attended. The Roman Catholics attend Mass regularly and there is very little attention paid to politics. At home in Canada they were warring in Parliament over giving the soldiers the vote. In the trenches no one cared. What did it matter to a man who was appointed poundkeeper or member of Parliament, at home in Canada, if tomorrow a shell should take his own head off. The petty affairs and jealousies that affect politicians at home and give them spasms and sleepless nights do not interest the man who sleeps on his arms in a dugout with the thunder of cannon shaking down the clay on his face. Religious controversies are also forgotten.

The men of this war are not inspired with religious enthusiasm like the men of Cromwell's time or the Japanese and Russians. There is religion of a deeper kind. The Bible is constantly in evidence. The Protestant and the Roman Catholic sleep side by side in the consecrated ground of Flanders. Both deserve the brightest and best Heaven there is, for they were all heroes and gave their lives for the cause of justice and humanity. In the church yard at Estaires, close by the wonderful church steeple which no German shell had so far been able to find, they buried the dead heroes of Neuve Chapelle in long trenches, three and four deep, with the officers who fell at the head of the mounds. In the corner of every farmyard and orchard you will find crosses marking graves, black for the Germans, and white for our soldiers.

In the presence of constant death, of wounds and anguish, it is wonderful the spirit that pervaded our men. They were reconciled with death and, often when I took a wounded Canadian by the hand and expressed regret that he was hurt and suffering the answer always was, "Its all right, Colonel, that's what I came here for." We all realized what we were fighting for, and the destruction wrought upon the poor Belgians has been so great that we all felt if we had a hundred lives we would cheerfully give them to rescue stricken Belgium and aid brave unconquerable France.

The Canadians that survive this war and return home will have a higher viewpoint, and there will be very few reckless drunken men among them. The "rough-neck" swearing soldier has found no place in this war.

With our brigade was Canon Scott of Quebec, an Anglican clergyman with a stout heart and a turn for poetry. He never tired of going about the billets among the men. There was no braver man in the division and his influence was splendid. Everybody loved him, and he was an ornament to the church to which he belonged. He reminded us often of the old fighting Crusaders.

On the evening of our arrival at Ypres I visited the Cloth Square a short distance away, and reviewed the ruins of the fine Gothic building known as Cloth Hall. This building was one of the glories of Flanders. In every niche over its hundreds of pointed windows there was a full-sized statue of some noted Count of Flanders and his wife. But the place was one great ruin, the inside having been blown out, and now it is turned into an horse stable. The town itself was resuming some of its wonted activity and workmen were busy mending the scars of war in the tiles and brick of the houses of the city.

Ypres was, in days gone by, the capital of Old Flanders. Within its walls there was an Irish convent, and in this convent was shown one of the few colours ever taken from a British regiment. Clare's Irish Regiment in the service of France, it is said, took this flag at the Battle of Fontenoy.

We were now among the Flemings proper, and they are a fine race of tall people, some with light brown eyes and flaxen hair, a rather odd combination. They are very clean and very friendly, worthy descendants of the warlike Belgae. They worship King Albert, who they say is the greatest warrior and king that Belgium has ever seen. The Belgians of today will not rank him second to even Claudius Civilis, the companion of the Roman Emperor Vespasian, nor to any of those heroes of Tacitus, who took up arms for Belgian liberty against the Romans, nor yet to Charlemagne, the great conqueror of Middle Europe.

We were to garrison Ypres for four days, and then we were to take over the piece of trench occupied by another battalion in our brigade, the Canadian Scottish. Our position in the line was the extreme point of the great salient of Ypres that has been held so valiantly for months by the British, French and Belgians.

Chapter 20

The Historic Salient at Ypres

On April 17th we received orders not to gather in groups on the street if hostile aircraft were seen, and also that officers were to keep close to their billets. Three of my companies were moved out to farms in the outskirts. They had been billeted in a big factory, and if a shell had come in many would have been killed. I went out to see Brigadier-General Turner at noon. His headquarters were located at a large farm northwest of St. Julien. I found General Alderson and several of his staff there, and the matter of the defence of the Canadian line was discussed. From this point with my field glasses I could get a good view of the greater part of the salient at Ypres.

Let me here explain the line of the salient of Ypres held by us. South of Ypres, about four miles away, at St. Eloi, the opposing trenches ran straight south of Armentieres, a city named after Thomas de Armentieres, envoy of Flanders to Philip of Spain of Armada fame. From St. Eloi the German line was bent northeast running to what is called Hill 60, and from there northeast past Chateau Hooge to the village of Zonnebeke. From there the line ran almost north across Gravenstafel ridge to where Stroombeek Creek crossed the road from St. Julien to Poelcappelle, thence the line ran northwest past Langemarck to Bixschoote, on the Yperlee Canal which runs northwesterly. The British held the southern face of the salient as far east as Zonnebeke. The Canadian Division replaced a French division on the extreme toe along Stroombeek brook almost to Langemarck. From there on to Bixschoote two French divisions were garrisoning the northern face until they came in touch with the Belgians.

Roughly speaking the whole British front from north to south on the whole Flemish frontier is only about forty miles. All the Ypres salient is historic ground and every foot is rich in sentiment. Every farmhouse, every field bore the scars of war,—the houses and barns with their broken tiles, the fields with almost every hundred feet, a "crump" hole where a shell had fallen and exploded! Some of these holes were ten feet deep and thirty feet across. Life was cheap in this great salient and the Canadians were given "the post of danger, the post of honour."

There was no strategical reason why this salient should be held so far east of Ypres. If we kept our artillery west of the canal where they could not be enfiladed, the shells would not reach where the Canadian battalions were holding the trenches six miles away. If the guns were brought into the salient they could be bombarded by German artillery from each flank as well as the front. If the infantry line was broken at any point the whole would be compromised. There was the danger also of the canal in the rear with only a few pontoon bridges. The canal would be filled with our guns and dead. Very few of our men could escape. There were no troops but ours and the French on the left between us and Calais. Two weeks after the Battle of St. Julien the salient was flattened to conform with sound strategy.

The weather had been very fine and it was a bright clear day with clouds scudding across the sky, such as we see in Flemish pictures. Everywhere tall lines of elms and stubs of pollard willows filled the landscape. The cattle were grazing in the field and everything looked very peaceful. The larks were soaring and singing on high. Every now and then a muffled roar alone told us that there was war. Somewhere along the horizon to the south I could see the famous Hill 60, and east of it the Zillebeke ridge where, on October 31st, Moussey's Corps, with a division of the French Ninth Corps, made a great stand against the Germans and foiled their attack by calling in the cooks and transport men and dismounting their cavalry. There again in the evening of November 6th our Household Brigade under Kavanagh saved the situation that cost the British Blues and Second Life Guards their commanders. Along the same ridge towards Gheluvelt Cawford's Brigade came out of action reduced to its brigadier, five officers and seven hundred men.

A little to the north, on the afternoon of October 31st, the Worcesters made a famous stand, and on November 10th the Prussian Guard was wiped out by the Black Watch on the same spot. They tell how General French told the Black Watch that they had many famous honours on their colours that told of many glorious days, but that the greatest day in the history of the Black Watch was that on which they met the Jäger Regiment of the Prussian Guard and the Jägers ceased to exist as a unit.

Every little farm was dotted with graveyards where the British and French had buried their dead. On the way back to Ypres, Major Marshall and I took a short cut across the fields and ran into a battery of 4.7 British guns, Territorials. When they saw us coming they loosened up for our special benefit, and the first thing we knew the answer came back in the form of a heavy German shell that came within a few hundred yards of the British batteries.

That evening the British blew up Hill 60. Captain Frank Perry had been told off to assist the British engineering officers in this work. The explosion was followed by a most terrific cannonade and rifle fire which continued all night. This was a hot corner. During the night my slumbers were disturbed with the whistling of German high explosive shells in our vicinity.

On Sunday, April 18th, Canon Scott preached a sermon to the men. During the day several shells burst in the town and some of them not far from our billets. The inhabitants had begun to flee.

About eleven o'clock at night Canon Scott wandered into my billets. He had been holding service with the men and had lost his way. I was afraid he would get killed or drowned. He was so zealous, and such a charming character, he made an ideal chaplain. No hour was too late, no road too long for him. His son was wounded with another corps and would lose his eye.

Early in the morning Sergeant Miller of the headquarters staff called me to witness a duel between a German and a British aviator. It was a beautiful bright morning, with not a breath of air stirring and not a cloud in the sky. Away to the north the two aviators were at it, circling about each other like great hawks. The British aviator was the smarter of the two, and he finally got the Hun, whose machine started for the earth nose down at a terrific speed. Both of the German air men were killed we learned later. It was certainly a thrilling sight.

The next day, the 19th, more shells were thrown into the town. One shell fell into the billet where Lieutenant Frank Gibson was quartered. It killed an old man, his wife and daughter, a beautiful girl of seventeen. The back of her head was blown off. Lieutenant Gibson got a splinter of shell in the calf of the leg and had to be sent to the hospital to have it cut out. The Germans continued shelling the town all day. When they get beaten they always start shelling the nearby towns and work their spite off on the inhabitants. The blowing up of Hill 60 seemed to have stirred them to an extraordinary degree. Towards dusk I went down the Menin road to watch the bombardment.

Some of our batteries, hidden in the hedges away on my right, were sending shrapnel across the German lines beyond Hill 60. I could watch the flight of the projectile and its bursting in a sheet of flame over the enemy's line. The opposing guns were hard at it, while away in the distance the rapid rattle of rifle fire told of the tragedies that were being enacted near the crater that Captain Perry had blown in Hill 60. Away to the south a momentary flash like sheet lightning on an autumn evening would light the horizon with a baleful gleam, and after a long interval the muffled roar of a "Grandma" would mingle with the twang of the bursting shrapnel. Truly as one British Tommy, who watched the battle, said, "Hell was let loose that night." As I returned to my billets along the ancient moat that at one time defended the city, shells passed over my head and a dozen or so aimed no doubt at the tall chimney of the ancient *magazine de gaz* fell within a few yards of my quarters.

On the evening of April 20th we were to take up the line of trenches held by the Sixteenth. The Germans still continued to shell Ypres, (which is pronounced Ep-r-r, E as in fee, two syllable r-r, the R sounded the Scotch way with a burr aspirate).

Shortly after luncheon Captain Warren and Lieutenant Macdonald came to the orderly room to ask some questions about the order in which we were to march into the trenches. An officer from each company had gone into these trenches the night before and looked them carefully over. The left section was given to Captain Osborne, the right to Captain McGregor and the centre to Captain MacLaren. The position consisted of seventeen half moon redoubts and they were not at all strong. Captain Alexander's company was to be in reserve with headquarters at St. Julien. As the officers had received orders not to go away from their billeting area, and had to receive permission to do so, both Warren and Macdonald asked me if they could go up to the Cloth Square to buy some comforts to take down into the trenches for the men. I gave my consent, but warned them to be careful and take cover from any shells that came along. About ten minutes later Lieutenant Macdonald arrived back breathless. He asked quite coolly, "Where is Major MacKenzie? Trum's hit with a piece of shell."

I immediately called the major, who was in the next room, and we learned that "Trum," as Captain Warren was affectionately called, had been badly wounded. He and Macdonald were standing in a grocery store at the north side of the square when a "Jack Johnson," as the huge seventeen inch shells fired by the Germans from the Austrian howitzers they have brought up to shell this town are called, fell into a building in the south side just opposite. The shell wrecked the building into which it fell, killing an officer and seventeen men. A piece about an inch square flew fully two hundred yards across the square, passed through a plate glass window, missed Macdonald by an inch, and struck Warren below the right collar bone piercing his lung. "They have got me in the back, Fred," were the last words he said. He was carried on a stretcher to the hospital a few hundred yards away, and the surgeon made an examination of his injury, cutting his clothing away. In a moment we saw there was no hope for him. It was only a matter of a few minutes. Canon Scott heard that he had been injured and hurried to the hospital. He had only time to repeat the prayer for the dying as poor Warren passed away in Major MacKenzie's arms. His death was a great loss to the regiment.

I left the arrangements for the funeral with our quartermaster, Captain Duguid. He was to be buried the next night at the Place D'Amour.

Truly, this was a war of attrition. One by one we were losing the gallant young officers that came over with us to Flanders. Darling was wounded, Sinclair wounded, Warren killed. Sinclair had had a dixie of boiling water spilled on his leg while in the trenches and had received a very severe burn.

In the evening Captain Perry arrived from blowing up Hill 60. He had escaped as usual without a scratch. Perry bore a charmed life. I suppose it was because he lived so much in the north country in Canada among the miners who always carry a stick of dynamite in their boot legs. At the Rue Pettion billet he escaped the "coal box" that entered the next room in which Captain McGregor slept. The shell made pulp out of McGregor's clothes and belongings, but Perry was not scratched, although not ten feet away from where the shell burst. At Hill 60 he assisted the British engineer to run several mines under the German trenches. He was the last man out of the tunnels when they were loaded with several car loads of dynamite, and his was the grimy hand that touched the button that sent half the Hill and about eight hundred Germans into the air. He had a narrow escape from being buried alive.

Captain Perry had a terrible experience after the mine was blown up. As soon as the mine blew up the Germans turned all their artillery

THE ORIGINAL SALIENT AT YPRES

on the crater to prevent the British from taking possession till they could bring up reserves. The place became a living hell. Perry, after examining the crater with a lantern, found a German counter mine with a candle still burning in it. It had been vacated. He started to make his way out through a communication trench to make his report when he ran into a British brigade coming in and had to lie down in the trench and let the brigade pass over him. He was mud and sand from head to foot.

Chapter 21

The Red Cock Crows

On the afternoon of the 19th I was very busy closing out my correspondence. I always made it a point while I was out of the trenches to answer all the letters I had received, and that usually occupied three or four hours every day while we were out of the trench line.

Previous to this our battalion has alternated with the Royal Montreal Regiment in our tour of trench duty. The rule used to be for each battalion to be three days in the trenches, and then three days out. In these trenches we were changed around. The 16th Canadian Scottish were to alternate with the 48th Highlanders. The 16th reported to us that the trenches were very bad, and we were to go into them the next night. This evening Majors Marshall and MacKenzie were out visiting company billets, and my adjutant, Capt. Dansereau and I went into a small Flemish restaurant to have our dinner. While we were seated at the table an officer of the French Flying Corps and several of his men came in for something to eat, and we engaged in conversation. The French officer, whose name is well known, and who was afterwards killed, was a small perky chap with black hair and eyes. His cheeks were hollow, as like most of the top-notch aviators he had had his teeth pulled out.

Many of the aviators have all their teeth drawn because when at very high altitudes it is very cold, and the nerves of the teeth become affected and give them most intense pain.

These officers told us that the French Flying Corps was going to leave that night for a district further south where there was going to be some "nibbling" at the German front. He told us further that the Germans were moving a great number of guns into the Ypres section, and that he had an idea that as soon as the Canadians and British took over the salient we would be "jolly well shelled," if not attacked in force. This was very cheerful news, and sure enough the next day they began shelling the city with big Austrian siege mortars, a shell from one of which killed Captain Warren.

In the evening of the 20th I rode out to the company billets to see that everything was in readiness for the battalion to take over the right section of our line from the 16th. The companies were to march into three sections independently, shortly after dark, and the idea was to have the relief over as quickly as possible. I found the men and officers in excellent spirits. Captain McGregor was to take the right section of our line, Captain Alexander the left and Captain McLaren the centre. They started off a little too early in the evening, and I had to send couriers to halt them and wait for the darkness. It was a beautiful spring evening, bright and warm. The larks were still soaring and singing in the sky, and the sun in the west was going down in a sea of gold and amethyst. South of us at about Hill 60 the guns were growling, the only sound at the moment to remind us of the war. But there was something else of ominous portent noticeable. Simultaneously, northwest, east and southeast of our line three huge German captive balloons reared their heads for all the world like golden hooded cobras.

Away, twenty miles to the south, in the sky could be seen the snaky outline of a zeppelin. The Germans were taking observations. When I reached the headquarters' line of trenches in front of our brigade headquarters, a few hundred yards west of St. Julien, I sent the horses back with Smith, my groom, and stood by the roadside to watch the companies go by. First came Major Osborne, who was to take the left, with his tam-o-shanter bonnet cocked on the side of his head, as jaunty a Highland officer as ever trod the heath in Flanders. His company swung after him, marching like one man. The trenches had certainly not taken anything out of them, for if anything they looked steadier and sturdier than they did the day they left their billets in Hazebrouck to take their first march in France.

Some distance behind came Captain McGregor, his two hundred and forty men tall as pine trees, with Lieutenant Langmuir and Lieutenant Taylor at the head of their platoons, both well over six feet. Next came Captain McLaren, always staid and correct, his company well pulled together, going so fast that a word of caution had to be given to them. Last of all came Captain Alexander, whose turn it was to be in reserve. His company was to occupy and act as part of the garrison at St. Julien, there to cover themselves with glory.

When I reached the village I found that Major Leckie was occupying the reserve headquarters of the 16th, and across the road was Colonel Meighen of the 14th or Montreal Regiment. The south section of the village was ours and the north was for the reserve corps of the battalion holding the left section of the line. The house in which we were quartered had at one time been a small restaurant, but the village had several times been shot up. The walls almost to the ceiling were plastered with blood. There was hardly a house in the village without several shell holes in the roof. Terrible tragedies had been enacted here. The gardens had a full crop of black and white crosses.

Colonel Meighen had a very swell house, the windows looking south towards Hooge and Hill 60. He came over and welcomed me to St. Julien and showed me his trench diary and plans of the trenches. Colonel Meighen was a very thorough and painstaking officer, very much loved by his men. Several companies of his battalion were French Canadians and they fairly worshipped him. He was a model trench commandant, never tired of strengthening the works, and always ready himself to do anything that he asked of his officers or men. He had made an excellent battalion out of his corps, and as we had alternated with them in the trenches until this turn, we knew their worth. His second in command, Colonel Burland, was also a keen and efficient officer. The commandant of the 14th was not a "fusser." He was always cool and collected and his example permeated his whole staff and officers. Captain Holt, his adjutant, was one of the hardest working officers in the division, cheerful, obedient and alert. He was a model staff officer.

Major Leckie turned over the trench diary to my adjutant. He reported that the 16th were hard at work fixing up the trenches which were in a very poor condition. His brother, Colonel Leckie, was down at commandant headquarters in the supporting trenches. Major Marshall went down to take over from Colonel Leckie, and I stayed at report headquarters to report back as quickly as possible that the trenches had been taken over. The 16th Battalion did not take very long to get out, and one by one our Captains reported their companies in place.

The battalions in the trenches reported that the front was quiet, and it was added that there had not been a casualty in our section among the French troops for a month.

My sleeping bag was placed in a corner of the only room with a sound roof in the house, and I slept soundly in spite of the blood-bespattered wall which told of a desperate struggle in this room during the great battles of the previous November.

In spite of the fact that the French had not had a casualty for a month, the map told me we were in the hottest corner in the whole of Flanders. I did not feel at all nervous, as a matter of fact after a person has been under shell and rifle fire for a few days he ceases to be nervous. Nerves are for those who stay at home. At first the heart action quickens a little with the sound of the explosions and the crack of the Mauser bullets, but after a while the nerves fail to respond and the action of the heart becomes slow and the beats below normal. The explosion of a "Jack Johnson" in the next room will not give you a tremor. Why should it? Jock will say, "If you are going to be kilt, you will be kilt ony-way." That is the everyday religion of the trenches. "When your time comes you will get yours, and all the machine guns and shells in Germany can have no potency if your time has not come."

War tends to make us all fatalists, and the officers have to be continually on the alert to keep the men from becoming careless.

In the morning I tried to arrange to go down to Ypres to the funeral of Captain Warren. Major Osborne wanted to go also and take a firing party with him, but much as he would have liked to acquiesce, General Turner had to refuse, for we were in a dangerous corner and no one could be spared. Lieutenant Drummond, his brother-in-law, was permitted to attend. Captain Duguid, the quartermaster, with the assistance of the engineers, had a metallic coffin made for him and they buried him in the Canadian burial plot.

That morning I learned of the death of Captain Darling in London. We had expected that Captain Darling would be convalescent shortly after he went to England, but about a week before news had come that gangrene, the terrible disease that took so many of our wounded, had infected his shoulder, and a number of serious operations had to be performed. Still we had hoped that his splendid physique would pull him through. But it was not to be, and the two comrades that had been the pride of the regiment died within a few hours of each other.

The whole Empire did not possess two kinder or braver men than Captains Darling and Warren. It is only when men go down into the valley of the shadow of death together that they learn to appreciate each other. In the trenches soldiers are true comrades, backbiting, lying and slandering is left to the slackers and "tin soldiers" who stay at home. Both these young men were in the flower of their youth, both

The Famous Road To Ypres

left young wives, both were men of means, brought up amidst wealth and refinement. They gave up a good deal to go to the war, and their example and their lives should fix a tradition not only for their fellow officers of "The Red Watch" but also for the whole Canadian Army. They did not hesitate to "take their place in the ranks," and they died like the heroes of Marathon and Salamis.

Early in the morning a German aeroplane, an albatress, came over St. Julien. The German aeroplanes have a large, black maltese or iron cross on each wing. The allies have a red, white and blue rosette. Shortly afterwards the German artillery started to shell the southern section of St. Julien. They threw a few shells at the remains of the church, then they started after a house and large barn south of us, about half way to the village of Fortuin. The barn was a large structure covered with a couple of feet of rye straw thatch beautifully put on. In a moment there was smoke and we saw some Canadian artillerymen running towards the barn which was apparently full of horses. One after another the beautiful artillery teams were chased out of the burning structure which the Germans continued to shell. The horses were turned loose in the field and proceeded to enjoy themselves like colts, and although the Germans fired shrapnel at them they did not hit one. In a moment the "red cock," as the Germans say, "was crowing on the roof." The flames rose to a great height and in a few minutes there was nothing but the charred rafters left.

The trenches reported everything quiet for the rest of the day.

That afternoon along with one of my signallers, Sergeant Calder, I made my way to commandant headquarters at the northern extremity of Gravenstafel ridge, northeast of St. Julien. I met Colonel Meighen, who showed me a line of trenches east of the church which his battalion was putting in order. When I got down to commandant headquarters General Turner came along with his Brigade-Major, Colonel Hughes. They were looking over the position with a view to having some dugouts and rifle pits established about five hundred yards south of my headquarters to support our right in case of trouble, the intention being to put a company in reserve there. I found commandant headquarters located in a dugout in the rear of a ruined windmill. The charred timbers of the mill lay scattered about, and all that remained of the dwelling house was a heap of bricks and some tiles still sticking to the roof.

A line of short irregular trenches ran across the front of the slope. Behind headquarters the hill sloped back to Haenebeek brook, northwest and southeast. Five hundred yards behind the Gravenstafel ridge ran the road from Zonnebeke to Langemarck. On this road immediately in our rear there was a ruined blacksmith shop and several old farm engines. Some of the implements bore the name of Massey-Harris, which brought back visions of Canada, and was another evidence of our coming world-wide trade, the possibilities of which first struck me when I saw the name of another Canadian manufacturer, Gurney & Co., on a heater alongside the tomb of William Longsword in Salisbury Cathedral.

A few yards south of the blacksmith shop a dressing station had been fitted up in the ruins of another farm house at a cross-road which subsequently came to be known as "enfiladed cross-road." In front of the blacksmith shop a clear spring of water ran out of a pipe and the water was cool and good. I quenched my thirst from the steel cup taken from a French Hussar's helmet. The man who wore the helmet was no doubt sleeping peacefully beneath one of the crosses that were strewn thickly over the little cemetery of St. Julien. These little graveyards were to be found in all the fields and gardens. It was wonderful how the French soldiers cared for them. Wherever a soldier of France lay there you would find a cross, with his name and the legend that he fell on the field of honour. The graves were usually decorated with tile and flowers, some real, some artificial. France thus silently worships the memory of her gallant dead.

Chapter 22

German Gas and Turcos

"Be careful there," said Capt. McGregor. "The French were short of sandbags here and they have built several dead Germans into the parapets." I was examining our new trenches in the twilight and my nose had been assailed by that peculiar odour which emanates from the dead.

"Get plenty of quicklime down here tomorrow," I suggested. "Build some traverses where they are laid."

"You're pretty heavy, don't step too hard. Dead Germans there." Lieutenant Langmuir was then piloting me along his section.

"Out in front, there on the left, there is a dead French officer caught in the German wire. He has been hanging there since last November. The Germans have left him there. There is nothing now but a blue coat and red trousers."

This certainly was the worst corner in the way of trenches I had seen since we came to Flanders. Behind the ditch rows of crosses, black and white, stood up a few feet away, ghastly reminders in the half darkness of the toll that had been paid to take and hold the trenches. The defenders here were buried where thy fell.

Earlier in the day I went down to the front line and had leisure to examine the commandant's headquarters, which had been held by our gallant French Allies since November, 1914. It was a dugout in the rear of a ruined windmill, and contained several pigmy rooms. There was a room for the signallers, another for the adjutant and one for the commandant. The French officers had left behind them excellent maps of the German position showing their trenches, also panoramic sketches showing the roads, villages and houses opposite, with compass points. These sketches were the work of their gunners. No wonder the 75's were so deadly. Their efficacy is in their recoil and the "graze" fuze they use. Their high explosive shells strike the ground, bound in the air and burst about thirty feet forward from where they strike. In this way they form a curtain of fire filled with splinters of steel, over the German trenches.

I turned a copy of the panoramic sketch over to Major MacDougall of the Toronto Battery, when he went into the loft of a ruined house some distance away to check up his guns as they fired on the Poelcapelle road in front of us.

I slipped quietly into a fire trench on the forward slope of the ridge to observe the guns at work also. I had sent word down to Major Osborne in the forward trenches to clear the men out of the redoubts on either side of the road so that if a shell fell short it would not hurt anyone. The Canadian "observing officers" were always very careful in "registering," as they called it. They began by sending their shots well over the German parapets, and gradually coming closer, instead of firing a shell short, another long and dividing.

While we were observing the Germans replied to our guns, and very nearly got Major MacDougall. Poor chap, he was subsequently assassinated by a German spy or sniper behind in billets. His clothing was stolen and worn by the assassin who was caught and suffered the death penalty.

Major Marshall came along to see what was going on and stood for a minute at the head of my trench. The Germans spotted his Glengarry and began shelling my trench with "Jack Johnsons," and Major Marshall had to clear out. I stayed until they got tired of shelling and then had a good look at their lines through my field glasses. The ground sloped gently down from where I stood in the sap-head for about three hundred yards to our forward line of redoubts. Away to the northwest the double line of parapets disappeared in the trees and hedges around Langemarck. Just short of the village the Third Brigade (ours) took up the defence. The trenches here for about five hundred yards were held by the Royal Highlanders of Montreal. Major Osborne held several half moons on the far side of the Poelcapelle Road. Then our battalion lines continued southerly, running for about eight hundred yards till there came a gap which occurred between us and the Winnipeg Rifles. Immediately behind our line ran Strombeek River, (we would call it a creek). It marked the bottom of the slope and crossed the line of trenches held by the "Little Black Devils," as the men of the Winnipeg Battalion were called.

The line of the Second Canadian Brigade trenches then ascended

The Break in the Salient

the Gravenstafel ridge. On the east side of the ridge the land sloped up towards Poelcapelle and Roulers. This slope was not very steep, but sufficiently so to dominate the little valley in which were our forward line of trenches. All along the enemy's lines were various clumps of trees, each one of which no doubt concealed several batteries of artillery, referred to in the conversation of my friend of the flying corps. High above the trees and the distant red tiled roofs of Roulers I could see the spire of the Gothic Church of St. Michael. Beneath these walls on June 13th, 1794, a fierce struggle took place between the Austrians under Clerfait and the French troops under Marshal Macdonald, in which the French Republican troops of the latter were victorious. Beyond Roulers lay Ghent, Antwerp and Brussels. The high ground in front was strongly held by the enemy, for this was the key to the advance on Brussels and Waterloo.

My examination of our position ended. I began to retrace my steps to St. Julien, but the Germans spotted me in some way and followed me across the fields with salvos of high explosive shells. I could hear the shells coming as the field was dotted here and there with "crump" holes or craters where shells had fallen. I promptly ducked into a hole till the "whistling Willies" fell and sent showers of mud and flying steel over my head. I observed that sometimes these "crump" holes were very small, and found that after all in this war a small man had some advantage over me. I made my way back to the village, carefully reconnoitring all the trenches on the way, for I had a premonition that we might want to use them some time soon.

After dusk I returned again to commandant headquarters and went into the front line of trenches along with the ration party. There was lots of work to be done to strengthen our position if we were to hold our trenches as we had been ordered to do.

We started down the old disused mill road in the twilight of a lovely spring evening. Behind us the moon hung a silver bow almost on the horizon. It was going to be one of those nights, clear, but with objects not distinguishable at any great distance. Major Osborne met me at his dugout, which was on the east bank of the creek, and together we went on to the left of our line where his men were busy digging fire trenches in the rear of the half moons. Here I saw for the first time a line of French trenches. The French lines were held entirely different to ours. We usually built solid parapets of clay and sandbags high enough and strong to protect a man standing up, but the French usually do not allow this to be done. They had adopted their favourite method of entrenchment here, namely, a series of low parapets built in the form of half moons. My battalion held seventeen of these half moons and our brigade, I understood from our Brigade Major Lieut. Col. Hughes, held far more of the line than it was intended we should hold. About three hundred yards of our right line, some seven half moons, were to be turned over to the Second Brigade on the next relief.

I went over his section carefully with Major Osborne. All the young officers were hard at work bracing up the parapets, joining them together and rapidly erecting formidable defences. I consulted with them all as I passed along the line from left to right, Macdonald, Fessenden, Daniels, Taylor, Bath and Smith, and all were of one opinion, *viz.*, that the half moons should be turned into small redoubts, and a line of parapets built as quickly as possible connecting them.

The French parapets were not built to be held, as we were ordered to hold our line. They build low parapets so the men will have to crouch behind them, and they will want to go forward and take the other fellow's line in order to get better quarters in the German trenches.

This corner had been the scene of some hot fighting at some period during the war, for in my tour of the trenches that night I encountered a dozen little graveyards a few yards in rear of the parapets.

Back and forward I went, and the entire line was canvassed and discussed. Lieutenant Fessenden, one of the most brilliant graduates of the Royal Military College, had a particularly hard spot to deal with, and was handling it in a manner worthy of any of the great Belgian engineers. Fessenden had a brother in the British army. No lieutenant in the whole allied army was a better student of the art of war, or a more fearless man, than this rosy-cheeked boy of twenty-two.

"Sandbags, and more sandbags!" was the reply of Lieutenant Macdonald, when I questioned him as to the requirements of his section. He was on the extreme left, and if anything happened on that side he was sure to be enfiladed. He was quite cool about it, however, a worthy namesake of the great Marshal who had fought so valiantly beneath the walls of Roulers a few miles away.

Lieutenant Smith, always cool and dour, a thorough Scot, was a man to be trusted in a tight place. Captain McKessock had a long talk with me about the machine gun positions. He had reconnoitred his ground very carefully, and had found several places back of the lines where he could mount a gun and rake the German lines if they advanced to the attack. Captain McKessock was one of the men who had sacrificed a great deal to do his share in this war. He was a captain in the 95th Battalion when the war broke out, and he brought a large quota of men to Valcartier. He joined the 48th and insisted upon having command of the machine gun section. It was pointed out to him that it was a subaltern's position, but he wished to have it, and his wishes were gratified. He left the position of crown attorney of a large district, with an income of ten thousand dollars a year, to go to the front, leaving behind him a wife and family. Such devotion to duty is exemplary. He understood his guns thoroughly, and is one of the few men I have met who had studied the tactical employment of the gun as well as its technical operation.

When I came to Captain Daniel's section he was waiting for me. Daniels was a very handsome man, an engineer of note, a graduate of the Technical Department of Mines in Queen's University. He, too, gave up a splendid position, as manager of a large mine in Cobalt, to go to the war. He was a very competent engineer and knew his work thoroughly. As we passed along his parapets we could hear the Germans talking, and a party of them out in front of their parapets were driving in stakes for their barbed wire. There was not much firing going on, and as we had several parties out in front engaged on the same task, we decided to leave our Saxon friends alone for the time being until ours got back under cover. We could see their ghost-like forms close by from our listening post. If we opened fire on them they would likely get some of our patrols.

Lieutenants Taylor and Langmuir were both busy at their sections. Langmuir was one of the "finds" of the 48th. He joined us at Long Branch by coaxing me very hard to give him a commission. I hesitated on account of his youth, but finally consented because I recognized a gleam in his hazel eyes that told me that if the occasion arose he would be a man of high courage. He was tall and slim with a bright colour on his cheeks, and several of my older officers said it was a shame to take him along, he was so young that the hardships would kill him. I took him nevertheless, and though he knew very little about drill or military matters, he studied night and day so hard that it soon became known he was one of the best instructors in the battalion. He developed into a strong well built man, over six feet tall with broad shoulders and a commanding presence. He had a splendid grip on his men, who worshipped him and would follow him any place.

Captain McGregor never tired of singing his praises. He was admired and loved by everyone, an ideal officer and a gentleman worthy to lead a Highland platoon or regiment anywhere. Taylor, who was with McGregor, looked up his captain for me when I came to his section. Lieutenant Taylor was a student at Oxford University when the war broke out. He threw up lectures and joined our battalion as a supernumerary. Our officers had almost all known him before. Standing over six feet tall, with the shoulders and chest of a young giant, Taylor was a man to be noted anywhere. He was famed both at home, in Canada, and abroad as a student and an athlete. He pulled a good oar, played a splendid game of football, hockey and lacrosse. He was an all round star, "a born leader of men," as Lieutenant Alex Sinclair, himself a well known athlete, said to me when he was pleading Taylor's cause for a commission. Both Taylor and Langmuir were very fearless men. They were constantly out in front of their lines at night reconnoitring the German lines and boldly trying to get a look into the German trenches. I had to check them several times and warn them against taking any unnecessary risks.

Daniels had a very hard section of trenches at Neuve Chapelle. He had gone out on the "devil strip" at night, reconnoitred his whole front and mapped it for an advance.

I arranged with Lieutenants Mavor and Fessenden to have a sketch of the line made showing the work proposed to be done. On our right there was a wide space between ourselves and the Winnipeg Battalion. This open space was protected by wire entanglements, but McGregor and Mavor both contended that it was a dangerous spot. I told them that it was the intention to give several of the redoubts on our right to a Company of the 8th Battalion, and that the order was expected to come through the following evening. Lieutenant Mavor accompanied me out to commandant headquarters. On the way out we met a working party of the Canadian engineers going in with Major Wright at their head. I could not help remarking about the commanding figure of Major Wright, who looked like a giant in the uncertain light, a paladin out of the pages of ancient or mediaeval history. I made my way back to St. Julien that night, not by any means satisfied with our military position. The Germans could certainly shell us jolly well if they liked, for so far only five of our own batteries had been put in position behind our lines. But the French had some ten batteries of 75's on our left rear and that was assuring.

The way in which our fire trenches were sighted at the bottom of the Gravenstafel slope did not commend itself to me. It is very difficult to get a good position for trenches. If you go on top of a ridge, the enemy's guns will pound you to death, and if you lift your head they will get you with rifle fire on the sky line. If you dig in on the forward slope they will look into your trenches with their guns. If you go to the bottom of the slope, the enemy on the high ground on the other side can command your trenches. In rear of the crest, the old Wellington position is the best. Our supporting line held this position, but I felt that on the forward slope towards the enemy a few rifle pits would give us a chance to get at them behind their lines. This was to be attended to as soon as the work on the forward trenches was completed. This Ypres salient had only one thing of military value to commend it. It afforded a position in which troops could be massed to break through and advance on Ghent and Antwerp.

I suspected that when the proper time came that was what would happen here. "Sentiment should have no place in business" is a hackneyed expression. War is a business, therefore sentiment should have no place in war. In war there is usually too much sentiment. We cling to impossible positions because we have won them and held them. We attack villages and redoubts that we should go around, and out of which the enemy would run the minute they found us on their line of retreat. We fail to support because we think it is a corps duty to hold their own line, which they may be able to do, but out of which if they had been supported they might launch a counter attack at the worn and shaken enemy which might bring us a notable victory. The principles of war which guided Wellington and his staff apply to this war. I often wished I had brought my *Napier's History* of Wellington's campaigns with me.

When we got back to St. Julien the staff told me that the Germans had registered pretty nearly all over the place during the evening, and that it was a case of shells from north, south, east and west. During the night I called up the various sections of our line and they all reported that the Germans were very quiet.

While I was doing the rounds of the forward trenches I could not help noting the roar of waggons and limbers along the whole German line in front of us. The night was very calm, and whilst it was quite usual to hear a lot of waggons about rationing time, still on this occasion the whole German line seemed to be in motion. I had never heard anything like it before. Something extraordinary was certainly happening. Either the Germans were changing the army in front of us, or else I thought they had got tired of holding the line in our immediate front, and anticipating a strong offensive of which rumors were abroad, they were preparing to retreat to the Rhine. I reported the occurrence to headquarters that night.

In the morning of the 22nd of April Lieutenant Drummond of the Royal Highlanders came to see me and told me he had attended the funeral of Captain Warren.

The Germans were shelling our billets and dugouts in St. Julien pretty heavily, and I was asked to look up some places outside of the town into which I could put some of the men and build new dugouts. I selected several places along the banks of Hennebeke brook where the ground was soft, and the shells would bury themselves and not explode, and started the men digging the dugouts. The particular spot which the Germans had chosen to shell that day was the "Cross Roads" and church of St. Julien. All of the church was gone but a piece of the spire. The graveyard in the rear of the church was torn all to pieces with "coal-boxes," and the coffins and remains of dead civilians and soldiers had been unearthed. These graves had already been carefully repaired by our men under Pioneer Sergeant Lewis under heavy shell fire.

Some distance east of the church a line of fire trenches had been cut. These were to be occupied in case of an attack. The shelling continued all day. In the afternoon about four o'clock my adjutant and I visited the supporting trenches and dugouts at the forward lines. We had a chat with Major Marshall and some of the officers over the telephone, and repeated the orders given to me, that if we were attacked we were to hold the trenches till support came, for if we gave any portion of them up we would have to take them back ourselves with the bayonet.

Lieutenant Dansereau was returning with me about five o'clock to St. Julien to see what progress had been made on our new dugouts, when a very heavy cannonade and rifle fire broke out along the northeastern face of the salient along the section held by the French troops. The rifle fire seemed to grow heavier every minute and a strange yellow haze grew over the distant line of the French trenches. I remarked about the haze to the adjutant, and we both concluded that either the French or Germans were using some new form of gunpowder that caused the greenish haze.

For weeks we had become accustomed to heavy bursts of infantry fire, but these bursts had usually died away. This seemed to continue longer than usual. As we neared St. Julien I met Captain Alexander, and ordered him to tell his men to get their rifles and ammunition and "stand to." The Germans immediately began shelling our dugouts near the church with "coal-boxes," and in a minute they had put a shell into one of them and four men were killed. As I passed up the main street I warned the men and told them to be in readiness to take their places in the trenches in front of and at the northeast corner of the village.

I went to the battalion headquarters and ordered out the orderlies, and in a few minutes the French troops began streaming back without arms or accoutrements. To my horror I found that they were *Turcos* and not the regular French troops which we had thought were holding that part of the line. Lieutenant Dansereau spoke French to them, but many pretended they did not understand.

Almost immediately the bombardment of St. Julien became fiercer and the number of *Turcos* coming back greater. We hurriedly gathered as many as were armed of them together and sent them up to assist our companies in the St. Julien trenches. By this time the rifle fire was very intense and the gas so thick that it choked us, so I ordered every man to go to the trenches. I sent messengers to General Turner, V.C., to inform him of conditions and where we were.

Chapter 23

The Battle of St. Julien

It did not take us very long to realize that a great disaster had befallen our gallant Allies who held the northern face of the salient. The *Turcos* in broken French explained that the Germans had sent asphyxiating gas from their trenches, and that the gas had killed one quarter of their men. For weeks we had been warned that the Germans were going to use asphyxiating gasses against us, but no one had ever dreamed that they would be so inhuman as to use gas that would kill, but they had done so, for the *Turcos* told us that many of their men had fallen dead where they stood.

The gas used was chlorine gas which is one of the by-products of the process whereby common salt is turned into soda, salt being a combination of soda and chlorine. When the salt is heated along with an acid the chlorine gas is liberated, the soda remaining. This soda is used in manufacturing soap. The chlorine is generally combined with lime to make chloride of lime or bleaching powder. In the chemical works of Germany the amalgamation of chlorine and lime was omitted, the chlorine being liquified under pressure in tanks. This liquid chlorine was a cheap preparation used largely for bleaching linens and cloth of various kinds manufactured in the districts in which we were fighting. The bleacheries were silent and there was no longer any use in the cloth industry for the German chlorine gas, so the Germans having plenty of it on hand no doubt decided to use it against the Allies.

We had staid a trifle too long in the village of St. Julien while the streets were filled with this deadly gas. Some of our orderlies could hardly escape and several of the headquarters staff had to be sent to the hospital. I had taken on a pretty stiff cargo of it myself. When it is first breathed it is not unpleasant, smelling not unlike chloroform, but very

Sniping Through a Port Hole

soon it stings the mucous membrane of the mouth, the eyes, and the nose. The lungs feel as if they were filled with rheumatism. The tissues of the lungs are scalded and broken down, and it takes a man a long time to recover, if he ever does fully recover after having some of the "upholstering" of his lungs destroyed. We did not then quite realize the horror of this new form of cowardly and inhuman warfare, but we should have known that the Germans consider war a game without an umpire or a referee.

Messages came promptly from General Turner, V.C., of the Third Brigade to hang on, that the Canadians were going to try and hold the Germans back until help came. We all knew we could depend on General Turner, V.C., and his Brigade-Major, Lt.-Colonel Garnet Hughes. We knew that we were fighting a rear guard action and that this was no time to think of running away. We hardly realized, however, that the Battle of St. Julien which had just commenced was to be one of the greatest battles in the history of the world, that the Canadian casualties were to be as great as the casualties of the British at Waterloo, that the total casualties of the combatants before the fight was ended were to number close to seventy thousand men, and that the Canadians, by brave fighting and losing sixty *per cent.* of their men for three days, were to hold in check five German army corps, or a total of close to a quarter of a million men.

The brunt of the fighting fell to the lot of the Third Canadian (Highland Brigade). Through their lines ran the frightened and disorganized *Turcos*, groaning and shrieking in agony and fright. The French artillery men, finding their lines broken and confronted with the deadly wall of chlorine gas which rolled slowly over the ground turning the budding leaves of the trees, the spring flowers and the grass a sickly white, destroying every living creature in its path, blasting and shrivelling everything over which it swept, cut their horses loose and fled, in many cases two of them clinging to one horse. Ten batteries, it is said, were lost in this way, a gap of nearly six miles was made in the French line through which the Germans poured firing rifles, machine guns and cannon at the fugitives. A Turco Division, and part of a French Division had fled. A remnant of French troops belonging to the "Iron Divisions" held on next the canal.

To meet this situation, the most alarming which had confronted a British General for centuries, there was for the moment only the reserve troops of one Canadian Division. These consisted of the 7th Battalion of British Columbia under Colonel Hart McHarg, which was in billets between Fortuin and Ypres, the 10th Battalion Calgary and Brandon under Colonel Boyle in billets in Ypres, and the 16th Canadian Scottish under Lt.-Col. Leckie billeted in Ypres and the farm cottages towards La Bryke to the north.

General Turner, V.C., of the Third Canadian Brigade, took prompt measures to ensure the safety of the line and the fighting part of the action was in sure hands. Not a moment was lost. Orders were sent down to the commanders in the trenches to hang on, and the 16th Battalion, Canadian Scottish, was ordered to "stand to" its arms on the outskirts of Ypres. Aid was asked from the 2nd Brigade, and the 7th and 8th Battalions were placed at the disposal of the Third Brigade Commander.

As there was only a very gentle breeze the gas did not clear out of the way very quickly, so that the victorious march of the Germans on Ypres was considerably checked. The Huns had a wholesome dread of the Canadian rifles and they advanced cautiously, firing "flares" in the air to mark their advance to their artillery. The flares flamed white in the dying sunlight.

The situation, as far as the Canadians were concerned, was that upon us there devolved the necessity of fighting a rear guard action. The word was passed from officer to officer. We knew we had to fight to the last. In a rear guard action every man has to be sacrificed. Behind us holding the other sector of the salient was the 27th and 28th British Divisions. If we gave way they would be slaughtered almost to a man, and the German road to Calais, forty odd miles away, only two short marches, would be open.

The Germans were spending millions of rounds of ammunition. The streets of St. Julien were covered with a curtain of shell fire, whilst the air was filled with the weird sound of the rifle bullets as they rattled a deadly tatoo on the few tiles that remained clinging to the charred and battered roofs. The air was thick with spent particles of steel and lead that rattled on the pavement and tiles as my Adjutant, Sergeant Miller and I made our way out of the burning shattered buildings through dense clouds of asphyxiating gasses that blinded us to the trenches at the east side of the village where Captains Alexander and Cory held their ground.

So far, so good. The fleeing *Turcos* had not spread panic in the ranks of the Canadians. Every man was prepared to die rather than give up the trenches. As we made our way to Captain Alexander in the gathering dusk we passed through a company of the 7th Battalion going into reserve behind St. Julien. As we reached the trenches we learned that the 7th Battalion had received orders, and were going to fill the gap between the defenders of St. Julien and the trenches held by the Royal Highlanders of Montreal and the 48th Highlanders of Toronto at the toe of the salient.

One of the first men to greet me when we got to the trenches was Captain Alexander, cool and imperturbable. He always had a pleasant word for everybody and a kind heart for his men. During the small hours of the morning the 7th Battalion slipped quietly past us, also a company of the Buffs. They quickly lined the St. Julien, Poelcapelle road and began to dig themselves in.

All through this trying time I was accompanied by my adjutant, Lieut. Dansereau, and Sergeant Miller. We all realized that the situation was very serious, but they were both very cheerful and Miller was in the best of spirits, cracking jokes with the men.

When the shelling of the village began, my men showed me a bomb proof cellar which they suggested that I should occupy. I examined it, but something compelled me not to stay in it. Inside of ten minutes it was destroyed by a couple of "coal boxes."

One of our signallers, Bell, tried to hang on to the telephone at our centre in St. Julien village, although two shells burst in the building and he narrowly escaped death. The signalling section under Sergeant Calder soon had the line connected up with our trenches, and Bell was ordered to leave St. Julien, which he did reluctantly although he had suffered a lot from the gas and had been slightly deafened by the explosions.

The chirpiest soldier in the whole outfit was Signalling Sergeant Calder, who was one of the shortest men in the regiment. The breadth of his shoulders and the burr on his tongue got him enlisted in the first instance. As he was stringing the wires to the trench he had to duck several times. "Here is where I shine by being a 'sawed-off,'" he informed me. We were soon in touch with commandant headquarters, and from Major Marshall I learned that our forward trenches were still untouched. As the night closed in the Germans redoubled their shelling of St. Julien. The charred church spire was lit up with the high explosive shells, and several fires broke out in the village and made the night hideous. Shrapnel broke constantly overhead spraying our trenches and several men were wounded. Several poor wounded *Turcos* had taken refuge in our trench. One of them, an under officer, informed Lieutenant Dansereau that the *Turcos* would stick with the

British till the last. He added as an aside that he wished Algiers was as prosperous as Egypt. So much for this son of the desert who in this terrible hour envied the Fellah of Egypt who was permitted to follow his ordinary avocation as farmer, in the midst of all these warlike times, undisturbed by conscription or his British rulers.

As dawn came the German fire increased and my adjutant pulled a note book out of his pocket and began writing in it with a big blue pencil. I asked him if he was going to try and send a message through to headquarters. "No, sir," he said. "I am afraid I will not come out of this alive, so I am writing a message to my friends, I have reconciled myself to death."

I told him I felt sure that we were going to come out all right, that I had a "hunch" that we were, and that some time we would read that memo together under happier circumstances, and it would bring back memories of the Valley of the Shadow of Death through which we were passing together.

He shook his head doubtfully, and when I laughingly showed him a German horseshoe which I had picked up on the field when we first saw the gas and which I still carried in my overcoat pocket, he smiled but was not reassured.

However, the fact that he felt that we were both going to be wiped out did not dampen his courage. Strange to say my prophecy about his last message came true, for we read it together and laughed over it in Montreal, Canada, months later as I had predicted.

Before dawn several of my runners or signallers returned from brigade headquarters with the story of the fight around the farm house where General Turner, V.C., and Major Wright of the engineers had rallied the cooks and orderlies to the defence of the place. They told us how the 16th Battalion, the Canadian Scottish under Lieut.-Colonel Leckie and the gallant 10th Battalion under Lieut.-Colonel Boyle, had hurried from Ypres to the aid of their comrades. These two battalions reached the reserve trenches in front of Wieltje about eight o'clock, when they were ordered on to 3rd Brigade Headquarters and preparations made for them to counter attack the advancing Germans who had seized the wood northwest of St. Julien.

The counter attack was launched at midnight, the 10th on the right in two lines, and the 16th on the left. Major Lightfoot led the front line of his battalion, the 10th.

"Come on, boys," he said, "remember you are Canadians." The line advanced with great spirit, less than two thousand Canadians against a hundred thousand Germans. It was the biggest bluff in history but it won. On and on went the Canadians, 10th and Highlanders, one moment with the bayonet the next moment firing. The Germans, who were busy digging in south of the wood, saw the Canadians coming in the twilight, and only waited to fire a few shots and then they started to run. Lightfoot was down, but the line went on. Major McLaren fell, but the lines never wavered. They drove the Germans into the wood and clear through it on the other side. If there had only been plenty of supporting troops the German victory would not only have been stayed but the charging Canadians would have gone through the German army that night.

The British howitzer battery which had been lost was retaken, the French guns were recaptured and a great victory was in sight.

When the Germans were caught they began to throw down their arms and cry for mercy. The gallant Canadians gave it, but in the hot rush of the charge they did not wait to disarm their foe. The second lines merged into the first and the fight in the dim forest became Homeric. Then the cowardly Germans whose lives had been spared, plucked up their courage. They picked up their rifles and began like the Arabs in the desert to shoot the men in the back who had spared their lives. Colonel Boyle went down, killed almost immediately. He had led his troops on through the forest by voice and example, armed only with a riding crop. The Germans were driven beyond the northern edge of the forest. The charge by this time had spent a good deal of its force, and as the flanks of the charging lines were not protected, and men were falling on every side, it was deemed advisable to withdraw to the southern edge of the wood and occupy the line of shelter trenches which the Germans had begun to dig. This was one of the most gallant charges in the annals of the Empire. The fame of the gallant charges of the Canadians in St. Julien Wood will live forever in history, engraved in letters of gold.

Considering that the brave Canadians met a foe that outnumbered them over twenty to one, that they drove the enemy ahead of them, foot by foot, exacting fearful toll, their success was phenomenal and had a tremendous effect upon the conquering Huns, who had fancied Ypres was within their grasp. The German Emperor, it was said, had come especially to the western front so as to be able to make a triumphal entry into the last city left to the King of Belgium, Ypres, and to be on hand when his guards and marines from the Kiel Canal, who were present in large numbers, did the goose-step down the Rue

Royale to Calais. The courage of the Canadians proved his undoing.

The struggle in the Wood at St. Julien will go down to history side by side with the fight at Albuera and the hand-to-hand struggle at Inkerman. It was a soldier's battle, and many brave men fell. When roll call was held in the morning only five officers and 188 men of the 10th responded, whilst the 16th Canadian Scottish could only muster five officers and 260 men unhurt. The command of the 10th, owing to the death of Colonel Boyle, devolved upon Major Ormond, who gallantly held the position gained during the next day and until Saturday morning, when he was relieved and sent as support to the 8th on Gravenstafel Ridge where I met him and his remnant at Enfiladed crossroads, the hottest part of the line.

The brigade bomb throwing unit assisted in the charge on the St. Julien Wood, and few of them lived to tell the tale. One of them belonging to the Red Watch returned, Pte. Adkins, a boy of nineteen, and from him I learned many of the facts I have recounted.

In the meantime what steps were being taken to succour the hard pressed 3rd Brigade? A portion of the 45th French Division was still hanging on to the extreme left of the French line. They had fallen back to try and conform with the general retirement on their right, but they pluckily determined to try and extend their ground by a counter charge near Pilken and regained some ground.

West of the Yperlee Canal at Vlamertinghe the 1st Canadian Brigade was in billets. Two of the battalions, the 2nd and 3rd, were sent to aid the stricken front. The 1st and 4th were kept in divisional reserve west of the canal. The 2nd and 3rd marched through Ypres and up the St. Julien road. It was there they got their first real baptism of fire. They advanced in open order and the German guns gave them "the curtain of fire." The 1st and 4th were later sent, first to the banks of the Yperlee Canal and subsequently to take part in the counter attack along with the rest of the Canadian Division. By three o'clock in the morning all the Canadian troops that were in reserve were up and at it, "hammer and tongs," driving back the Germans and trying hard to reconstitute the broken line from St. Julien to Pilken.

In the counter attack some very brave deeds were performed by the Toronto Regiment. As they marched down the stone road to St. Julien they came under the intense shell fire, "the curtain of fire," which the Germans were directing against all the approaches to our position along which reinforcements might come. Here and there a shell would fall in the ranks, but the regiment would only pull itself together and keep on. East of Wiltje a big shell fell and when the smoke cleared away Macdonald of the machine gun section, Ross Binkley, Broughall and Bickerstaff, four of the most popular young men in the battalion, great athletes and football players, had paid the price. As they neared the 3rd Brigade Headquarters they were put into the headquarters trenches. Later on two companies were sent to fill in the vacant space between the right flank of the 10th and the corps that held the village of St. Julien. The companies that advanced were the Body Guards, the Mississauga Horse and the Royal Grenadiers, and they behaved splendidly.

As morning dawned the situation as far as we could learn was as follows: The British section of the salient had not been attacked beyond some desultory shelling. The section held by the Second Canadian Brigade had remained untouched also. This section ran from Gravenstafel northerly. First, the 5th Battalion on the right, the 8th battalion on the left. Then the 15th Battalion (the Red Watch) less one company, held the line along Strombeek creek as far as the Poelcapelle road. The 13th Battalion (Royal Highlanders of Canada) carried on till their line almost reached Langemarck. Their left was very much in the air. The line then bent back towards the Poelcapelle-St. Julien road, and in the gap there was a company of Buffs sent to try and fill in the opening. They stood almost back to back with the 13th. Then came three companies of the 7th Battalion. A company each of the 14th, "The Red Watch," and the 13th with some *Turcos* were holding the trenches in front of the village of St. Julien. The Third battalion had succeeded in getting into touch at St. Julien and continued the line to the 10th south of St. Julien Wood.

The 16th Canadian Scottish continued the line with some supporting companies of the 14th on their left. Here a gap occurred, defended by a few groups from the 2nd, and further along astride the Ypres Pilken road the 1st and 4th Canadians were fighting like heroes. The Canadians during the night had reconstituted the line, but at great cost. The troops in this front line all came under the command of General Turner, V.C., of the 3rd Canadian Brigade, as senior officer present. His experienced eye recognized the weak places, and his staff, headed by Lt. Colonel Hughes, was there ready to lead the units to their proper places. Each Canadian unit as it came opposite its place had been ordered to attack, and after advancing some distance they were ordered to dig in, which they did.

The irresistible bayonet charges of the Canadians had misled the

Germans, for their advance was paralysed and they had for the moment lost the initiative.

Here is where a great military mistake was made but not by the Canadians. The German staff came to the conclusion that there must be thousands of supporting troops behind the charging Canadians and made the biggest mistake of the war. But the Canadians had not accomplished this bluff without much loss of life.

One of the first officers of my acquaintance to fall on the evening of the 22nd was Lieutenant Drummond of the 13th Battalion. I had spoken to him in the morning. When the *Turcos* had come streaming across the field, tearing through his company of Montreal Highlanders, he, together with Major Norsworthy, gallantly tried to rally these men, along with my adjutant. Drummond fell, together with his comrade, each a victim to a German bullet. No braver lad, no more ardent Highlander ever donned the tartan of the Black Watch than Lieutenant Guy Drummond. When he fell Canada lost a valuable and useful citizen. His training, education and charm of manner, coupled with his intense patriotism, marked him for a great career. Major Norsworthy, his friend and comrade, fell by his side.

Further along the line held by the Toronto Regiment, Captain George Ryerson fell at the head of his company. "Happy" George, his comrades all called him, for he was worshipped by his men as he always wore a smile. No man ever saw a frown on the captain's face. Lieut.-Colonel Boyle had made the supreme sacrifice at the head of the 10th. Major Maclaren of the same battalion had been wounded in the charge at St. Julien Wood and was killed outright by a shell in the ambulance on the way to Poperinghe.

Word drifted through to me that our transport billets at Ypres had been shelled and that Sergeant-Major Grant, "Soldier Bill," as he was called by our men, had been dangerously wounded on the way down to the trenches with ammunition. Macdonald, a gallant corporal of the quartermaster's department, had also been badly wounded and much regimental property destroyed and lost.

We passed a very disagreeable night. The trenches were wet and unpleasant and the incessant shelling made it impossible to move. Several wounded *Turcos* in the trenches kept moaning like fretful children. Every time a shell burst there was a hideous chorus of groans and wails from them. Finally an exasperated Highlander shoved a rifle butt threateningly in front of the groaning figures and the noise was stopped. It is a strange thing, but I have never heard a Canadian groan when wounded.

As the east reddened the sentries called out to the troops to "stand to," and I watched the men as each one stood up in the trench and watched the sun rise. Many of them saw it that morning for the last time. Shortly after the order came to "stand down."

The quartermaster succeeded in getting some rations through to us. Captain Duguid and Capt. Jago never failed. During the remainder of the fight they fed the whole brigade.

My forward line reported "all well," and we were cheered by the knowledge that the advance of the Hun had been checked, and regardless of numbers we felt we could hold them.

As the men were ordered to "stand down" I watched them one by one start cleaning their rifles, getting ready for the stern business ahead the coming day. Their conduct so far had been splendid, and as I thought of them in this critical hour standing in the gap for the Empire, I realized that a new figure had risen in the lurid battle-swept horizon of Europe, that of the Canadian soldier, young, athletic, tense, alert and indomitable, a figure that will now live as long as history and song is written. Unconsciously there rose that morning in my mind the majestic words of the great Milton:

> *Methinks I see in my mind a noble and puissent nation rousing herself like a strong man after his sleep and shaking her invincible locks.*

Those soldiers of ours that had barred the Hun were well worthy of the Homeric age fit to follow old Cromwell and his Ironsides. That night had witnessed thousands of gallant deeds that pen may never tell and to which neither crosses or medals could begin to do honour.

CHAPTER 24

Hanging On

"Stretcher for Captain Cory."

A cry went along the line of the trenches, and two stretcher bearers jumped up on the parapet and ran towards the Poelcapelle Road, along which Captain Cory's platoon held the trench.

A groan went up from the whole line. We all thought Cory had been hit. He was a universal favourite.

Only a few minutes before as dawn broke my officers in the front trenches came to me to report and have a cheery word. Captain "Bob" Cory, Captain Alexander, Lieutenant Barwick and Lieutenant Jones all reported and stopped for a moment's chat.

While we were at Cassel, Captain Cory had obtained leave of the general officer commanding, the blessing of his own commanding officer and the good wishes of his brother officers, and had gone to London for two short weeks and there married Miss Telfer of Collingwood, Canada. She reached England with her sister, Mrs. (Major) Porter, too late to become a bride before the regiment started for France. Captain Cory would not transfer and stay in England, so the first opportunity that came he was granted leave. Marriage had quieted him down a lot and I kept cautioning him, for the sake of the wife he had left behind, to be careful.

Barwick and Jones wanted leave to take their platoons down to the forward trenches to assist Major Osborne. Cory said that with the *Turcos*, and the other two platoons of the company, he could hold the trenches at the northeast angle of the village, so I consented to their leaving. It was a very brave offer, and it showed excellent spirit on their part to wish to go and participate in the defence of the peak of the salient which was considered the most dangerous part of the whole line.

As Captain Cory was on his way back to his position one of his men was hit with a machine gun bullet and they called for a stretcher. I started to go down the line to where he was, but was told he was all right, that it was one of his men that had been wounded.

My signallers reported to me that all night long the fighting had continued in front of St. Julien, the Germans trying to force an entrance at the northwesterly side between the village and the wood. The village had been shelled continually. During the night several limbers of artillery came clattering down the road, dodging shell holes, dead horses and men, followed by the wakeful German guns, as the gunners knew that these limbers held ammunition for the Canadian artillery in the first line. The Germans seemed to have a weird sense of what was going on on our roads. The 10th Battery under Major King was at the cross roads at Kersselaere. During the night Major King gallantly ran one gun by hand well forward on the left of the Royal Highlanders to try and stop the advance of the victorious Huns.

It was Major King's ammunition that came rattling down the ruined streets of St. Julien during the night, and when the "coal boxes" fell at the concrete bridge over the Hannebeek creek where it crossed the road not far from the ruined St. Julien church, the horses and several of the riders fell to rise no more. Nothing daunted, the non-commissioned officer in charge returned for help to man-handle his precious load down to the guns at the trenches. Captain D.S. Gardner of the 7th took a squad of about thirty men and they manned the limbers, and amidst a perfect hail of shells and bullets drew the ammunition down to Major King, who lost no time in firing it point blank into the Germans that were advancing on Kersselaere cross roads. They were mowed down in heaps by the shrapnel. The German advance was stopped at this point and the gun was later taken out safely.

Throughout the battle no Canadian guns were lost.

As usual with the morning sun, there came from the east two large German aeroplanes with the ominous black crosses on their stiff outspread wings. They flew low and seemed particularly interested in our breakfast bill of fare. The warning whistle was blown as they approached and everyone lay down in the trenches as still as death. The Germans seemed to satisfy themselves that there was nothing in our trenches, for after they returned to their own lines they stopped shelling the church and graveyard close by which up till then had been their favourite target. When they stopped shelling the church and graveyard the scene was dreadful. The walls of the church and rafters were torn to pieces. But it was the cemetery that presented the most grewsome sight. Graves, ancient and modern, were torn open and coffins and corpses were strewn in all directions. Our dead had been disinterred a second time. I set a party to work under Sergt. Lewis to repair this damage.

We learned in the morning that some British troops had been sent to the assistance of our severely pressed left flank. This detachment was under the command of Colonel Geddes and consisted of the remnants of seven mixed battalions from the 27th and 28th divisions that had held the southern face of the salient. They were detachments of the 3rd Middlesex, the 2nd East Kents, the 1st South Lancasters, the 2nd East Yorks, the 9th Royal Scots, the 5th R. Lancasters, the 2nd D. of C. Light Infantry. The 5th Lancasters and Royal Scots were Territorials, the rest of the detachment were regulars. This brigade went to the assistance of the French remnant left at Pilken, and they helped to reconstitute the line after a gallant charge in which the French and Canadians joined, closing up a gap at this point.

Along towards noon, Colonel Loomis, who had his headquarters west of the village of St. Julien, sent for Captain Alexander. I told Alexander to take a couple of men with him in case anything happened to him as the shelling in the village was very heavy. He did so, and was gone about an hour. He returned alone looking very grave, and I asked him what was the matter. He told me that on the way out his men had fallen at his side, killed by a shell.

About eleven o'clock we noticed very heavy shelling and gas fumes rising in the direction of our front trenches east of Kersselaere. There was a pretty stiff breeze blowing, and shortly after we saw the gas our guns began firing and there was a terrific burst of rifle fire. We recognized the "chop" of the Ross rifle and knew that our men were in action at the extreme angle of the salient. Major Marshall telephoned me from his headquarters that the Germans were gassing and that they were following up the gas with an attack.

I was very anxious but soon learned that the German attack had been beaten off, for their artillery as usual began working off their spite on the farm houses in our rear. I also learned that although the shelling was very heavy we had escaped so far with very few casualties. About noon I began to realize that I had not eaten anything since breakfast the previous morning, when my meal had been disturbed by the German shells and the tragic death of the sentry at our headquarters. Someone handed me a tin of "bully beef," and I ripped the top off with the trusty hunting knife which had been my faithful companion on every expedition I had made into the unknown wilds of Canada for the past twenty years, and I finished that tin of beef with apologies to "Fray Bentos."

In the afternoon I started down for the front line of trenches to see how they were getting along there. Capt. Dansereau accompanied me. At first he insisted that I should not go down into the "devil's corner," as they called it, and said he would go down and look it over and come back and report to me. However, when he saw I was determined to go he got his revolver and insisted on coming along. I bade goodbye to Capt. Alexander and the brave lads that were holding the St. Julien village trenches. Many of them would "return to Lochaber no more."

We made our way down to commandant headquarters. On our way we passed in the rear of the 7th Battalion and noted that the British Columbians knew how to use their shovels and grubbers. They were busy in spite of sniping and shell fire fortifying the line of the Poelcapelle Road for some distance east of the St. Julien and in rear of Kersselaere village. Colonel Hart McHarg was there directing the men. When we got to headquarters we found Major Marshall quite cheerful. Lieutenant Shoenberger wore his customary grim smile as he told me how our men had driven back the attacking Germans a few hours before. The Germans had "gassed" them twice, but the wind was too high and it blew the deadly fumes over the parapets. The men waited till the Germans emerged from their trenches three or four deep to charge. Then our whistles blew, and hundreds of them were cut down and piled on top of each other before they broke and ran back to their trenches. One machine gun got about 200 of them.

They told me that Major Kirkcaldy of the 8th Winnipeg Rifles had come over from their headquarters on the Gravenstafel Ridge to reconnoitre. Orders had come through that after dark the 13th Battalion, whose left flank was much exposed to enfilade fire from some machine guns, were to retire, pivoting on our left flank at the Poelcapelle Road and linking up with the 7th and Buffs. They were to dig in, trenching the line in rear of Kersselaere. Part of the 7th Battalion, which was virtually in support of them, were to hook up with our supporting trenches, thus forming two lines. The orders were that the 48th Highlanders were to hold their original trenches and protect, and the 7th were to conform. We were all warned to hold our trenches at all costs.

The order to conform and to consolidate, which reached the 7th, sent Lieutenant-Colonel McHarg out to reconnoitre his front about five o'clock in the afternoon to find out the most favourable place to build the parapets. Lieutenant Matheson of the engineers had arrived and Lt.-Colonel McHarg, Lieutenant Matheson and Major Odlum proceeded down the slope from their lines towards some ruined houses in their front, which they entered, and from the back windows of which they immediately saw the enemy lining the hedges not one hundred yards away.

When they started back uphill the Germans opened fire on them and Colonel McHarg was instantly shot through the stomach. Major Odlum made his way out and sent Captain Gibson, the battalion surgeon, down to attend to the wounds of their commanding officer. Gibson stalked fearlessly down to where his colonel lay, picked him up, got him under better cover and dressed his wounds, and that night after dark they got him out. There was much gloom and sorrow among the British Columbians that night for they all loved their colonel and they knew that there was very little hope for him. He died the following day at Poperinghe. Thus died one of the bravest of the Canadians, a splendid soldier, the champion sharpshooter of America, for that matter of the world. He had always displayed great coolness and daring, and British Columbia will always cherish and revere his name.

The command devolved for the time being upon a worthy successor, Major Odlum.

At dusk I checked up the casualties over the telephone and I learned that we had only a total of forty-seven for the strenuous twenty-four hours, and that most of these were in the trenches of St. Julien. Lieutenant Vernon Jones and Lieutenant Barwick came along with their men, and they helped to take double rations and ammunition to the left flank company commanded by Major Osborne. They were ordered to close the rear of the redoubts with sandbags so as to save their men from enfilade fire which they were sure to get in the morning, as soon as the enemy had discovered that the 13th had retired to take up a new line.

During the attack at noon the 13th had their line pierced at one point and a machine gun belonging to the Germans was brought through and put into position in a farm house surrounded by a moat in the rear of their lines. From this farmhouse the Germans were giving them all kinds of trouble, and it was to relieve this pressure chiefly that they were ordered to retire. The suggestion to bomb the Germans

A Narrow Escape

A shell entered the tree above these officers' heads, but failed to explode.

out was not practicable. Our guns were too few to cope with the powerful German artillery, although well served.

Company Sergeant-Major De Harte came up from the trenches along with the ration party at eight o'clock and told me the story of the gassing and bombing in the morning. When the Germans sent their gas over the wind was too high and it blew over the top of the trenches. The 48th waited until it passed over, then as soon as the gas and shelling ceased they manned the parapets knowing that an attack was coming. The whistle blew and the Ross rifle rang out a deadly hail that tumbled the Germans in heaps and sent them scurrying like rabbits for shelter.

The Huns gave us no more trouble during the afternoon and the men were confident of their ability to cope with any force that might come against them. Word came through to be sure and hold our trenches at all costs as help was coming. This message was sent direct to the trench line. Major Osborne asked me what would happen if the ammunition ran out. I told him the standing orders of the trenches were that we must use our side arms. Our standing orders read as follows:

> All ranks must realize the exact nature of the duty they are called upon to perform for the moment and must not exceed this duty. This duty is to hold the trenches at present handed over to their care at all costs against all comers, and on no account to give up the line. If attacked the men must continue firing and remain at their posts. If the enemy endeavours to rush the parapets the men will use their bayonets. Any of the enemy who make their way into the trenches must be bayoneted. The regiment is provided with ample supports in the rear. Any of the enemy who gets beyond our trenches will be taken care of by the supports. Each man must fire low and steadily.

As the night closed down the heavens were lit with the German flares and the lurid flashes from their guns. I took a long look over the battle line and I confess I thought our chances of ever getting out were very slim. The German flares crossed each other in the heavens behind us. In our left rear, and all around to the right rear, I could see the angry red flashes of the thousands of guns they were directing against our devoted defenders. I began counting the batteries, but after I had reached a hundred I concluded they had enough. Almost every calibre of gun was being used against us, from the great seventeen inch

Austrian siege mortars they were firing at Ypres and Poperinghe behind us, to the nine, seven, six, five, four and three-inch high explosive shells that were filling the air with their fiendish notes.

Bayonets, brawn and bull-dog courage were all we had to match against all the resources of chemistry and mechanics of our enemies. They might poison us, destroy us or take a bit of the line here and there, but take the city of Ypres—not that summer, not so long as a Canadian arm was left to defend the stricken salient.

At twelve o'clock that night I checked up my sketch of our position after having a bowl of soup in Major Marshall's dugout. The second brigade line was untouched. So was the 48th. The 13th were withdrawn from their trenches and were digging in along the slope on our left flank. One company of the Buffs, one of the 5th and two companies of the 14th were mixed up in the line here, along with the three companies of the 7th that were consolidating their trenches along the Poelcapelle Road towards St. Julien where they linked up with the 48th, 13th and 14th Companies of the garrison. From the left flank of St. Julien, the 3rd Toronto Regiment, two companies, joined up with the 10th and 16th at St. Julien Wood. Then came Geddes' British Brigade, and on their left the 13th British Brigade under Brigadier-General R. Wanless O'Gowan. This brigade arrived in the afternoon from Hill 60. It was made up of what was left of the tired 1st West Kents, 2nd King's Own Borderers, 2nd York Light Infantry, 2nd West Riding, 9th London, all from the 5th Division that had lost half their officers at the crater blown up by Captain Perry. Next came the 1st and 4th Canadians, and then the French troops held as far as the canal.

There had been little or no change during the day. The honour of holding the dangerous angle of the great salient at Ypres had fallen to the lot of the Canadians. The Red Watch held the danger point, the toe. It was our duty to hang on and die to the last man until help came and the French line was reconstituted as it was when the French *Turcos* broke before the deadly gas. Like typical Highlanders we were the "Forlorn Hopes" of the Empire.

It was away after two o'clock in the morning when the shelling died down a bit in our front. I threw myself down in the dugout and fell asleep. I slept with revolver ready and boots on and got in a few winks. I was awakened at about a quarter to four by loud talking and the roar of guns. I jumped up and turned out to get a glimpse of what was going on in the trenches in front. I met Capt. Dansereau, who told me the Germans were again trying to gas the 48th. True enough, in the grey dawn a heavy yellow pall hung over our trenches and there was a sweet pungent smell of chlorine in the air. The two platoons that were in dugouts were at once sent to their stations in the supporting trenches. Major Marshall and Capt. Dansereau went into the trenches with them, while Lieutenant Shoenberger and I remained at the dugout trench at the telephone. There was a slight lull in the cannonading for a few minutes, then the German guns began to speak in louder and more insistent tones. I looked around the salient, shaped like a man's right foot, of which we were the toe, and hundreds of batteries seemed to be turned on our trenches, both front and supporting.

Again and again salvos of "coal boxes" fell in succession along the parapet. Talk about Neuve Chapelle, we were getting our own back with interest. All the German batteries were concentrated on our parapets and the trenches held by our regiment. Pandemonium reigned along the front line of trenches. The Germans followed up their gasses again with intense rifle and machine gun fire. Up and down along the parapets of the redoubts the shells kept dropping, throwing up huge pyramids of black smoke fifty feet in the air. These blasts resembled rows of black trees or fountains. How anything could live in that seething vortex, created by the bursting high explosive shells, is a mystery. Many a brave Highlander would see the lone shielings and the misty mountains of Canada no more.

All this time the Germans were industriously shelling the dugouts and supporting trenches where our supports were located and along the Gravenstafel Ridge. Huge shells fell like hail. Those that failed to burst in the air exploded the minute they struck the hard untilled clay of the fallow fields and fragments flew in every direction. One fell on the roadway about twenty feet away from me. Two men who were standing under cover of the broken wall of the windmill crumpled up like green leaves in a forest fire. They were done for. They were giving us a double "curtain of fire" as well as the death dealing gasses.

A piece of the same shell struck Lieutenant Shoenberger, my signalling officer, who stood close beside me, and he fell. He said never a word, but in a trice had his knife out, cut off his *puttee* and looked at his ankle. The bone was broken. Before I could give him a hand he had his first aid bandage out and tied up the wound himself. I offered to send a man with him to the dressing station a quarter of a mile back, but he said he would crawl down on his hands and knees all right and that every man would be needed in the trenches. He was quite cool and collected and did not show any sign of fear. I felt very sorry for him.

Nearly a century ago Admiral Lord Cochrane, a man of wonderful scientific knowledge, advanced a project to the British Government for a terrible and unseen agent which could be used against an enemy, and which was so destructive and powerful it would render their armies helpless. That secret was asphyxiating gas. His plan was on the field of battle when the wind was favourable to build large fires with tar and damp straw behind which an attack could be prepared. Then sulphur was to be thrown on these burning piles so as to produce gas, which blowing over the enemy would render them helpless. This would not produce a poisonous gas. It would only be an asphyxiating gas that would knock a man out for a while. Still the British had refused to use this secret.

In 1913 German scientists at the German Headquarters Staff had experimented with sulphur, chlorine and bromine fumes. They reported on sulphur gas: "This gas thus produced acts as an irritant on the lungs and eyes, and thence it is adapted to render the enemy incapable of resistance, but is not poisonous, and in that way its use in war is not contrary to international right." They had in view Article 23 of the rules of conducting hostilities promulgated by the second Hague Conference to which they had subscribed, which specifically prohibits "the use of poisons and poisonous arms" and "the use of arms, projectiles and material destined to produce useless suffering." The Germans could have used sulphur gas just as well as chlorine gas, but sulphur was not poisonous, and would not kill; chlorine and bromine would.

We had just learned that they were using red phosphorus in their shells, and that any particle of that chemical that got into a wound would set up gangrene from which hundreds of soldiers died in terrible agony. We had surmised that they were in the habit of dipping their rifle bullets in red phosphorus solution because where they struck the men's clothing they invariably started even the wool clothing burning. That was the case at St. Julien Wood where, according to the stories brought back by the men, they had foully crucified a sergeant belonging to our brigade on a barn door. He belonged to our bombing section.

The sun was shining a red rim on the horizon in the east. The sickly green clouds of the gas appeared denser in some places than others. The wind was just right for the infernal curtain that gradually drew over the trenches. The thickest pall was blown against the right of our line between McGregor's company and the left of the 8th Battalion, where there was an open space protected only by a small trench and barbed wire. Of those on our right hardly a man was left to tell the tale.

All those who stuck to the trench and did not use wet *bandoliers* or handkerchiefs died. Some tried to get out, only to fall stricken with the deadly vapour before they had gone many yards. Among these was Lieut. Taylor, an Oxford scholar, one of the best athletes in the First Division. He won out of the trench only to die on the Gravenstafel Ridge. Company Sergeant-Major Hermitage and his brother Sergeant Hermitage were stricken down also but managed to crawl out. The latter lost the use of his vocal chords for some time. They were burned with the fatal gas. Lieutenant Mavor, who was in this section, fell, but they managed to get him out before he succumbed. Some of the men fell back to the left to a communicating trench which they held till the German infantry attack came when they rallied to the parapets and drove the Germans out with their bayonets.

A very dense cloud of gas was directed against the centre of our line and Captain McLaren was one of the first to fall. Some of his men succeeded in getting him out. For days his life was despaired of, and his lungs were scarred forever. Lieutenant Maxwell Scott, of Abbotsford, kindred of the great Sir Walter, author of *Waverley*, one of the finest officers in our battalion, fell from the effects of the fumes. They succeeded in getting him out also. His life was dispaired of.

The only thing the soldiers had to stave off the poisonous gas were their wet handkerchiefs or wet *bandoliers* where they happened to have them. Pads and masks were not then known or issued.

My lungs were sore for months from the gas we got at the village of St. Julien and here, which was a second dose.

When the German attack came many of the men had fallen. Others were too weak to fight, but there were still some left and they counter attacked and drove the Germans out of the trenches with the bayonet. The fighting was very strenuous while it lasted. It was a case of butt or point whichever came handiest. I noticed a number of men straggling back through on our right and went over to see what was the trouble, thinking that they were retiring without orders. I found, however, they were all badly gassed and wounded so they could be of no further help. Those who were able to shoot were halted and put into the supporting trenches, over which the Germans were putting a curtain of fire filled with asphyxiating gasses which smelled like ten thousand "camphor balls turned loose," as one man said, as he turned sick with the gas and smell.

When the Germans were driven off they again turned their guns and rifles on the brave few who were hanging on. Captain McGregor went down with a wound in the head, but he still kept on using his rifle till a second bullet laid him low. Lieutenant Langmuir, revolver in hand, fell after he had killed eight of the foe. He had more than evened the score at the head of his platoon. Smith and Macdonald fought like lions. Again and again they charged the Germans with the bayonet. Lieutenant Bath, a quiet and mild mannered youth, greatly distinguished himself. Captain McKessock was operating his machine guns like mad. One of the guns he turned over to "Rolly" Carmichael, the tallest man in the regiment, a daredevil who did not know the meaning of fear. With a wound in his shoulder McKessock took one gun out of the forward line, mounted it in rear of a ruin about two hundred feet behind its original position and began ripping holes through the German ranks that were appalling. He was finally overcome from loss of blood. Major Osborne, badly gassed, fought on with a wound in the shoulder till a bullet caught him in the face. He was put into a communication trench from which he directed his men.

The line held against the first attack. Although the Germans broke through in several places they were driven back and paid a fearful price for their daring.

The gasses rolled to the supporting trenches and made life unbearable. The pungent smell was awful. Shells and rifle fire were forgotten in the scorching livid breath of the chlorine. Scores of men died where they stood. Some tried to crawl away. The bearers brought some out from the front line, but when I examined their pulses I found them dead. Poor fellows, their features were distorted and their faces livid. Blood-tainted froth clung to their lips. Their skins were mottled blue and white. They were a heartbreaking sight to behold.

Chlorine gas killed! No wonder the poor ignorant *Turcos* fled. But the indomitable "Red Watch" held on.

The sun rose from a lurid red sea in the east. It was now daylight and five German aeroplanes of the Albatross pattern rose in the German lines and started boldly across our territory. Our machine guns spoke against the flying observer, and I knew that Captain McKessock's guns had still a few kicks left. The stream of wounded and gassed men continued. Many of them could hardly make their way along on their hands and knees. The gas affected some of them so they did not recognize anyone. They afterwards fancied they had been in the front line for days.

The poisonous gasses affected the brain as well as the lungs. Then we realized the full enormity of the gas attack of the enemy. It was not a gas that would knock a man out that they were giving us, but a poisonous gas that would kill.

It was half past six o'clock before the German infantry again tried to force our redoubts.

The gas, shell fire, enfilading fire and machine gun fire they fancied had again done their work, and they ventured out of their trenches and charged against the centre of our line. They broke through between some redoubts in Captain McLaren's line, but the men rallied and drove them out again with the bayonet. The "chop chop" of the Ross rifle told us that there was still plenty of fight in the front line.

The Royal Highlanders on our left and the "Buffs" were attacked at the same time. The German machine guns in the farmhouse were playing havoc with the men in the shallow "dig ins" which they had made the previous night, but the Highlanders held on like grim death. Shells filled with asphyxiating gas were fired at us, and whole squads of men in the supporting trenches were wiped out at each salvo, which consisted usually of four huge shells.

A message from Major Osborne stated that there was a possibility of a shortage of ammunition and he asked for orders and supports. I was sorry to have to tell him that the 48th were to "hold on to the last, and if ammunition gave out to use the bayonet, to hold the redoubts to the end. If the Germans broke through to drive them out with the bayonet."

Orders were issued that the wounded were to get first aid, but were not to be carried out. We needed every rifle and man, and could no longer spare stretcher bearers.

Help was expected, but it was just as dangerous to retire as to hold the forts. We were holding the enemy back and any minute the British might come.

I do not know whether my message got through to him, but I do know that he and his fellow officers carried out the orders.

The Automatic Colt 45, which all the Canadian officers carried, is a good weapon at close quarters. Its bullet would stop an ox, but there is a limit to the rounds that can be fired. In a hard close scuffle, there is nothing like a stout rifle and a long sharp bayonet. I picked one up that had been dropped by a wounded man. It was an excellent weapon, better at close quarters than my claymore. The knowledge learned in the old Toronto Fencing Club of how to lunge and parry was to stand me in good stead during that awful morning. The *arme blanche* is not to be despised, and when you are at it hand to hand you are relieved from shell fire.

I afterwards gave the rifle to Sergeant Coe, the bravest of many brave men, who carried it when he fell at the head of his platoon in the immortal charge on the orchard at Festubert.

About nine o 'clock the German aeroplanes again came along and took another good look at our position. A white flare was dropped over the bit of trench held by Major Marshall, a platoon of forty odd men with a machine gun and crew, that had again and again raked the German trenches. About twenty howitzers immediately opened fire on that unfortunate trench, and how any of them escaped was a mystery, for they seemed to get the range to a dot. Company Sergeant-Major Vernon, one of my best non-commissioned officers, had his head completely blown off with a piece of shell. Sergeant Angus Ferguson, veteran of India, Egypt and Africa, was shot in the arm and leg. He was left for dead. Later the diabolical Huns captured him, and on his raising an objection to having his leg amputated gave him his choice of that or being shot. They amputated his leg above the knee without even administering an anaesthetic, but he lived to return to Toronto and tell the tale.

A number of the machine gunners were killed and wounded. Lieutenant Dansereau, my adjutant, was struck in the head with a piece of shell and everyone thought he was finished. Word was brought to me to that effect, and I felt as if I had lost my own son. Sergeant Flood of the machine gun section stood by his piece as long as possible, but finally a shell smashed the mount and this piece of trench became untenable. The pitiful remnant of the platoon, now consisting of seven men with Major Marshall, had to find a place to the right of the supporting trenches where they kept on fighting. The Germans had broken through on our left and were trying to force our supporting trenches.

Major Marshall and the few that were left with him spotted a platoon of the enemy advancing in their front about one hundred feet away, led by a man who they thought carried a white flag. He wore a blue coat and looked like a French soldier. They thought at first that it was a bunch of *Turcos* or of Germans wanting to surrender. They opened fire, and the man with the white disk turned and started running back and they saw that the other side of the disk bore the ominous black cross. He was a marker for their artillery. He did not run far. Marshall had a rifle and bayonet and knew how to use them. On our left Lieutenant Colonel Burland of Montreal took charge of the 14th and fought rifle in hand. He greatly distinguished himself.

All this time a miserable Hun was playing on our trenches from the left rear with a machine gun.

Between our forward position and St. Julien, a short distance northwest of the Poelcapelle Road, a number of farm buildings had been seized by the Germans when the *Turcos* fled the first night, and they had placed their Maxims in the upper windows and were trying their level best all the time to get us in the back.

Chapter 25

All that was Left of Them

"Look out!" called Lt.-Colonel Burland of Montreal to me.

"You make the hair stand up on my head. That 'blighter' has followed you up and down with his machine gun all morning, and it is a mystery to me how he manages to miss you."

"Well, you're a machine gunner too, and you know he traverses the Maxim after me by patting it on the cheek. I just step short two paces and he goes on."

This answer brought a roar of laughter from the grim warriors in the trenches. The sorry part of it was that that "blighter" in trying to get me had shot several other men.

All morning long the Germans had been trying to take St. Julien. The German artillery south of Zonnebeke sent a storm of shell, raking the rear of the trenches held by our troops from end to end with high explosives. In front of the trenches machine guns hidden in barns and houses ripped the top of the parapets of the hastily-formed trenches held by the Toronto Regiment.

Here Lieutenant "Bill" Jarvis of Toronto died the death of a hero. Medland, another of the Toronto boys much loved by his men, was hit. They were in a trench that was very much exposed which formed the connecting link between the battalion which held the wood north of brigade headquarters and the line of the 3rd Brigade before St. Julien.

"Bill" Jarvis, as he was affectionately known by all ranks in his battalion, had been struck the day before with splinters of shrapnel in the ankle. He was not disabled, and instead of going to the hospital he tied his emergency bandage over his wounds and "carried on." With a half dozen men he was ordered to clear a bunch of German snipers out of a house. When he got there he had only one man left, but the job was done and thoroughly done at that. Fearless to a fault, up and down the line he went during the night of Friday and Saturday morning. He was cut across the chest with a fragment of shell and had a bullet wound through his shoulder, still he refused to leave. Finally he sat down in his trench never to rise again. During the night he had carried a number of wounded to the dressing station but neglected to have his own wounds dressed. He fought as gallantly as his ancestors fought at Chippewa and Lundy's Lane. A stern sense of duty kept him in the trenches when he should have been in the hospital. He gave his life for others. There was mourning among the sailing fraternity in Toronto, and Ridley College, Canada, half masted its flag in memory of the famous Cadet Captain who gave his life so freely on the Plains of Flanders.

All day long the tide of battle surged back and forward along the front line of trenches. Dearly the Germans were made to pay for every foot of frontage. Again and again they charged and were driven back. Then the hell of shell fire would be redoubled and preparation made for a fresh attack. With only a few guns in support it was very difficult to hold our own. When would the supporting troops and artillery come? For two days and two nights we had fought against odds of at least ten to one in men and fifty to one in artillery. The tragic monotony of it all was awful, but the honour of the Empire rested in our hands and it was our duty to play the game to the last man. Every few moments the shell fire and machine guns of the enemy would claim a victim.

Two brave men, Sergeant Coe and Private M.J. O'Connor, signallers, went into the machine gun trench, which was on our extreme left behind a hedge, to bring out Captain Dansereau's body. I also told them to bring back any papers which were left in the shelled and ruined dugout. Through the hurricane of shot and shell that tore the earth up in all directions they made their way. When they returned they told me that the bit of trench was almost filled with dead but they could not find my adjutant. When they went to the dugout to get my papers they found it wrecked and the maps and papers gone. Then I knew that my adjutant must have recovered consciousness sufficiently to get my papers, among them some maps, and that he must have got out, badly wounded as he was. He was the fourth officer of my staff to be wounded, and Major Marshall and Dr. MacKenzie were the only two left of our headquarters staff.

Early that morning while we were in the midst of some very strenuous fighting a message came down from headquarters to the effect that it had been reported that the "48th Battalion had been gassed and compelled to retire." The "fusser" and liar lives even on the battlefield. This story had been told by some runaway to give an excuse for his own cowardice.

I sent a message back that this report was untrue. Our telephone lines and telephone station had been blown up by a "coal box," so we had to depend upon runners to get messages through. One of these, Pte. M.R. Kerr, later on sent me a message from the hospital to the effect that he had taken a message through for me but had been struck by a shell on his way back with the receipt and had to be taken to the hospital. He apologised for not returning to report the message delivered. I recommend him for the D.C.M.

The left flank sections of the 8th had been gassed when the Germans tried to get through between that battalion and ours. Some of their supports had come to their assistance and had driven the enemy back and reconstituted the line. They were supported by a remnant of the gallant 10th. In the early morning of Saturday this undaunted battalion had been withdrawn from St. Julien Wood where they had earned undying glory. After rallying about two hundred and seventy men they marched down to our assistance but were diverted to our right. We heard shortly after noon through runners that two battalions of British troops, the Yorks and Durhams, were on their way down to assist us in a counter attack, but these corps did not arrive until later in the afternoon. They were raw troops only out that day from England. In coming down to Fortuyn they came in open order and the German "curtain of fire" took heavy toll.

After the first attack the Germans settled down to a steady diet of shelling and machine gun fire. I noticed men coming back to both flanks of our supporting trenches, so I went over to rally them and put those that were not incapacitated in with the few of our platoons that were left. In the rear of the right flank of the 7th I saw some men gathered behind a ruined house at a place we called Enfiladed crossroads and went over to see who they were. The moment I stepped out of my trench a German machine gunner got after me and I could hear the "*swish swish*" of the bullets a few feet in front of me. I realized that death was very near, so I stepped short and let him get his range a little ahead of me. His gun followed me for a hundred yards. I found Captain Victor Currie there trying to get the wounded away from the dressing station. Major Odlum, with a few of the remnant of the brave

THE SALIENT FLATTENED

7th, came along.

Some of his men who were gassed were coming back and he was getting a trifle alarmed about his front companies as the enemy were launching attack after attack on St. Julien on his left. I told him to tell his companies to hang on till the last on the left and at the same time to take all the stragglers and put them into the trenches in rear of his left company as support. The ground on his right which I had crossed was badly enfiladed. Lieut.-Colonel Burland came along, having put all the men he could muster into our supporting trenches. He had been struck on the chest with a spent fragment of a "coal box" which had bowled him over, but he was still full of fight. When I started back across the Kerrserlaere Zonnebeke road for our trenches a short distance east, a devilish machine gun again got after me and followed me to the shelter of the dugout in which a number of the wounded had been placed. As I entered the door of the dugout half a dozen bullets pattered on the timber prop of the low doorway not a foot from my head. After seeing to the comfort of the wounded I started back along the trench, and my old friend the "German gunner" again took a crack at me. He certainly had it in for me that day. He caught a sergeant of the Royal Montreals a few feet away from me and he fell, shot in the spine. But a Merciful hand protected me. My hour had not come.

The companies of the 13th, 14th and 7th on our left were hanging on to their trenches like demons. The men in our forward trenches, subjected to a torrent of shot and shell after driving the enemy back and losing half their number, were still fighting valiantly. From a sap at the rim of the ridge I could see our torn trenches still occupied by a few intrepid men. I could hear the "*chop chop*" of the rifles as they drove off the Germans, who had now resorted to open formation to try and win our forward trench. Six ranks deep the German marines had come on to take our trenches. We did not know at first that we were opposed to the German Navy but we were. The marines had been brought down from the fleet to take our trenches and see some fighting. They paid a good price for their curiosity. One of our machine guns is credited with putting over four hundred of them out of business.

Behind the German position I could see the fields filled with great masses of troops formed up ready to be launched against us. God help the heroes that day in the forward lines! Few of them would return to Toronto or the green plains of Canada. I did not know then that the German Emperor was standing on the slope behind Poelcapelle watching his hosts trying to break through the thin Canadian line. Every time the foe fell back discomfited they turned the full fury of their thousands of guns on our front line. Volleys of shells fell in rapid succession along the thin French parapets. One would think that no human creature could live in the tremendous blasts and the showers of steel fragments from the high explosive shells that flew screaming through the air in every direction like mad things.

But the bond of an iron discipline still held the Canadians, not a sound came from the tortured trenches. When the guns were turned upon the parapets and a perfect deluge of bullets would rip through the sandbags and send the clay clattering down the osiers of the hurdles and willow gabions, there would come no response from the Canadian trenches, not a shot would be fired. Plucking up courage the Huns, with much hesitation, would emerge from their "funk holes," as our men called their trenches, port arms and start across the "devil's strip," hoping that the whirlwind of shells had despatched the last of the "white devils" from Canada. But no! They would only make about ten yards when the "warning whistles" of the dauntless Canadians would sound, and then the roar of rapid fire would rise.

It was not for idle pastime our men had practised night and day with dummy cartridges going through the motions of loading and firing. The attacking lines would fall in whole sections, in many cases one bullet killing two or three men. The rifle fire of the Canadian marksmen was exceedingly deadly. Every bullet found a billet. Groans and cries from the dying and wounded Germans would reach us. We could hear distinctly the hoarse shouts of their officers as they ordered "*Vorwarts, Vorwarts, Schneller,*" while the poor unfortunate privates dismayed by the deadly blast would groan "*nein, nein.*" Then we would hear "*Wir sollen Ihr lehren Ihre Canadian Schwein! Uns Neuve Chapelle, zu sagen.*" "We'll teach you Canadian swine to boast about Neuve Chapelle."

Then like one man they would turn and dash madly back to their parapets, leaving the trampled clay of the devil's strip heaped with writhing figures of wounded and dead.

Again and again we scanned the fields in the direction of Fortuyn to see if help was coming. If this process of attrition continued much longer there would be no front line. Meanwhile the German guns searched every foot of ground behind the crest of the Gravenstafel ridge. Every inch of ground that could afford a particle of protection, or was not quite visible, was torn to pieces with their "hiex" shells.

"Why are they throwing away so much good ammunition?" my men would ask me.

I knew but did not say anything. On account of the brave way in which our forward lines were fighting, the Germans fancied we had thousands of men in support. If they only knew they could have steam-rollered us. It is part of the game of war to impose on the enemy and we were carrying out that tradition. It was the biggest bluff Canada ever played.

About noon the Germans began blowing the troops out of the trenches on the right of our supports. I went down again with Lieut. Colonel Burland to the enfiladed crossroads to see what troops were there, and to learn if any word had come through from headquarters. I stopped at the field dressing station and ordered them to get the wounded away as quickly as possible as the enemy were shelling their quarters, evidently with the intention of destroying them. I met Major D.M. Ormond of the 10th who had retired some of the men on his left. He was asked to put his men back into the trenches below the crest of the ridge and hang on. He wanted us to go back with him but that was impossible. He was under the orders of the 2nd Brigade. I told him to direct any of his men who were slightly wounded, but still able to fight, to a line of trenches east of Hennebeke Creek, my idea being that the Germans were having such a tough time with the forward lines that as long as they suspected the crest was held they would not come on. Any troops seen going back to the crest would be taken for reinforcements. I knew that there must be an observation station not far from the German "machine gunner" that was following me and that this station would warn the enemy in our front that we still held the ridge in considerable strength.

This theory proved to be correct, for the supporting trenches then held by us on the ridge were taken over and held by the British troops for days afterwards.

It was late in the afternoon when the din and rifle fire in our front trenches ceased. Not a man came back, so I knew that everyone had stood to his post until overwhelmed. About the same time, five o'clock, a blood-stained order reached me to retire the remnant to the Divisional Reserve trenches. By this time the relieving troops could be seen advancing in open order a short distance away. The Germans were still attacking the line held by the Seventh on our left along the Poelcapelle road. I watched them attack in open order at about three paces interval through a turnip field, the officer following behind with a drawn sword. Every time they reached the margin of the turnip patch, which had not been dug up and which was producing a perfect miniature forest of seed shoots, our guns and the 7th rifles would open on them and they would run back for cover. Again and again they persisted until finally the artillery ceased to fire.

As ordered I sent Major Marshall back to the headquarters trenches with what was left of the supporting platoons, some seventy men, and taking several scouts with me we endeavoured to convey the order to retire along the line of front trenches. We were fired on and three of my scouts were hit. It will be remembered that the forward line extended about a thousand yards and consisted of a series of redoubts.

A wounded man told us that the redoubts at the east of the line, which had been surrounded by hordes of Saxons and marines for a long time, had been rushed when the ammunition ran out. Our men fought to the end with their bayonets.

The scouts sent down to the right were fired upon and only one of them returned. The Germans fired on Sergeant Coe and myself and tried to intercept us, but some of them would not intercept anybody any more. We got away with whole skins. Not a man or an officer in the redoubts remained unwounded when they were taken prisoner. Those who were not hit had been weakened with gas. It is no disgrace to be wounded and taken prisoner in a rear guard action.

Help was now coming in some strength and the situation was saved. I could see battalion after battalion coming down the Fortuyn road in extended order, and I knew that in a short time there would be an advance of these troops north-easterly towards the Poelcapelle road, closing the dangerous space held by the remnant of the 7th Battalion and taking over our supporting trenches and the crest of the gap along the Gravenstafel ridge to the 8th Batt.

The first troops to arrive were the Suffolks and the 12th London Regiment. A few German sharpshooters had crawled through the forward lines and were firing from the crest in two places. On our left the valiant 13th fought in their shallow fire trenches to the last man. Two companies of the 7th hung on to their trenches at the Poelcapelle road until they were overwhelmed by the onrush of Prussians, Saxons and Marine battalions that surrounded them on all sides. The company of "Buffs" that was in support behind the extreme right of the 13th was wiped out. I sent runner after runner along the front trenches but they were fired on and two of them failed to return. I could still hear the row and fighting in front of St. Julien, and the machine guns were going fiercely. I was the last man back. I had borne a charmed life all day, and certainly had a lot to be thankful for.

As we started out for St. Julien I sent some runners ahead of me to notify Captains Alexander and Cory to break off and retire to general headquarters line of trenches as soon as the British troops took over from them. The messengers came back and reported that the village was in the possession of the enemy and that they had been fired upon. Only an hour before I had received a message from Captain Alexander telling me that they were having a pretty tough time, that they were glad to know that I was still safe and that help would be very welcome.

We made several attempts to get into St. Julien but found the Germans held it in considerable force. It was some days later that we learned that Alexander and Cory and a devoted few had held on to the trenches at the northeast angle of the village, although surrounded all that night and part of the next day, Sunday.

On Sunday morning the British troops about daylight launched an attack to recover St. Julien. Four battalions, the Royal Irish Fusiliers, the Dublin Fusiliers, the Seaforth Highlanders and the Warwicks, with the Northumberland brigade in support, tried to retake the village. They found the remnant of the garrison very much alive in the northwest corner although surrounded by the Germans. They, however, failed to carry the village and save the Canadian garrison.

The 48th had suffered terrible losses along with the other battalions of the 3rd Brigade. The question may be asked why did we hang on. Why did not the Canadians retire when they found the Germans were in such force and determined to take their trenches? Instead they stuck to their redoubts and did not budge. They fought back to back when surrounded and refused to give up, driving the enemy back scores of times, until only about 100 of the 800 in our forward trenches were able to raise a rifle. They had lived up to the best traditions of a Highland Regiment. Had we retired, or had the corps at the angle which connected us retired, Canada would have been disgraced forever.

General Alderson, a couple of weeks later, after he had reviewed the whole situation answered all critics by issuing a general order to all the Canadians from which I quote.

I think it is possible that you do not, all of you, quite realize

> that if we had retired on the evening of the 22nd April, when our Allies fell back before the gas and left our left flank quite open, the whole of the 27th and 28th Divisions would probably have been cut off, certainly they would not have got away a gun or a vehicle of any kind and probably not more than half the infantry. This is what our commander-in-chief meant when he telegraphed as he did that 'The Canadians had saved the situation.' My lads, if ever men had a right to be proud in this world you have.
>
> I know my military history pretty well, and I cannot think of an instance, especially when the cleverness and determination of the enemy is taken into account, in which troops were placed in such a difficult position. Nor can I think of an instance in which so much depended on the standing fast of one division. You will remember the last time I spoke to you, just before you went into the trenches at Sailly, now over two months ago, I told you about my old regiment, the E. West Kents, having gained a reputation for not budging from their trenches, no matter how heavily they were attacked. I said I was quite sure that in a short time the Army out here would be saying the same of you. I little thought, we none of us thought, how soon those words would come true. But now here, today, not only the Army here, but all Canada, all England and all the Empire are saying it of you.

The Canadians held their trenches like the West Kents. The German papers subsequently said that they (the Canadians) fought till their ammunition was gone, then they fought with their bayonets, and still unconquerable they died in the trenches they had dug. Every writer on this battle has given them unstinted praise.

The manner in which they held their trenches fighting to the last with small groups of men, taught a new lesson in tactics to the Allies which later on bore fruit at Verdun.

Chapter 26

Digging in With General Snow

"Kar-r-umph!!! Bang!! Puff!!

"Kar-r-umph!!! Bang!! Puff!!

"Kar-r-umph!!! Bang!! Puff!!

"Guess the Germans are handing us the wrong bill of fare this morning. Coffee and iron rations," said Sergeant Coe as he bent over and took a look into the tin basin on the Flemish stove in the kitchen of one of our billets, where we were both striving to get hot water for some tea.

Three "coal boxes" had landed in succession in the upper storey of the house with a great rattle of tile, and as each one exploded huge puffs of black smoke and cinders flew out of the cracks in the stove, turning the water in the basin into a black decoction not unlike coffee.

We started a fresh fire. Sergeant Coe calmly remarked that lightning never struck twice in the same place. He was right.

Major Marshall had met me at dusk, in the rear of St. Julien village to tell me that he had sent the men into headquarter trenches at Wiltje under Sergeant "Jock" Thomson, and that he could not find out anything about Captains Alexander and Cory.

No officer in the division was more conscientious in his work and duty than Captain Alexander. Every man in his company worshipped him. He was absolutely fearless and always wore a pleasant smile when the danger was greatest. For his gallant defence of St. Julien, on my recommendation he was subsequently decorated with the Military Cross, although he had been made a prisoner of war. Capt. Cory, also on my recommendation, got his promotion to major.

On the way out I had passed a number of British regiments in extended order advancing to try to restore the lines for which we had fought so dearly. Seeing them going forward under shell fire in extended order told me at once they were green troops. When I reached Fortuyn I saw a battery of our artillery loaded and hooked up in the shelter of some farm buildings ready to withdraw.

I was then sent for to report to a British *aide-de-camp* in a "dugout" what the situation at Gravenstafel Ridge was. I told him briefly that my front trenches had been blown up, that I had retired all that was left of my supports,—some seventy all told,—on orders from Canadian Headquarters,—and that the British troops could easily make good our supporting trenches below the crest of the ridge without any difficulty.

After this I left the "report centre" and was passing through a territorial regiment which was advancing in open order when a man called out from the ranks, "Is that you, Colonel Currie?" I recognized him at once, and he asked me how his brother was. I knew them both well in Canada. I was sorry to have to tell him that his brother, who was with my regiment, was missing, either dead, wounded or a prisoner. He told me he had been rejected in Canada for being undersized and that he had gone to England and joined a territorial regiment. Their battalion had only just arrived from England and they were getting their baptism of fire. Truly the world is very small.

It was dusk when Major Marshall and I got back and we could not locate our contingent among the mixed units that were snatching a wink of sleep in the reserve trenches. We had partaken of very little food ourselves for about forty-eight hours, so we found our way back to our old billets in the outskirts of Ypres to get some bully beef and biscuits.

The shelling still continued. Every minute a shell would break close by and pieces would rattle against the wall of the house. I arranged that Major Marshall was to go in the morning and gather up the men in the reserve trenches and get them together, while I went to look up any stragglers in the city and send them forward. I was also to find the transport, which had been shelled out of their quarters at Ypres, and arranged with them to send food to us that evening. I then wrapped myself in my cloak and fell asleep on the floor to the weird sound of the German shells passing overhead.

The next day was Sunday, but no peal of bells was heard that morning calling the worshippers to early mass in the churches at Ypres. The civil population had fled. If there were bells ringing their notes were drowned by the fierce explosives that were following each other through the crooked streets in rapid succession. When old Vauban fashioned the moats and ramparts he never imagined they would be bombarded with seventeen inch shells from guns that had a range of twenty-four miles.

I was up by four o'clock. Major Marshall snatched a hasty breakfast and started so as to be in the trenches when the men "stood to." Coe, my signallers, and runners, all that were left of them, tried to get some breakfast when we were interrupted by the "coal boxes" just referred to. We persisted, however, and finally got the tea. Then we sallied out to see if any of our strays or wounded had reached Ypres.

We found that our transports and quartermaster stores had been pretty badly smashed up, and that what was left of them had been moved back about a quarter of a mile from the canal. It was absolutely necessary that they should refit at once and get rations down to us that night, so we went up to the stone bridge on the canal which we had crossed so gaily a few days before with ribbons and tartans flying.

From a couple of sentries that had been left at the lock by their regiments when they marched into action, we were informed that a few of our men who were slightly "gassed" had gone back to the transports. I made my way back, leaving the guard on the bridge. At the transport headquarters I found some thirty-five men who had been partially gassed. They were sent back to the headquarters trenches.

I learned that our division had been badly cut up, but that the Canadians[1] were given credit for having saved the situation.

Our transport and quartermaster stores and baggage had been terribly shelled in their quarters at Ypres. On the way out a shell had exploded in front of our mess-cart occupied by Captain Mabee, the paymaster, and had killed the horse and smashed the rig. The gas fumes had overcome the plucky paymaster and he had to be sent to the hospital.

What had happened to Major MacKenzie, our surgeon, no one seemed to know. The last seen of him he was giving aid to stricken men in a house in the outskirts of St. Julien. We afterwards learned that for twelve days and nights he had served in the forward dressing station. Three times he had been shelled at the dressing station. The annals of the British medical service can show no better service, hero-

---

1. *The 1st Canadians at War*, two accounts of the First Canadian Division in the Great War, *From the St. Lawrence to the Yser With the 1st Canadian Brigade* by Frederic C. Curry and *"Crumps"-the Plain Story of a Canadian Who Went* by Louis Keen also published by Leonaur.

ism or devotion to duty. He was the soul of honour and efficiency.

As soon as I had finished reorganizing what was left of the transport and given instructions about rationing I went down to the headquarters line of trenches. The arrangements made for the rationing of our remnant kept the brigade from starving. Capt. Duguid drew double rations for 1,000 men every day and sent them in to us every night by by-paths and by mule pack.

My battalion got these rations. Sergeant-Major "Soldier Grant" had been badly wounded in the leg, and Quartermaster Sergeant Keith, a very brave and well-trained soldier, took his place. Keith had left an excellent position in Canada and a wife and several small children to follow the pipes. He had fought in the Camerons in Egypt and South Africa and was a splendid soldier.

Lieutenant Frank Gibson, son of Sir John Gibson of Hamilton, Canada, was in the clearing hospital at Poperinghe suffering from a wound in his leg, which it will be remembered he received at Ypres, when he heard from some of our wounded men that the battalion had been badly cut up and the officers gone. He left his cot, evaded the surgeons and came down five miles to the transports. Nothing would do but he must accompany me back to the trenches. Never did a young man show greater devotion to duty and forgetfulness of self than did Lieut. Frank Gibson. I asked him if he felt able to take over the duties of adjutant and signalling officer and he immediately consented to do so. He was one of six graduates of the Royal Military College that held commands in our battalion. He later lost his life at Givenchy. Captain Perry, although badly shaken with the gas and the terrific explosions and fighting at Hill 60, insisted also on accompanying me. We proceeded to the trenches which ran in front of the headquarters of the 3rd Brigade, but owing to the fact that this line was subject to the most intense rifle and cannon fire all day it was very difficult for us to assemble the scattered Highlanders.

During the day the Germans bombarded the headquarters of General Turner, V.C., of our brigade close by. Huge shells fell in the house, and the shock from the explosion and the effects of the gas had knocked out Staff Captain Pope. The gasses acted on him, and many others, like chloroform, so that for a time he lost his reasoning power and appeared to be delirious. He had to be carried away. Captain Harold Macdonald, one of the staff captains of our brigade, was struck with pieces of shell and narrowly escaped with his life. He was literally filled with splinters. One in the cheek, one in the eye, one in the shoulder, the right lung and in the neck. His wounds were dressed by Captain Scrimger of the 14th Battalion. They managed with considerable difficulty to get him out of the burning building, and for this action Scrimger won his V.C.

General Turner, V.C., and Lt.-Colonel Garnet Hughes had to move their headquarters to a dugout close to the burning building. They had clung tenaciously to this building which was in the fighting area and only about six hundred yards south of St. Julien Wood. General Turner had borne the brunt of the fighting from the evening of the 22nd. He had not had a moment's rest night or day, all the troops along the broken section having been placed under his command.

On Sunday evening General Alderson was superseded by General Plumer.

At dusk we succeeded in gathering together most of our men that were about brigade headquarters. Major Marshall had a detachment in the trenches south of the storm-swept St. Julien Wood at Wiltje. When we reached the much-shelled village we found General Hull in charge and Colonel Burland and Colonel Loomis in a house on the north side of the road waiting for orders. The Third Brigade Sergeant-Major soon brought orders to the effect that the remnant of the 3rd Brigade was to march out by way of La Bryke.

During the morning and afternoon a number of attacks had been launched by the British against the village of St. Julien. The stalwart Irish and Highland Regiments had forced their way a number of times into the blood-soaked streets of the village, only to be driven out again with a murderous machine gun and howitzer fire. There was not much of the place left. Every house had been set on fire and the pavements were a shambles. Highlanders, Irish Fusiliers, Canadians and Huns had fought it out in the crooked streets hand to hand. As the shades of evening fell over the scene the German still held his ground, but our artillery had come up in increasing numbers and were raining deadly gusts of shrapnel over the tile and pavements, making it impossible for any creature to live in the place.

We learned that fragments of the 2nd Canadian Brigade still held their trenches near Gravenstafel Ridge, that the valiant Suffolks were still in part of our supporting trenches, and that the Hun had made no progress along the line of the Poelcapelle Road east of St. Julien. The Red Watch had not held in vain. The Hun was just as far away from Ypres and Calais as ever.

We waited until long after midnight for General Turner, V.C., and his staff, and when they did not appear we decided something must have happened to them. Silently in Indian file the brigade slipped quietly through Wieltje, led by one of my signallers, Sergeant Calder, who knew every hedge, ditch and by-way in the Ypres salient. It had been the custom, and a good one, with our signallers, as soon as we got into a new area to bicycle and walk all over it so that they could readily find their way about in the dark. Sergeant Calder took us as straight as a gunbarrel across fields and ditches to the stone road that ran from the unfortunate headquarters of the 3rd Brigade which we could still see was a lurid mass of flames in the distance. We gave General Turner and Col. Hughes up for lost.

Along each hedge we passed we were halted by English "Tommies" who, busy as moles, were digging in. The Germans would find that a tough crop had grown up during the night in the shell-stricken field of the Ypres salient.

Every minute or so there would be a burst of rifle fire along the German lines. They were beginning to show "nerves" and signs of exhaustion. They had paid a terrific price so far for the few blood-soaked acres they had won.

As we reached La Bryke we met at the crossroads two British staff officers on horseback who wanted to know the way to Wieltje and General Hull's Headquarters there. One of them was Brigadier-General Riddell, who was killed a few hours later not far from St. Julien at the head of the brave Northumberland Brigade. He was shot through the head while personally conducting an attack to recover St. Julien.

When we reached La Bryke we found that Captain Duguid, our quartermaster, had fortunately brought down double rations for a complete battalion. This enabled us to ration the whole brigade. He had done the same thing on the Friday night previous. The transports of the other battalions had been all shot up, but Captain Duguid had used mules as pack animals. We waited for several hours for orders and the general did not turn up. The brigade sergeant-major, who had brought us his orders, said he would remain at La Bryke and notify the general if he should come while we went back to the transport to spend the few hours of darkness left. It was necessary for us to go through and past the bridges over the canal before daylight, otherwise we would be spotted by aeroplanes and shelled.

It was dawn when the tired battalions made their way into the field in which all that was left of the transports of the four battalions was packed. They had hot soup ready and it was a case of bivouac on the green grass with the heavens as a blanket.

Very soon afterwards General Turner, V.C., and Lt.-Colonel Hughes, his staff officer, arrived. They both warmly congratulated me on sticking it out at the hot corner. General Turner, V.C., told me that the Canadians had been given credit for saving the situation, and that my battalion, though it had been almost wiped out, had not died in vain. He was completely worn out, so I gave him and his officers a place under a piece of tarpaulin after they had had something to eat. They had not had any rest or sleep since Thursday morning, and in a few minutes everyone was fast asleep except the transport men.

I had not been in the Land of Nod half an hour when I was roused by the trample of a horse and the voice of a horseman enquiring for me. I was up in an instant and found a staff officer looking for General Turner. I refused at first to awaken him unless the matter was urgent, but when I was assured that it was, I roused him and he opened his message. It was an order to take the brigade back immediately to La Bryke to go into support of the Lahore division under General Snow, which was to attack that afternoon together with some French troops.

The men were all dead tired and sound asleep on the ground. They had not had any sleep since the previous Thursday night, and now they were to be roused to go at it again, digging in with General Snow.

Rations and ammunitions were issued and off we started. We crossed the Yperlee Canal by a foot bridge and climbed the steep slope once more into the deadly salient. As we passed down to the bridges in Indian file several of our men were struck by shrapnel bullets. When we crossed over the canal we were led to the west of La Brique and halted in a ditch, where we promptly dug in. The Indian guns were in front of us. About an hour after, just as we were well dug in, we were again moved further east and put in behind some hedges and some more Indian batteries.

Again we dug in, making a good job of it. The troops in front of us were apparently attacking and the din of the shell and rifle fire became terrific. We all thought we would be at it again in a few minutes, and the men began tightening up their *puttees* and looking to their rifles and ammunition. Some began eating their rations, for as one poor fellow said they might as well enjoy them because they might not need any more after a few minutes.

The attack in our front died away and pretty soon another order

The Muster of the 48th Highlanders after Battle of St. Julien—
212 out of 1,034

came and we started down behind hedges and ditches back to Wiltje. The Germans were shelling the village for all they were worth and the church was burning, so we gave it a wide berth and slipped in behind the village and proceeded to dig in again. Every few minutes the Huns would start shelling Wiltje and we would come into their "Zone of influence." The shells that missed the roofs of the houses from the north would pitch over into our lines and we had to duck and count ten when we heard them coming.

While we were being jolly well shelled in these trenches an incident occurred which was of extraordinary interest. I remember reading when I was a boy how at the siege of Toulon, while Napoleon was dictating a message to a young soldier named Lannes a British shell struck the parapet and threw sand all over them and also on the written message. The writer coolly shook the sand off the paper, remarking that they would not need any sand to blot the ink. This soldier showed such bravery that he subsequently became a Marshal of the Empire. That afternoon after we were dug in I was dictating a message to Sergeant Venner of my signalling staff who had his telephone in a "dig in" alongside of mine. He was half way through when a big "coal box" shell exploded a few feet away emitting a terrible stench, a cross between marsh gas and camphor balls.

The smell was overpowering. Venner dropped his pencil and clapped his hands to his face saying, "Wait a minute, Colonel, the smell of that shell makes my head ache." I looked at him and saw he had turned very pale. Looking more closely I noticed blood trickling down the side of his face between his fingers. I snatched his Glengarry off his head and sure enough a jagged piece of shell had cut through the Glengarry and ripped a gash in his scalp about two inches long.

I pulled the piece of steel out and said, "No wonder the shell makes your head ache! You are wounded."

In a trice I had my scissors out, and cutting the hair away from the wound I put some iodine into the cut, Corporal Pyke, his assistant, helped to bind Sergeant Venner's wound with his first aid bandage. After he was fixed up he pulled out his book to finish the message, but I ordered him to clear out and go back to the dressing station. To my amazement he dissented.

"Not a bit of it, sir," he boldly replied, for the first time in his life disobeying my orders.

"Go on, sir, please, and finish the message." "I am all right."

I was so surprised that I finished the message and he stoutly refused to go to the hospital and worked on the signal wires till the battalion was permanently relieved a week or so later. I recommended him for a decoration, also a few other brave officers and men who did not get them.

Chapter 27

Twelve Glorious Days

"They've got me in the back, Colonel! My poor wife and children!"

This was the startled exclamation of one of my men who occupied a "digin" about ten feet from mine. He turned pale.

The Germans were shelling us with high explosive shells from the north rim of the salient. Huge "coal boxes," coming from the direction of Pilken, were falling in the village of Wiltje on our front. With a *twang* like a giant steel bow a shrapnel shell had burst overhead. They had commenced to spray us in the back with shrapnel from the direction of Hill 60, and one of the bullets that pattered like hail on our clay parapets had struck him.

I had ordered all the men to keep on their overcoats, as the stout woollen cloth of the Canadian great coats will stop the German shrapnel bullets and a lot of high explosive splinters, American experts to the contrary. The thick overcoat and the pack is the next best thing to a coat of mail.

Sergeant Lewis and I jumped out and pulled him out on to the banquette of his trench and in a minute had the overcoat and jacket off him. His shirt followed and there, sunk into the flesh of his back about half an inch from his spine and almost half an inch deep, was the black shrapnel bullet. I picked it out with my pen-knife and handed it to him with a silent prayer of thanksgiving.

"There's the bullet. You're worth a dozen dead men yet," I said.

The look of relief on his face was worth seeing.

"Will you let me have the bullet as a souvenir?" I asked.

"Yes, Colonel."

He was not the only man relieved.

We dressed the wound with iodine and put a pad and a piece of plaster over it. He put on his clothes and I told him to go back to the dressing station, but he refused and kept on fighting.

We held the narrow trenches all afternoon and evening. Fierce fighting was going on all around us and we spent a very disagreeable night dug in in Mother earth.

My men endeavoured in every way possible to make me comfortable. Sergt. Coe requisitioned a long bolster pillow from a ruined *estament* in Wiltje for me to sleep on. Another man brought in a few fresh eggs that some Flemish hens had laid in a henhouse in the outskirts of the village. The occupants of Wiltje had all disappeared. Some of them were dead in their cellars, which were not proof against the high explosive shells.

Towards dawn in spite of the lurid glare of bursting shells and the roaring of the flames in the burning houses, the Flemish roosters crowed lustily, typifying the Belgian as well as the French nation.

Dawn came at last but it brought no cessation of the terrible artillery fire. The fighting along the line to the north still continued. The British troops were holding their own and dealing lusty blows at the enemy.

This was the situation as outlined by Corporal Pyke, one of my signalling staff who had gone away to the right to see what was going on in the old "hot corner." A British Division had taken up the supporting trenches of the 2nd Canadian Brigade along the crest of the Gravenstafel Ridge. They had our supporting trenches east of Hennebeke Creek along the Kerrselaer Zonnebeke highway to the ruined houses at Enfiladed crossroads where I had met Captain Victor Currie and the officers of the 7th and 8th Battalions.

The 2nd Brigade, all that was left of them, had been kept hard at it in this section and were still in reserve behind the 28th Division. The line of the 28th Division ran thus from Gravenstafel to Fortuyn, which was still held by us, and along west to where the headquarters trenches crossed the St. Julien-Ypres Road at Vanenberghem, from thence almost due west to a part of the Yperlee Canal near Zwaante. The east bank of the canal was held by the French and Belgians. The Germans had crossed the canal the night of the 22nd at Lizerne and had been driven back at the point of the bayonet by our allies.

Strung along from Gravenstafel Ridge in the following order were the following British Battalions: The Hants, the Rifle Brigade, the 12th London, the Suffolks, the Northumberland Fusiliers, five battalions, the 5th Durhams, the Somersets, the E. Yorks, the Yorkshire, two battalions, two battalions of Yorks and Durhams, the 5th S. Lancasters, the 1st R. Lancasters, the Lancaster Fusiliers, the Essex, the 1st Irish, the Monmouths, the 2nd West Riding, the London, the Royal Kents.

General Hull commanded the 1st R. Warwicks, the 2nd Seaforth Highlanders, the 1st and 2nd Fusiliers, the 2nd Dublin Fusiliers, the 7th Argyle and Sutherland Highlanders.

Colonel Geddes' detachment held the line from our old general headquarters to where they linked up with the French troops who were coming up in some strength. The 1st Canadian Brigade was back west of the canal, protecting Brielen, while our brigade was again south of Wieltje.

All the Canadian troops had fought with great valour and had lost over half the effectives of each battalion. It was my misfortune that I could not chronicle the many deeds of individual bravery performed by my countrymen. I could only describe what was taking place in my own vicinity and in my own corps.

The shelling continued all day of the 27th. There was a chilly wind blowing but the sun shone very brightly. I had a fairly comfortable section of trench and tried to snatch a wink of sleep in the bottom of it during the afternoon. I had not been sleeping long when General Turner, V.C., our brigadier, came up and I made room for him alongside of me. His dugout a couple of hundred yards in the rear of us had been hit several times by German shells and he had a very narrow escape. When he jumped in alongside of me he picked up several spent splinters of shell that had fallen on my greatcoat as I slept. He laughingly remarked that everybody said I bore a charmed life and the shells never bothered me, so as his dugout had become untenable he had come up where he could find a quiet "restful" place.

He informed me that since the battle began on the 22nd he had seen and sustained more rifle and shell fire than had been his lot during the whole South African campaign. He and his hardworking chief, Lt.-Colonel Hughes, had not had any rest since the previous Thursday.

Sergt. Coe made the General comfortable in the bottom of the trench beside me, and in a few minutes he was sound asleep with the shells still beating their infernal tatoo in the heavens over us.

A number of French troops had come up and so had the gallant Lahore Division consisting of Indian troops, and they had attacked the Germans and driven them back some distance towards Pilken.

No jauntier soldier ever trode the plains of Flanders than the brave

Ghurkas. Short and swarthy with that peculiar elastic step and well set-up figure which can only be obtained by a rigorous course of physical setting up drill of the old style with "thumbs behind the seams of the trousers," the Ghurkas are in a class by themselves. Their battalions are led by pipe bands. The weird music of the Highland Glens seems to have the same potency with the Indian Highlanders that it has with the Scottish and Canadian. In a charge at close quarters the Ghurka uses a peculiar shaped knife with a blade as heavy as a butcher's cleaver and keen as a razor. Like the Highland Pipers who play

Mo dhith mo dhith gun tri lamhan
Da laimh 'sa phiob 's laimh 'sa chlaidheamh.

My loss, my loss, without three hands
Two for my pipes and one for my sword,

the Ghurka bewails his great loss, also that he has not three hands, two for the pipes and one for his "*crookie*."

That evening orders came through that we were to march out again and we followed the old line along the hedges and ditches back to our transport. We found that our transport had been moved further back to a field on the Ypres Poperinghe Road to avoid shelling. We were all thoroughly done out when we arrived and we had a good sleep.

Next morning we had roll call and counted our losses. It was the saddest moment in the history of our regiment.

The "roll call" showed killed, wounded and missing, seventeen officers and six hundred and seventy-four men, a fearful total of six hundred and ninety-one out of a battalion of nine hundred and twelve effectives. Seven officers and one hundred and fifty-seven men, all of them gassed and wounded, were taken prisoners. The rest had paid the price of Empire. As the wounded I had sometimes pitied had always said, "That is what we came here for," but it was very hard to be reconciled to the loss of the flower of the regiment. Of all our officers only Major Marshall and myself were left unhurt. How we escaped the Lord alone knows. His mercy was very great. How jealous we had all been of the lives of the men. What care we had all bestowed on their drill, their discipline, their health and equipment. We were all a happy family, no quarrelling, no disputes either among the officers or men. Everyone tried to live up to the best traditions of the old Highland Regiments that oftentimes went through campaigns without a crime. When we reached France not a dozen men in the battalion had entries on their conduct sheets. We all fondly hoped that our efficiency, our courage and power would be reserved for some great day when we would march triumphantly through the German trenches, charging with our bayonets and clearing the road to Brussels, the Rhine, and Berlin.

But our day came differently to what we expected. Still we did our duty. Had we come to grief through any blunder or fault of mine or any of our officers there might have been cause for regret and heartburnings. Our orders were very simple—to hold the trenches at all costs until relieved. We carried out these orders and held the line. When finally ordered out we left nearly four hundred dead in the trenches.

Often during our days and marches in Flanders, in admiration of the men of my regiment and the other gallant men of the First Canadian Division, there would recur to me the words spoken at St. Helene by Napoleon of the men of the Army of Italy:

"Another libeller says that I conquered Italy with a few thousand galley slaves. Now the fact is that probably so fine an army never had existed before. More than half of them were men of education, the sons of merchants, of lawyers, of physicians, of the better order of farmer and *bourgeoise*. Two thirds of them knew how to write and were capable of being made officers. Indeed in the regiment it would have puzzled me to decide who were the most deserving subjects, or who best merited promotion, as they were all so good. Oh! that all my armies had been the same."

A new form of "casualty" had been written into the records of the hospitals and dressing stations, "suffering from" and "died of gas poisoning."

If there is a law of compensation which evens up injustice, if there is an avenging Deity, then the German nation is doomed to die and be forgotten. Cowardly methods of attack will ultimately sap the vigour and courage of their men, and they will curse the day when their ruler wrote them into the history of the ages as a race of cowardly poisoners, unfit even to stand alongside of the Red Indians or the savages of the Soudan.

The tortures inflicted by savages of burning and flaying alive are not comparable to the torture of burning lungs with tissues seared as with a red hot iron. The agony which often ended in gangrene of the lungs was worse than a thousand deaths from pneumonia and the suffering is very long drawn out.

I know whereof I speak as to the torture of scorched lungs, and my case, I am thankful to say, was not as severe as many of them.

On the 28th all the Canadians were west of the canal having a little rest which was enlivened constantly by salvos of high explosive shells sent by the Germans into our vicinity. Every village and farm building for miles back were being shelled.

In the evening we were ordered to prepare to go back into action again. We started out at dusk and followed the familiar paths back down to the engineers' pontoon bridge and then along up the highway in the rear of La Bryke. We were shelled and several men hit with shrapnel while we waited for some transports to get out of our way on the west side of the canal.

When we got to the east and began climbing the slope we were halted again while a battery passed us on the way out. The battery looked very weird against the skyline as they came down the roadway and passed us. The feet of their horses and the waggon wheels were muffled, and they appeared for all the world like the ghostly horsemen out of some old world tale.

We met some English soldiers who told us that the gallant Col. Geddes, who had taken charge of this section and whose corps was the first to come to our aid as we were trying to stop the first mad onrush of the Germans, had been killed in the morning by a shell that entered his headquarters.

We turned to the left and steered straight north to a point in support of the French troops who were in position on the east bank of the canal opposite Brielen. Further along the road we found some transports and a French Battery stuck. A huge German shell had fallen in the road at this point and blown a crater in which a good sized house could easily have hidden. The hedge had to be cut to allow of a passage, and it took some engineering to get this tangle straightened out. After a little manoeuvring we found our trenches, and as the Germans began shelling the highway immediately in our rear, following the transport waggons along the road, it did not take us long to dig in. Someone remarked that the Germans have underground telephones along the roadways.

That morning our base company, under Captain Musgrove and Lieutenant Muir, reached us. A few days later at Festubert Musgrove was to lose an arm and Lieutenant Muir was to be killed. They were full of ginger and cheered us up considerably.

During the night we consolidated our trenches. The shelling continued all the next day. Thousands of French troops continued to arrive and it looked very much as if a general offensive was going to be organized against the Germans on our front.

On the evening of the 29th we moved into trenches at Number Four Pontoon Bridge and remained there until the 4th of May. Day and night the shelling continued. Many stirring and some even humorous incidents occurred during these twelve glorious days of fighting.

Chapter 28

Winning Another Championship

"Jump down into the trench quick, Colonel! That shell may explode," called Captain Musgrove.

"What shell?" I enquired, as I had not heard any "whispering Willy" arriving, but something seemed to have covered my clothes suddenly with mud and splinters of wood and bark.

"Look up over your head. It is a wonder it did not stun you. And please do move out of there for a while at least, for fear it may be still alive."

I glanced up at the pollard willow over head, against which I had been leaning to steady my field glasses as I watched our artillery "strafe" the Germans who were attacking the Ghurkas. Captain Musgrove stood by my side when the shell arrived. It struck the hard red clay about twelve feet directly in front of me, ploughed up the earth about three feet and turning upwards entered the tree directly over my head. The shell, which was a large one from a four-inch howitzer, entered the willow bole, burying itself in the soft wood all but about half an inch of the base.

These shells are fused with what are called detonating fuses that burst when the shell touches anything. It should have exploded when it struck the ground in front of us. If it had we would have had about one chance in a thousand. Again, when it struck the tree it should have blown up. The "kickback" would have certainly killed or wounded us both. But a Merciful Providence caused that shell not to function.

I climbed down into the trench. Next day when the Germans were quieter, Colonel Leckie photographed us. It was a marvellous escape.

On the evening of the 29th we had moved a short distance to our left and again dug in in four lines in rear of the French and as guard over Pontoon Bridge No. 4. The canal here passed north between high banks and a schooner, that had doubtless plied between the North Sea ports and Ypres, had been sunk in the middle of the canal and furnished a pier for the bridge which the engineers had perfected.

Along the banks of the canal were shelters and places where previous troops had "dug in" and the place looked like a huge rabbit warren.

Our batteries were in action along the banks and they were very skilfully hidden. I looked them up and found some old friends from Ottawa, Lieut. Colonel Morrison, the commandant, amongst them.

We had tried to preserve the Belgian buildings in the same condition as we found them as much as possible, but since the Germans were setting fire to all the barns with thatched roofs we decided to annex some straw from the roofs to put in the bottom of our trenches.

The trenches in our front were being unmercifully shelled by the Germans all the time, and about three times a day the Germans and the French would exchange front trenches. Divisions of French troops kept coming up. They carried on in the most casual way. The cooks took soup down to the front line trenches in broad day. They did not seem to care for shot or shell.

The French always moved in single file with men about three yards distance. We learned to like and admire them. They are great soldiers.

The Germans would shell the French troops out of their trenches and then charge and take the low parapets which the French built. After a short rest the French would fix their terrible long four-cornered bayonets which they call there knitting needles, charge the enemy and recover their parapets again. This game of see-saw went on for several days.

The second morning we were at the bridge a handsome well set-up French officer came past our lines and stopped to chat. He wore the gold medal of honour given by the *Czar* which he had won a few weeks previously for conspicuous bravery. He was very proud of it. We all envied him his good luck. He went on up to the front line. About an hour later he passed us again, lying in an ambulance hand-cart very severely wounded. Poor fellow, he was in a bad way but still cheerful.

When the Germans got tired shelling the French they would start in and give it to us. Three and four shells would follow in close succession. They would search up and down the fields and hedges with their guns showering shells on everything within their range.

The gallant 16th Canadian Scottish were dug in about fifty yards in front of us. Colonel Leckie was in a dugout at the extreme left, and alongside of him was another dugout in which were some of his staff. A large German shell fell in the staff dugout during the night, completely obliterating all traces of four men who were sleeping in it at the time. A part of Lt.-Colonel Leckie's dugout was torn off at the same time and he had a very narrow escape.

The same night while I was dozing in my "digin" I was awakened by heavy breathing on my right as if a man was dying. It was pitch dark, so I called the sentry and told him some one was hurt.

Sergeant Miller, who was close at hand, jumped up and with an electric torch we started to search the line to find out who was wounded. In the second "digin" on my right we found Corporal Kells very nearly gone. A large five-inch shell had fallen in his "digin," slicing a large piece of flesh off the calf of his leg and stunning him. Fortunately the shell had not exploded. He had almost bled to death when the peculiar heavy breathing of a man suffering from bleeding attracted my attention. We bound him up and had him taken back to the dressing station. He subsequently died from the shock.

One morning about daylight I was wakened in my narrow cell by a lot of earth tumbling down on my face. I fancied a shell had fallen on my parapet, and after clearing the dirt out of my eyes and ears I lay awake listening to the seventeen-inch Austrian batteries which were shelling some place very heavily. The guns were apparently in a position not far from Pilken. I could hear the "*Kerr-Rump*" of four guns of a battery firing in rapid succession, then a pause, and I could hear the huge projectiles go roaring on their deadly mission till the sound ceased. I waited for the report so I could count the time to find out how far away they were ranging, but I noticed a very strange thing. I could hear no report from the explosion of the shell. Evidently it was falling too far away for me to hear it. A few days later we learned that they had been shelling Dunkirk, some twenty-odd miles away.

The second day we were at the bridge, the Germans were searching diligently for us with their shells when I was called to the telephone which was located in the next hole in the ground to mine. I found Corporal Pyke in charge of my wire. Pyke was a brave cheerful lad, a splendid operator and telephone expert. He was thoroughly posted in wireless work and used to rig up an attachment to our telephone by means of which he could read all the wireless messages that came over the wires from the ships of the Navy in the Channel to the naval batteries that were working behind our lines which were called the Admiral Churchill batteries. If there were any German wireless men in the neighbourhood they could also get these messages. Pyke could hear the Germans working on their lines but could not get their code.

As I hopped over to see who wanted me, and crawled into the telephone hole in the ground a shell came whizzing past and ripped the earth from the parapet about a foot above Pyke's head. He never even ducked, but quite coolly remarked as he shook the dust off, "That sod is rather thin, Colonel. I guess it was only about six inches."

The urgent message that I was called to take was something to the effect that clean socks, underclothes and a bath would be ready for my battalion at a certain date.

I told headquarters to cut out commercial messages for a few days.

Our batteries were earning a great reputation for themselves. They were posted on the bank of the canal and alongside of them were some of the batteries of the Indian Division. Our guns were in action one evening when the major of one of the Indian batteries came along inspecting his observation wires. He watched the drivers of one of our batteries (Morrison's) take a limber of ammunition up to its guns through a perfect hailstorm of shells. He remarked to me that the Canadian gunners were magnificent, and that they did not have six drivers in the Indian Army that were as well trained and as good at their work as the Canadian boys who were driving the limber we were looking at. That was a high compliment from a regular officer as the Indian army knows its trade.

On the afternoon of the 28th, while the Germans were trying to destroy the Canadian batteries with heavy seventeen-inch shells, a German aeroplane came along flying low to check up the big gun practise. We were getting very tired of these German visitors so I ordered my battalion to fire on the flyer, using one thousand elevation and leading the birdman about five times his own length. In a few minutes we had the satisfaction of seeing him turn back with a tail of fire streaming from his gasoline tank. We had got his tank and he was on fire and trying hard to make the German lines. He fell in our lines and the aviator and observer were made prisoners.

Aeroplane activity in that section ceased for a time. The fighting, however, never let up night or day.

On the evening of May 2nd we were ordered to co-operate with British troops in our right who were heavily attacked with gas. There was a dull, heavy atmosphere and everything seemed favourable for the German poison plan. Our guns, however, were ready and they opened a fierce bombardment with shrapnel over the German trenches. It was here the shell incident described at the beginning of the chapter happened. A gentle shower came which dissipated the gas. Three times their infantry climbed out of their trenches and started to charge across the space intervening between the lines. The iron voices of the bursting shells blended into one note as the deadly spray of lead swept entire sections of them away. There was little left for the rifle fire to do.

The attack was beaten off easily. The German offensive for the moment was weakening. They had never fully recovered from the terrible punishment they had received during the first three days from the Canadians. They realized that a new element was barring the way to Calais and victory.

Canada had won many championships on the fields of sport, science, art and mechanics, and now another championship had been won on a sterner field, the field of battle in historic Flanders.

Chapter 29

An Appreciation of Valour

During the night of the 3rd and 4th of May our brigade was withdrawn from the salient and marched to a bivouac west of the Chateau Trois Towers in which our Divisional Headquarters were located all through the battle.

As we marched through the park the day was breaking and the birds were singing more sweetly than I had ever heard them before, even in Canada. They did not feel any more pleased than the few that were left of the gallant "Red Watch" and the other battalions of the Third Canadian Brigade.

The larks were now beginning to build their nests, and strange to say they did not pay the slightest attention to the shelling. The lark we noticed several times would continue to soar and sing higher and higher, intoxicated with the joy of his own song until he came in the way of an exploding shell. Then the beautiful song would be cut short and all that would be left of the spring-time chorister would be a bunch of feathers in the field or on the roadway.

We stayed a day in bivouac and enjoyed a good rest. About noon General Plumer, under whose command we had fought the last days of the battle, came to see us to console us for our losses and to congratulate us upon our stand during the trying hours of the 22nd, 23rd and 24th. His sympathy and kindness will never be forgotten by the men who survived the terrible struggle that ended the great German drive and spring offensive of 1915.

That night we started for Bailleul and made a long, tiresome march along the stone roads. The night was dark as pitch, but we made good time and got to our billets at daybreak.

That afternoon General Sir Horace Smith-Dorrien came to see us at our billets. He warmly congratulated me on the action at St. Julien and expressed much regret that so many good men were lost. At Cassel he had told us that the Canadians had brought him good luck in South Africa, and he felt sure they would distinguish themselves again under his command. His prophecy had come true. Nothing will destroy the confidence of the Canadian troops in the Chief of the Second Army. The hope expressed by every Canadian soldier who fought under him was that he would be their leader when they won their way across the Rhine.

The people throughout the Empire gave every evidence of their appreciation of the conduct of the Canadians. The press was loud in our praises and His Majesty the King was graciously pleased to send the following message to Field Marshal His Royal Highness the Duke of Connaught;

> Congratulate you most warmly on the splendid and gallant way in which the Canadian Division fought during the last two days north of Ypres. Sir John French says their conduct was magnificent throughout. The Dominion will be justly proud.
>
> George.

His Royal Highness the Duke of Connaught then sent the following message to the Minister of Militia for Canada:

> Canada has every reason to be proud of the gallantry of her sons who have nobly done their part in this great struggle for the liberties and honour of our Empire against the tyranny and injustice of Germany.
>
> As an English officer, I am proud of our Canadian comrades and feel that they have brought honour to the British Army as well as themselves, and that their heroic work will thrill the Dominion from the Atlantic to the Pacific.
>
> I deeply lament the long list of casualties and send our profound sympathy to every home which is plunged into sadness and sorrow by the tidings that reach us from hour to hour.
>
> Assuring you again of my heartfelt sympathy for the relations of all those Canadian officers, non-commissioned officers and men who fell so nobly on the field of battle. I am,
>
> (Signed) Arthur.

It has been impossible to describe the part the British troops played in this historic action which lasted over twelve days. Their valour was beyond question. This story deals with the Canadians and their British brothers did not begrudge them any glory which they may have received. The story of the British troops and their part in the fight will no doubt be written. I can testify to their incomparable valour. Braver men than those from London, Durham, Northumberland, and other parts of England who fought alongside of us never lived.

With reference to our comrades from the Indian Empire having fought alongside of them and seen their wounded and their dead, I can testify to their spirit of loyalty, their unquestioned bravery and all the qualities that are to be found in great soldiers.

The Empire contains no better men than the men of the Lahore Division and more particularly the Sir Hind Brigade, whose deeds have shed undying lustre upon the British Army. The lie factories that have been established by German gold, even in the heart of the Empire, have endeavoured to cast doubt upon the relative value of the Indian troops and the troops from other parts of the Empire. There was no truth in these stories. The army in Flanders was equally good all round.

With a national system of military service, such as they have in France, there would be no qualms of patriotic consciences at home, and fewer lie factories.

The Canadians can also bear witness to the splendid conduct of the French troops and the French nation. Our conception of the French people derived from books, chiefly novels of a questionable nature, are entirely wrong. The French soldier is cool and intrepid and they "carry on" their work without the slightest "fuss." The pose of the nation is an inspiration and speaks of solidarity and resolve.

Many of our preconceived notions of them were shattered. The men and women in all classes of the French people are kind, industrious, very moral and deeply religious. They are not at all like the hysterical neurotic creatures of the yellow French novels.

France is the most democratic country in the world. Far more so than the United States or Canada where in most cases every family tries to establish a peculiar cast, a special creed and a select circle of society all its own.

France has a national system of military service and every young man when he comes of military age has to learn the trade of soldiering, starting in the ranks. He does not begin his soldiering by being an honorary general. He reaches the commission rank by study and attention to his duties, not by having friends at Court.

Some people foolishly confound National Service with conscription. They are not the same at all. Where a country has conscription a portion of the population is liable to be drafted compulsorily into the army. When men are needed each parish or community is called upon to provide so many men, whether they know anything of military duties or not. The mayor or head of the community puts all the names of the eligibles into a hat. The required number are drawn by ballot and are supposed to go to war,—but seldom do. One of the beauties of conscription is that if you have the money you can buy a substitute. Conscription is the product of a very old form of civilization, for if in China, for instance, you are conscripted to be hung or be beheaded, you are at liberty to hire a substitute. Conscription thus bears very heavily on the poor, while the idle rich can always escape service.

With national service, rich and poor, prince, priest and pauper have to serve alike without exemption. When the nation is at war, every man, woman and child in it is at war. The males are divided into categories, and those who have youth and no responsibility have to serve in the first line. The only son of a widow, and the father of a numerous small family does not have to leave them to the mercy of public charity and "Patriotic Funds" and go into the front line to fight. There is a place for everybody.

The nation is mobilized and everybody knows that if a man is left behind at the counter, in the mill, or on the farm that it is so ordered, and that that is his place in the service of the State. The people who have experienced this form of service despise the volunteering system, first, because it bears unjustly on the brave and patriotic, and, secondly, because a paid soldier they say is a man hired to kill.

I asked the mother of a handsome lad of seventeen at one of our billets near Cassel when she asked me if the war was likely to continue another year, if she regretted if her boy might have to serve.

"Oh, no, sir," she said. "I fully realized from the first day that I rocked him in his cradle that he would have to fight for France. I am resigned and proud to give two sons for France."

That is the spirit of the French people, calm indomitable and persevering. The spirit that endures to the end and will prevail.

CHAPTER 30

Wanted, More and More of Them

When General Sir Horace Smith-Dorrien came to see me he suggested that I should take a few weeks' rest in England. I objected and said I wanted to be in the big British spring drive in Belgium. He replied that a few days' holidays would not deprive me of that honour, and that he considered the Allies might postpone the offensive until the autumn.

I accepted his suggestion and crossed to England. I met at Bologne an officer of one of the Scottish regiments and he was good enough to get me a pass and a military automobile to take me to La Toquet Hospital, where I renewed old acquaintances with Dr. Shillington, the clever surgeon in charge of the Canadian Hospital there and an old Ottawa friend. When I arrived in London I was notified to attend a medical board at the war office that insisted on giving me three months' sick leave to get my lungs fixed up. I refused to accept more than six weeks.

When I was up in Scotland enjoying a holiday and doing the Loch Lomond country, I received a telegram from Colonel Carson in London telling me that the Minister of Militia would like me to return to Canada for a few months to lecture to the officers in training and assist in recruiting.

In accordance with these instructions I returned to London where I received the following letter from my Brigade Commander, General Turner, V.C.:

> Dear Colonel,—Leave has been extended for four days as requested.
>
> The process of reorganizing is a heavy one.
>
> Your battalion will have lost its identity as the 48th Highland-

ers.

In forwarding recommendation for "Mention in Despatches" it has given me great pleasure including your name for the valuable services rendered at St. Julien.

According to medical officers and my own opinion you are entitled to a good rest or suitable staff employment.

You have done more than called for as a regimental officer.

With best wishes, believe me,

Yours Sincerely,

R.E.W. Turner.

The list of honours for the second battle of Ypres was out and my name had been omitted. I had, however, received notice at the same time that I had been advanced to the rank of full Colonel.

I was pleased, however, to see that Major Marshall, my second in command whom I had recommended for "mention in despatches," had received a D.S.O. He was a professional soldier and this meant much more to him than it did to me. He was later to fall in the front line trenches the victim of a German sniper. A great athlete, a splendid soldier, a universal favourite, Canada and the Empire could ill spare such a man. His solicitude for his men was such that I have known him to give his clothing to some ailing private. He was one of the bravest, truest and kindest of Canadians.

Only a few of the many deserving ones had received recognition, but where there were so many brave men and brave deeds performed it was very difficult to give honours and distinction to all. Officers did no more than the privates, signallers and bombers in the battle. All did their best.

I returned to Canada on board the S.S. *Hesperian*, which ship had the misfortune to be torpedoed next trip.

In Canada I did my best to stimulate recruiting. The "Red Watch" recruited two more fully-equipped battalions for the war—the 92nd and the 134th.

The story of the brave deeds of the men of 15th Battalion, the Red Watch, after I left Flanders will have to be reserved for a further volume. They covered themselves again with glory at Givenchy, Festubert, Hooge and Sanctuary Wood.

The reader may be inclined to ask the question if through all these troublesome times, the Canadian soldier ever lost faith in ultimate victory and the Empire?

The answer is that we had so many evidences around us of the organizing power of the Empire that it inspired us with faith and confidence. We knew what the navy was doing. The splendid manner in which we were supplied with food and clothing convinced us that the business genius and talent for organization of the Empire would sooner or later overcome lack of preparation and "red tape."

The deeds of our gallant Canadian comrades who fell at St. Julien will always be an inspiration for Canadians in future wars. They have given their lives as hostages for the Empire. They did not die in vain for they have given Canada "a place in the sun." The First Division lost over nine thousand out of about seventeen thousand effectives, at St. Julien.

The men who accomplished this were not "rough-necks" nor swaggering bullies, "muttering strange oaths and bearded like pards." They were good, quiet, clean-living, God-fearing young men, the athletic product of the schools and the Y.M.C.A's. They were typical of the Canadian race. With their red blood they etched the figure of the clean-cut intrepid athletic-fighting Canadian soldier indelibly into the history of this war. It was this noble figure which the officers of the First Canadian Division strove to create. It is this figure that will live in the battle scrolls of Europe.

It is the duty of Canadians always to cherish this tradition as well as to maintain their proper place in the world. It matters not under what system their services are required, if duty calls they should be prepared to arm and go. They will always be wanted where liberty needs defending, yes more and more of them.

www.ingramcontent.com/pod-product-compliance
Lightning Source LLC
Chambersburg PA
CBHW032040080426
42733CB00006B/144

* 9 7 8 0 8 5 7 0 6 6 5 0 3 *